W9-DGE-024

ROMANTICISM IN PERSPECTIVE:
TEXTS, CULTURES, HISTORIES

General Editors:
Marilyn Gaull, *Professor of English,*
Temple University/New York University
Stephen Prickett, *Regius Professor of English Language and Literature,*
University of Glasgow

This series aims to offer a fresh assessment of Romanticism by looking at it from a wide variety of perspectives. Both comparative and interdisciplinary, it will bring together cognate themes from architecture, art history, landscape gardening, linguistics, literature, philosophy, politics, science, social and political history and theology to deal with original, contentious or as yet unexplored aspects of Romanticism as a Europe-wide phenomenon.

Titles include

Richard Cronin (*editor*)
1798: THE YEAR OF THE *LYRICAL BALLADS*

Péter Dávidházi
THE ROMANTIC CULT OF SHAKESPEARE: Literary Reception in Anthropological Perspective

David Jasper
THE SACRED AND SECULAR CANON IN ROMANTICISM
Preserving the Sacred Truths

Malcolm Kelsall
JEFFERSON AND THE ICONOGRAPHY OF ROMANTICISM
Folk, Land, Culture and the Romantic Nation

Andrew McCann
CULTURAL POLITICS IN THE 1790s: Literature, Radicalism and the Public Sphere

Ashton Nichols
THE REVOLUTIONARY 'I': Wordsworth and the Politics of
Self-Presentation

Jeffrey C. Robinson
RECEPTION AND POETICS IN KEATS: 'My Ended Poet'

Anya Taylor
BACCHUS IN ROMANTIC ENGLAND: Writers and Drink,
1780–1830

Michael Wiley
ROMANTIC GEOGRAPHY: Wordsworth and
Anglo-European Spaces

Eric Wilson
EMERSON'S SUBLIME SCIENCE

Reception and Poetics in Keats

'My Ended Poet'

Jeffrey C. Robinson

First published in Great Britain 1998 by
MACMILLAN PRESS LTD
Houndmills, Basingstoke, Hampshire RG21 6XS and London
Companies and representatives throughout the world

A catalogue record for this book is available from the British Library.

ISBN 0–333–71638–8

First published in the United States of America 1998 by
ST. MARTIN'S PRESS, INC.,
Scholarly and Reference Division,
175 Fifth Avenue, New York, N.Y. 10010

ISBN 0–312–21001–9

Library of Congress Cataloging-in-Publication Data
Robinson, Jeffrey C.
Reception and poetics in Keats : 'my ended poet' / Jeffrey C.
Robinson.
p.   cm.
Includes bibliographical references (p.   ) and index.
ISBN 0–312–21001–9
1. Keats, John, 1795–1821—Criticism and interpretation.
I. Title.
PR4837.R54 1998
821'.7—dc21
97–31891
CIP

This book is printed on paper suitable for recycling and made from fully managed and
sustained forest sources.

10   9   8   7   6   5   4   3
07   06   05   04   03   02   01   00

Printed and bound in Great Britain by
Antony Rowe Ltd, Chippenham, Wiltshire

for

Jane R. Lilienfeld

and

Gerda S. Norvig

Contents

List of Plates

Acknowledgments

The influence, on this book, of previous scholarship seems to reside in categories either quantifiable or beyond measurement. Of the latter sort I count Marjorie Levinson's *Keats's Life of Allegory*, William Keach's article on Keats's 'Cockney Couplets,' and Tom Clark's book of poems *Junkets on a Sad Planet*; from an earlier generation, Lionel Trilling's essay on Keats in his letters, John Bayley's *Keats and Reality*, and Aileen Ward's biography of Keats. Jerome McGann's *The Poetics of Sensibility* appeared too late to hold a serious place in my thinking about Keats's poetics, but his book retroactively, as it were, belongs with these others.

The staff at the Houghton Library, Harvard University, and at the Keats House, Hampstead, have always been gracious and helpful, as has Bathsheba Abse and her assistants at the Keats-Shelley House, Rome.

Colleen Anderson has helped immensely and expertly with the preparation of the manuscript. My daughter Miriam Robinson also contributed to the preparation of the anthology-appendix. Thanks to you both.

I am particularly grateful to the John Simon Guggenheim Foundation for a fellowship (1993) that allowed not only for the writing of a draft of part of this book but also for the drafting of another book, *Romantic Presences: Living Images from the Age of Wordsworth and Shelley* (Barrytown, NY: Station Hill, 1995), the thinking for which affected the final versions of this work.

The following publishers and agencies have graciously granted permission to include the indicated material in the Appendix of this book.

Black Sparrow Press: 'Pegasus Jockey,' 'Endymion,' 'A Pocket Apollo' and 'It is Getting Late'. Copyright © 1994 by Tom Clark. Reprinted from *Junkets On a Sad Planet: Scenes from the Life of John Keats* with the permission of Black Sparrow Press.
The Ecco Press: 'Posthumous Keats' from *Summer Celestial* by Stanley Plumly. Copyright © 1983 by Stanley Plumly. First published by The Ecco Press in 1983. Reprinted by permission of The Ecco Press.

Alfred A. Knopf, Inc.: 'Voyages' from *What the Light was Like* by Amy Clampitt. Copyright © 1985 by Amy Clampitt. 'Oatmeal' from *When One has Lived a Long Time Alone* by Galway Kinnell. Copyright © 1990 by Galway Kinnell. Reprinted by permission of Alfred A. Knopf, Inc.

POETRY: 'There' by Mark Halliday. Published April 1992. Reprinted by permission of *Poetry*.

Princeton University Press: 'Scirocco' by Jorie Graham, from *Erosion*. Copyright © 1983 by Princeton University Press. Reprinted by permission of Princeton University Press.

Random House, Inc.: 'A Kumquat for John Keats' from *Selected Poems* by Tony Harrison. Copyright © 1987 by Tony Harrison. Reprinted by permission of Random House, Inc.

Weiser & Weiser: 'On Reading Keats in War Time' from *V-Letter* by Karl Shapiro. Copyright © 1944, 1987 Karl Shapiro by arrangement with Wieser & Wieser, Inc., New York.

Thanks also go to the University of Colorado for granting me sabbatical leave from teaching and institutional responsibilities during the same period.

Early versions of sections of this book have appeared in *The Wordsworth Circle* and *Studies in Romanticism* or have been given as talks at Brown University, the Modern Language Association Convention, the British Council at the University of Bologna where I was Visiting Professor in 1994, and the Keats Bicentennial Conference at the University of Bologna in 1995. Deep thanks to Giovanna Franci and Lilla Crisafulli Jones for their gracious and stimulating hospitality surrounding my visits to Bologna and for their support of my work.

I thank, for their conversations with me – perennial or singular or both – Martin Aske, Piero Boitani, Ed Dorn, Sidney Goldfarb, William Keach, James Kincaid, Marilyn Krysl, Peter Manning, Peter Michelson, Timothy Morton, Nicholas Roe, Terry Rowden, David Simpson, John Stevenson, Charlotte Sussman, and Susan Wolfson.

Marilyn Gaull's enthusiasm for this book, for which I am flattered and deeply grateful, has been instrumental in its publication. And Elizabeth Robertson has given unhesitatingly to a critique of the manuscript and a foregrounding of much of what is good in it. Her belief in the project helped me, at difficult moments, to sustain my own commitment to it.

I end by thanking, at last, Aileen Ward, the first scholar under whose guidance I thought seriously about Keats. She provided a 'space for our wandering' and set me on a path, by her example and our exchange, of a lifetime of engagement with this most engaging of English poets.

Every effort has been made to trace all the copyright-holders, but if any have been inadvertently overlooked the publishers will be pleased to make the necessary arrangement at the first opportunity.

'There are gods here, too.'

Herakleitos

'… my ended poet.'

Alice Meynell on Keats

1

Introduction

The subtitle of this work, 'My Ended Poet,' an epithet for Keats from Alice Meynell's passionate 1869 tribute poem, 'On Keats's Grave,' captures a central hypothesis of my book perfectly: the pervasive image of Keats as that poet who died-too-young has for generations guided his readers towards seeing his poems as closed, elegiac monuments; the view of the poet shaped the poetics by which he has been read.

Initially, however, I wanted to write a day-book of Keats, something that would break through predictable, traditional questions asked about him, in order to release what seemed to me the 'vernal' as opposed to the 'autumnal' energies of his poems. To make that point, I called it 'Keats and Sexuality.' But a year after having finished the day-book, I discovered by chance in Harvard's Houghton Library a collection of books of poems, each volume containing at least one poem on or to Keats and written after his death beginning with a single sonnet from 1823 and stretching to the mid-twentieth century in England and North America. Since then I've encountered many other poems (including Amy Clampitt's sequence and Tom Clark's book of lyrics) that dwell on the life, the poems, and the future of the phenomenon called 'Keats.' That the number of poems seems to have increased as his 200th birthday approached; that poets seemed, consciously or subliminally, aware of October 31, 1995, tells me that Keats still continues to hold his living hand towards the making of poems. My book, therefore, began to change into a register of Keats's *living* poetics (the sexual element from the original) as it has been both denied and affirmed by the praise poems that have helped to define his afterlife.

In 1995 I was thoroughly caught up in the spirit of the celebration – even the most sentimental eulogy had and still has for me a charm, the sense of connection to the poet of the empyrean. In an age when the operations performed at the periphery of poems may seem far more compelling than the conversations held in their presence, conversations that should renew the centrality and primacy of the poem itself at the same time that the poem disperses its energies and love among watchful persons, in such an age and at such a moment it is right to learn again the particular vitality of Keats's work, a vitality which I find first and foremost in his *poetics* and which, particularly towards the end of this book, I will reconsider.

Keats today is still by and large read as a fundamentally Tennysonian poet of closed forms and elegiac temperament. Open any of the standard books on Keats – by Stillinger, Sperry, Dickstein, Waldoff, or Vendler, for example – and you will discover in these elegant and well-argued studies a dominant drive to find the presence of a heroic closure to the poems. That is, each (of the 'best') of his lyrics – and the Odes being the *summa* of his shorter pieces – manages an impressive stay against the flux or mutability of the world and of his own vulnerable body. In the manner of Schiller's tragic heroines, the lyric subject 'endures' against its devouring enemies. Formally what counts in an assessment of Keats is his abandonment of his loose, hypothetically infinite string of enjambed couplets in his early poems and the embrace of and experimentation with sonnet forms (including the Odes): his genius is to make capacious the generic abstractions of the past but finally to stay within them, to have form reinforce the triumph of the ego against less socially definable versions of the self such as one finds in myth and in nature.

To critics of Keats in the past quarter-century this may seem a strange claim, given in particular the tradition of deconstructive readings of Romantic poems and the more recent historicizing of that apparently most ahistorical of poets. Deconstruction asserts that closure itself is problematic; historical research is recovering a wealth of contexts that locate Keats's poetry amid lively political, and literary-political, debate. To take several instances: Nicholas Roe has recently shown that Keats's Enfield School dwelt, since its founding, in a predisposition of radical dissenting politics that permeated its educational practices and that therefore, in all probability, colored Keats's experience there. Marjorie Levinson has argued for a Keats highly self-conscious about his marginal social position in poetic inheritance relative to more 'aristocratic' contemporaries like Wordsworth, Byron, and Shelley. As a result, he appropriates or quotes from the tradition in a pastiche foreign to the notion of originary genius or fount of inspiration that tradition posits as the Romantic lyric. In a similar counter to that notion is Jack Stillinger's work on multiple authorship, arguing that friends, editors, and publishers contributed to a number of Keats's final published versions of poems: where does Keats end and his friend Richard Woodhouse, for example, begin? William Keach has shown that the severe criticism heaped upon Keats's first volume of 1817 was largely disapproval of his 'Cockney couplets' that flaunted the orthodoxy of Pope's beautiful closed systems with a plethora of enjambment, slant rhyme, and internal full stops indicating to reviewers that 'loose' couplets went hand in hand with 'loose' reformist ('Cockney') politics. Christopher Ricks[1] located the center of Keats's poetic interest in a pervasive and irrepressible eroticism, more specifically, in the sense of embarrassment that might accompany the public (poetic) display of the erotic. Finally, feminist readings (e.g. those of Susan Wolfson and Margaret Homans)[2] of Keats's life, his poetry, and his readership have destabilized the sense of his identity as singularly, confidently, and stereotypically masculine.

It is precisely such destabilizations from traditional conceptions of Keats in history and in poetry that one expects would lead to a rethinking of his poetics, but – with the possible exception of Keach's work – this has not yet happened. Indeed, in Romantics criticism generally and that of Keats in particular discussions of poetics currently seem to be lagging behind cultural, political, and thematic studies. It's almost as if the release from traditional ways of seeing Keats in various cultural and historical contexts has been allowable as long as the poem itself remains secure amid the predictable forms, and assumptions about form, from the past. The final sections of this book will begin to alter the picture.

So how do we speak of the relationship between form and the elegiac temperament? Keats's poetry, first of all, refers often to death and the ending or vanishing of the images of persons and things; from one point of view his poetry shows his concern with fadings, vanishings, grievings, forgettings, and with the immediacy of oblivion as the spectral possibility of a world without poetry – what Wordsworth in *The Ruined Cottage* calls nature's calm oblivious tendency. This much is no news. The history of Keats criticism, of poems about Keats, of the cultural shrines to Keats all attest to the presence of the issue of oblivion in his poetry, and his letters, underscored by his early death. Moreover, for Keats to have died so young was to have played out the script for the truly 'authentic' poet: to die young for poetry, to sacrifice so obviously 'life' for 'art' is just what Chatterton and Burns did two generations earlier.

Keats, and Shelley a year later, rebel, as it were, against the pas-
sionately wished-for life in poetry, resolute and independent, urged
by Coleridge and Wordsworth and Charlotte Smith and Helen
Maria Williams who note with a mixture of admiration and dismay
the failure of social, psychological, and biological life to support the
poet's whole-souled entry into the collective imagination that is
poetry. Keats's life, references in his work, and a certain myth of
poetic authenticity have thus conspired to make him the poet of
death. But what is *not* necessary and yet what has predominated
historically is that we conflate his death-perfused world with a
poetics of closed forms and with what Keats, quoting Hazlitt, called
his 'morbidity of temperament.'

This, of course, is greatly overstating the case of how Keats is
read, and is not meant to overlook the view that Keats is a poet of
enormous energy. But the history of criticism would suggest that
when it comes down to reading a Keats poem, the reader will opt
for a traditional sense of British poetics – that, no matter how much
play or even 'hoodwinking' is in the writing, it is finally bounded
and defined by a sense of the poem's containment within its
borders: a poem represents an event now over, having, as Lionel
Trilling said about the Grecian Urn in Keats's Ode, 'pastness as one
of its attributes.'[3]

Stuart Sperry, in his standard book *Keats the Poet* that has
influenced many other readers, in effect argues that Keats's heroic
response to the pervasiveness of death in his world is to work to
create an aesthetic coherence as a counter to the entropy of his life.
Thus he is very interested in the way that the early (*1817* volume)
poetry develops from loose associative writing into rock-like structures. Of the early verse epistle 'To Charles Cowden Clarke,' Sperry
says: 'Since the poetic voyage, as he conceived it should have no
predetermined course, he could only hope that, while allowing his
medium, the rush of sensation, to bear him forward, he could from
time to time arrest and transform its flow of images into the
brighter, harder shapes and symbols of a crystallizing intention.'[4]
Or, '"I stood tiptoe" begins as an accumulation of disparate and
minute observations of nature which gradually achieve the cohe-
siveness and depth of landscape. ...'[5] Associations, accumulations
of detail, listings exhibit that winning quality of Keats, his generous
exuberance, but ultimately need to be abandoned or, more capa-
ciously channeled, for the higher concerns which demand a greater
coherence in the writing. Leon Waldoff, in the title of his book

Keats and the Silent Work of Imagination, gives a psychoanalytic turn to Sperry's work. Associations and accumulations of detail seem roughly equivalent to the powerful incoherences of the unconscious, which in Keats's situation means 'irrevocable loss and human mutability,' against which '[a]n important part of the imaginative effort in each of Keats's major poems goes towards working out a defense. ...'[6] Combining Sperry and Waldoff as representative of much of Keats criticism, a 'major Keats poem' is a closed form designed to foreground the heroic resistance of an expansive ego against the powerful and seductive but 'errant' pathways of youth and the unconscious, pathways ruled primarily by an elegiac combination of desire, longing, and severe loss.

Another kind of loss resides in the background of much of this criticism: the decline, historically beginning sometime in the eighteenth century, of the perceived power of poetry, what Sperry refers to as 'the relatively somber prospect for poetry that lies ahead.' In this light the Odes test 'imaginative inquiry [reaching] its limits.'[7] Visionary poetry according to this thesis is on the way out, and poets have come to feel that there is little left for them to do, a position articulated by W. J. Bate in *The Burden of the Past and the English Poet* but previously alluded to in his 1963 biography of Keats, and developed or echoed by Harold Bloom, Paul de Man, and Sperry himself.

But such a view of Keats's poetry does not square either with the history of poetry in the West (including non-Anglo-American writings) since the Romantics or with the particular inspiration Keats has afforded major modern and postmodern and Beat poets who have pursued open forms in their own work. The moments of Keats's legacy that seem to have appealed greatly to these poets are the twin notions of Negative Capability and the camelion poet:

> ...what quality went to form a Man of Achievement especially in Literature & which Shakespeare possessed so enormously – I mean *Negative Capability*, that is when man is capable of being in uncertainties, Mysteries, doubts, without any irritable reaching after fact & reason – Coleridge, for instance, would let go by a fine isolated verisimilitude caught from the Penetralium of mystery, from being incapable of remaining content with half knowledge. This pursued through Volumes would perhaps take us no further than this, that with a great poet the sense of Beauty overcomes every other consideration, or rather obliterates all consideration.[8]

As to the poetical Character itself, (I mean that sort of which, if I am any thing, I am a Member; that sort distinguished from the wordsworthian or egotistical sublime; which is a thing per se and stands alone) it is not itself – it has no self – it is every thing and nothing – It has no character – it enjoys light and shade; it lives in gusto, be it foul or fair, high or low, rich or poor, mean or elevated – It has as much delight in conceiving an Iago as an Imogen. What shocks the virtuous philospher, delights the camelion Poet. It does no harm from its relish of the dark side of things any more than from its taste for the bright one; because they both end in speculation. A Poet is the most unpoetical of any thing in existence; because he has no Identity – he is continually in for – and filling some other Body – The Sun, the Moon, the Sea and Men and Women who are creatures of impulse are poetical and have about them an unchangeable attribute – the poet has none; no identity – he is certainly the most unpoetical of all God's Creatures.[9]

Taken together the two passages point the way to a 'poetry of aperture.'[10] Rather than finding the purpose of the lyric to reside in the individuation of the self over and against the world, the conservation of the self, the negatively capable and camelion poets lose the self to the world in which they as fully as possible participate. Keats's preoccupation with 'easeful death' and with dying-into-life refers to this feature of open-form poetry.

I have been aided, indeed inspired, in my conviction that Keatsian poetics can been viewed differently, by poets from our own century and hemisphere, in the tradition of Whitman and Pound and William Carlos Williams and some members of the Beat Generation of poets and their followers. And here I am asking a more general question of reading: what happens to our experience of a major poet from the past if we emphasize less the poetics and values of late nineteenth- and early twentieth-century English poetry and aesthetics and more those to which we are immediate heirs? To read the past through the lens of more recent poetries and manifestoes forces the issue about how we read into the tradition – to what degree we acknowledge present biases and commitments. In this sense to read from the viewpoints of our best experimental poets is to assume a vantage of current *practice*, to take seriously the resonance of Keats in the work of recent laborers in poetry and claim it for ourselves as dedicated readers.

I divide this study, therefore, broadly into two parts. The first is a reception history and cultural history, focusing both on the range of praise poems written about or to Keats since Shelley's *Adonais* in the year of the poet's death, 1821 (notice, this is *not* an influence study), and on the shrines of Keats (the Keats House in Hampstead, England, where he lived in 1819–20; the apartment in Rome where he died; the English Cemetery in Rome where he was buried; the Houghton Library at Harvard University with its huge collection of Keats manuscripts, editions, and accessory documents). By yoking together poems and shrines I am insisting that to grant poets an interpretative authority is by no means to exclude them from their participation in more obviously public forms of cultural influence. The argument is that most of these materials helped significantly to produce the 'canonized' Keats: what poems we read and how we read them and, implicitly, what poems are not read and what is left out of our readings. But some of the poems – particularly more recent ones – lead us into a different emphasis, which then justifies the book's second part: a sketch of what I believe to be a more vital Keatsian poetics both in terms of familiar poems and of those that tend to be neglected or relegated to a minor place in his *oeuvre*.

To import poets as critics into the expectations of criticism creates certain dissonances and bewilderments in one's experience and sense of location. But this may be valuable since the problem of reading Keats has seemed to me, as well as to other readers and teachers, one of over-familiarity: we swallow his poems, life and career as if we have always known what they meant. (To be sure, this is changing with the advent of a new intensity applied to historical research.) Partly this has resulted in a kind of fetishizing of poems and career that denies the highly occasional and contextual, the highly volatile nature of reading and use of evidence. To counter this tendency I have resorted in this book to a collage format – with quick shifts of focus, content, even texture and genre. There is no smooth progression and building up of an argument because smoothness is part of the problem. Similarly, you may see much more of me than you may expect or wish, but that simply reflects that I am a non-insignificant factor in this reading of Keats. An essay, as we know from Montaigne and his many successors in this genre, is an experiment and an experience; as another essayist has said, it is a *walk* through one's materials. *Reception and Poetics in Keats* is a record of my walk through some of the materials that we call 'Keats.' As it is not an argument, I cannot guarantee an outcome in the increase of knowledge, except at the local level, for the reader, but then, I no longer know how to isolate precisely what constitutes the knowledge that literary criticism ought best to give. For example, shortly you will read about trips I made from Hampstead to Rome and back – the sites of Keats shrines; in this journey I try to find some meaning. But is it really *there*? Who is to say? The whole book works like this: a sequence of flights from topic to topic. Undeniably, however, they chart one reader at his reading.

And yet one of the subjects of the book – the openness of Keats's reputedly closed forms and the efforts of tradition to keep them closed – may be positively served by the open form of this essay.

The celebration of a great poet brings to bear a pressure upon the present. Two hundred years of poetic fame is described by the voices of the distant and recent past and by a sense of beginning to read again. The encounter with Keats today should be both mediated and, wherever possible, unmediated. I make no claim for comprehensiveness, either in reception history or in new readings, but offer a dynamics of recovery and renewal.

2

A Game of Shards:
Keats's 'Vitally Metaphorical Poetry'

As Hermes once took to his feathers light
When lulled Argus, baffled, swoon'd and slept
So on a delphic reed my idle spright
So play'd, so charm'd so conquer'd, so bereft
The dragon world of all its hundred eyes
And seeing it asleep so fled away: –
Not to pure Ida with its snowclad skies
        cold skies
Nor unto Tempe where Jove grieved that day,
But to that second circle of sad hell,
Where in the gust, the whirlwind and the flaw
Of Rain and hailstones lovers need not tell
Their sorrows – Pale were the sweet lips I saw
Pale were the lips I kiss'd and fair the fo[r]m
I floated with about that melancholy storm – [1]

Literary history: In the manuscript of the letter to George and Georgiana Keats (February–May 1819) containing 'As Hermes once . . ,' the sheet of paper having run out at line 12 of the sonnet, Keats wrote the final couplet in a one-fourth counterclockwise turn near the left-hand margin but through the text of the letter. What a surprise, to see the couplet floating free!

> Pale were the lips I kiss'd and fair the form
> I floated with about that melancholy storm –

There are two 'material' explanations for this up-the-margin event. The first, of course, is that it is a paper-saving device, as is 'crossing' a letter (writing over a letter perpendicular to the script already there), a practice familiar to readers of Keats's manuscripts. But in this long journal letter are instances of Keats placing the last lines of a poem on the next page: no paper-saving there. Second, and in no way denying the validity of the first explanation, Keats may have 'wanted' to play with the themes and images of his poem. To be sure, none of this gets into the *Indicator*[2] which published his poem in 1820 (and which, in fact, has 'worldwind' for 'whirlwind'). But at this moment, he may have delighted in the way that 'melancholy storm' crosses through the description (inspired by reading Dante's Paolo and Francesca section of *The Divine Comedy*) of his dream of floating with the woman in paradise, a description that directly precedes the sonnet copied out:

> [I floated about the whirling atmosphere as it is described with a beautiful figure to whose lips mine] were joined as it seem'd for an age – and in the midst of all this cold and darkness I was warm – even flowery tree tops sprung up and we rested on them sometimes with the lightness of a cloud till the wind blew us away again. – I tried a Sonnet upon it – there are fourteen lines but nothing of what I felt in it – o that I could dream it every night –

'Melancholy storm' seeps back into the dream, contaminates it, or – since it is ink we are talking about – stains it. Keats wishes the reverse had happened – that the dream might have flooded the poem, become the poem.

The poem is far more complicated than the dream. The dream, first of all, doesn't really evoke the somber beauty of Dante, but rather the summery wish-world of Leigh Hunt and his *The Story of Rimini*. The poem opens itself to the Renaissance original. Secondly, the octave concocts a drama of playful deceit upon a background of censorship of dreams, recalling Hazlitt's judgment (in 'On Poetry in General,' 1818) that modern poetry needs to counteract the intrusive role of the 'police' who do not even allow us to dream of a midnight murder. In the prose account of the dream there is a simple visual relationship between the foreground (warm pleasure) and the background (cold and darkness), but in the poem this clear opposition and others collapse. The tension of the simile of Hermes compared to the idle spright of the sleeping poet dissolves into a metamorphosis of the sleeper into the mythic figure so that the human scale of the former enters the outsized world of myth, implying a loss of boundaries that might indeed be registered by melancholy affect.

Pleasure and pain, happiness and melancholy: these are some of the pairs of terms in which Keats and the critical tradition have led us to read his poetry. Yet my surprise, and delight, at encountering this strange crossing in the manuscript offers, obscurely, a new unsettling response. This sonnet, and it is typical of many of Keats's poems, has a powerful centrifugal movement away from the human scale – what in other poems may be registered as *ecstasy* ('Away, away, for I will fly to thee...') – into another, utopian, space of literature and happiness, of collective comforts. Here that other space is registered by metamorphosis and metaphorization.

I look at the manuscript, with melancholy crossing the 'delightful enjoyment' of the dream and think, yes: the materiality of this event, the precise staining of the page, of the sentiment of the dream, the bizarre rightness, the sense of design, that accompanies the need – coming to the bottom of the page at line 12 – to cram the final couplet in somewhere, is stunning. It works so well that it seems a kind of spontaneous wit took over in the midst of the poem's melancholy. The alienation or exile of metaphor where 'one can always maintain a comfortable distance, a pathetic, dramatic, critical, aesthetic distance – the orphanlike serenity of one's own world,' vanishes into a 'deprivation of meaning and territory.'[3] For the moment the poem suddenly becomes a game of literary shards: Leigh Hunt, Dante, metaphor, kiss, warm, storm, melancholy, etc. The playful proximities of wit replace the melancholic alienation of metaphor. Whereas we tend, in Keats studies, to see melancholy as an outcome of happiness or pleasure as in Wordsworth's, 'We Poets in our youth begin in gladness;/ But thereof come in the end despondency and madness' or Keats's tragic early death coming too soon upon his 'flowering' of great poetry, an early winter following upon a luxuriant spring – the crossing of the letter suggests a correspondence, an eradication of diachronicity, of cause and effect, and the advent of a *scene* that includes both melancholy and pleasure, but redeeming each from a necessary relationship to the other and introducing, one might say, an element of chance, of foreignness into their mutual encounter.

Then, as if the poet corroborates my strange reading, I notice the first sentence that follows the copying out of the sonnet, to Georgiana: 'I want very much a little of your wit my dear sister – a Letter or two of yours just to bandy back a pun or two across the Atlantic and send a quibble over the Floridas.' Two pages before the poem Keats recounts the walk he took with Coleridge:

In those two Miles he broached a thousand things – let me see if I can give you a list – Nightingales, Poetry – on Poetical sensation – Metaphysics – Different genera and species of Dreams – Nightmare – a dream accompanied by a sense of touch – single and double touch – A dream related – First and second consciousness – the difference explained between will and Volition – so many metaphysicians from a want of smoking the second consciousness – Monsters – the Kraken – Mermaids – southey believes in them – southeys belief too much diluted – A Ghost story – Good morning… .

Codes, touchstones of whole monologues, signs. But Keats doesn't want to go into anything in depth – the pleasure and the point is the list, the names, the surface of names, all thrown together.

A few pages later, having just quoted 'La Belle Dame sans Merci,' he remarks: 'Why four kisses – you will say – why four because I wish to restrain the headlong impetuosity of my Muse – she would have fain said 'score' without hurting the rhyme – but we must temper the Imagination as the Critics say with Judgment.' Again, Keats's most famous nightmare poem, indeed a nightmare for his life, becomes a game of words and codes. Denial of the psychological power for him of his newly created poem? – perhaps, but it's a denial or disarming that seems central for his new poetics and for a more modern poetics which looks to language for its release of energy coming from the oddness of associations and correspondences and not to the depth, the 'distant deeps or skies,' that experience is supposed to provide.

So who is this Mr John Keats, the poet? Is he the poet of 'wild ecstasies' ('Ode on a Grecian Urn') or the poet of wordplay and puns and 'things all disjointed [coming] from north and south' ('Epistle to J. H. Reynolds')? I think he is both – not, however, because he planned it that way but because of the intensity of his genius pressing upon his extreme youth, his jejune mind, his love of the beautiful *and* of the real, and his 'morbidity of temperament' (a phrase he applied to himself but stole from Hazlitt). It is because of his absorption in the great epic, romance, dramatic, and lyric (generally vatic) poets of the classical and English tradition coupled with that outsider sense (see Marjorie Levinson's *Keats's Life of Allegory*) that apparently allowed him, on occasion, to view all poetries proleptically as quotation and an intuition that the ecstatic impulse in poetry (characteristic of Romantic lyric) might lead nowhere ('a burning forehead and a parching tongue'). The tongue: Keats, in thinking about nightingales, associated it with song, with the projection of the voice outwards towards the collectivity, the drive of the subject surrounded by the music of himself to lose himself in the history of songs and in what survives the hungry generations to return to human beings as consolation for their goings forth. But he also valued the tongue as an organ of touch – the high sensations of cayenne pepper, his 'palate affair' with claret, the feel of a slushy nectarine going down like a 'large beatified strawberry.' The moment of erotic privilege when the distance between two domains – the human body and the claret or nectarine – collapses as refined, beatified consciousness.

But if I were to stop here, with a Keatsian instance of intensities, I would only be restating a familiar pleasure that Keats, as both person and poet, brings. I am interested in revealing what I believe historically Keats brought to poetics, an advance in poetics realized triumphantly later in the century by Mallarmé, in our century the Surrealists, and more recently in America and Europe by poets such as Lorca and Vallejo, Pasternak, Zukofsky and Reznikoff, Lorine Niedecker, Charles Bernstein, Susan Howe, and others. Keats was not, by the way, the only Romantic to challenge the dominant poetics of Shakespeare/Milton/Wordsworth:[4] Blake and Byron, in their different ways, and the rediscovered Mary Robinson also refigure poetry away from metaphor as conventionally defined and towards what I will call *correspondence*: metaphor is a type of correspondence, a comparison of one thing belonging to one 'domain' to another of a different domain. It is one powerful instance of achieving the *visionary* in poetry, of defamiliarizing the world and thus making it evident in a new way, often in a challengingly more humane way. Or coming at it from the perspective of poetry's communal functions, Allen Grossman says: 'Metaphor is a device for reducing the unknowability of the fact by eroding its uniqueness.'[5] But some of the most experimental of modern poets have questioned its validity along the lines of Baudrillard, that its apparent extension into difference masks its burden in the poet's subjectivity, that it bespeaks, against our wishes, the poet's alienation from rather than his/her residing more closely in the suburbs of reality. As well as the poem's serving the needs of the *subject*, in its relationship to God, to other persons, to itself (the need to discover its dimensions, its sense of scale in relation to other beings in the universe), it may also serve the needs of the relationship between the subject and an autonomous reality which may be the poem itself. I think of Roland Barthes's notion of the *punctum* in photographs, a usually insignificant spot on a photograph apparently unintended by the photographer, apparently untouched by the ideology of photographer or the narrative line predicted by the concateination of images, yet one which touches the viewer all the more powerfully for its autonomy from narratives and predetermined meanings. Or, also in Barthes, there is his discussion of the tradition that includes Brecht's epic theatre: its emphasis on the meaning of a *scene* conveyed not by its relation to the diachronicity of narrative but by the juxtaposition of elements that dominant cultural narratives do not absorb; instead they display a fundamental principle of contradiction and yet correspondence that is the condition of a modern society in its relationship to the needs of each of its members.

What is called into question in such kinds of art is the authority of a subject to present anything but its own wishes and drives; the correspondence elicits the possibility of the artist's releasing a sense of a social reality that the narratives of subjects cannot predict but which exists in fact. Or, in the case of poetry, it may be an apparent jumble of words and phrases that reminds one of the arbitrary nature of the orders we impose.

I would suggest that the poetics implied here surfaces around the time of Romanticism as an expression of a sudden speed-up in the visibility and claims of diverse classes of persons and in the widespread availibility of the print culture. The poet acknowledges the overload on the person from these increases in voices and printed words and from the increased diversity of their sources and their targets by 'listing' (Mary Robinson, 'London's Summer Morning,' composed 1794) what is out there. For example:

> Now begins
> The din of hackney-coaches, waggons, carts;
> While tinmen's shops, and noisy trunk-makers,
> Knife-grinders, coopers, squeaking cork-cutters,
> Fruit-barrows, and the hunger-giving cries
> Of vegetable-vendors, fill the air.

The world is represented as a proliferation of elements (listed, one after the other, in the poem); at times the voice of the poet 'proliferates' as well, drawing on the voices of others present or past. Herein lies, I believe, the real significance of Keats's 'camelion poet' formulation, opposed, as he says, to the Wordsworthian ego-tistical sublime, capable of delighting in an Iago as well as an Imogen. The point, which I believe Keats understood in his poetry but may have only intuited in his letters, is not that the poet can enter selflessly into any object but that he/she can enter into multi-ple objects, more or less simultaneously – a principle that appealed greatly to Whitman and later to the Beat generation of poets.

The tradition has defined this poetic condition in terms of the subject, a kind of heroic divesting of self or selfishness for an object in the world. But all that is left of subjects is a profound, stimulat-ing delight in a world-abundance where world-scarcity or ex-clusivity (ideologically promoted) was thought to rule – the carnivalesque. The world evoked by such a poetic reaches beyond the dyadic penumbrae of subject to object (even when the object is God) and back. Or, the poet as subject performs the virtues of the host or hostess, beckoning *all* to come and eat at the table of poetry. In this sense there is in the correspondence a utopian element with respect to reality, as Ernst Bloch says, 'transcendent [of ideologies] without transcendence.'

Romantic poetry continually returns to the fundamentals of poetry in order to redefine or resituate them. Correspondence is the result, I believe, of what Shelley means by poetry's 'vitally metaphorical' nature and is similar to what Jerome Rothenberg, in his extraordinary anthology of world poetries, *Technicians of the Sacred*, describes as characteristic of the poetries of so-called tradi-tional societies as well as that of Surrealism:

a conscious placing of image against image [in Bantu combina-tions] as though to see-what-happens. Apart from its presence in song, this juxtaposing of images turns up all over in the art, say, of the riddle... . Poem as opposition or balance of two or more images is also the basis of the haiku, less clearly of the sonnet. In all these the interest increases as the connection between the images becomes more & more strained, barely definable.

He quotes Pierre Reverdy:

The image cannot spring from any comparison but from the bringing together of two more or less remote realities... .

The more distant and legitimate the relation between the two
realities brought together, the stronger the image will be ... the
more emotive power and poetic reality it will possess.[6]

If our views of Romantic poetry began less with Wordsworth (and
Milton and Shakespeare as forerunners) and more with Blake,
Byron, the parts of Keats about which I will speak later in this
essay, and some of the eighteenth- and early nineteenth-century
women poets, we would see that Romanticism has played a
significant role in pitching poetry towards some its most interesting
and experimental work of our own time; at the very least we could
feel the link to this moment in literary history coming less through
Romanticism's elegiac and closural impulses and more through the
comic elements of poetic aperture. Conversely, in this book I will
read Keats's Romantic poetics through the lens of the more or less
avant-garde poetics in modern Europe and America.[7]

3
Enshrinings:
Public Memorials and Keatsian Poetics

THE KEATS ROOM AT HARVARD

Right now, preparing to begin this section, I am reading with avidity Janet Malcolm's new book *The Silent Woman: Sylvia Plath and Ted Hughes*; it speaks to my Keats enterprise. Aside from the difference between suicide and death-by-consumption (a big difference, to be sure) the two lives resonate with each other: the early deaths and late, brief flowering of 'great' poems, the myth of death at the hand of malicious persons (the critics, Ted Hughes) and the preoccupations with finding, rooting out, and inveighing against the evil forces, the way that each poet remains, over time, stuck in youth and youthful thinking (of course) while everyone else – relatives, friends, citics, the world – grows older, how both poets think in rather jejune ways, being in fact young and excitable and in love with images, and yet one tends to honor them with maturity of insight. And then this disturbing sentence from Plath (quoted by Malcolm) that easily could apply to Keats because it points to his similar absorption in an inertia of affect (or an affect of such inertia): 'Perhaps when we find ourselves wanting everything it is because we are dangerously near to wanting nothing.'

The poetry of each may achieve its mysterious power in the neighborhood of this strange mixture of fullness and emptiness, fullness – desperate, critical, tenuous, extravagant – erected as a response to emptiness. Each poet is read avidly, but do readers understand the poems as loci of specifically fragile power? Is this why Keats and Plath have long seemed quintessential poets, their poetry ratifying the possibility of life as an awesome and compelling beauty of fragile power? We not so much see that beauty is beauty-that-must-die, in Keats's phrase, as we find the beauty of will and abundance supported by a greyness, a flatness, an inanition. A poetry that asserts this relationship while barely triumphing over its very possible negative outcome appeals as a ritual relevant to the modern world.

The phenomenon of shrines in Keats's honor and – roughly the same thing – poems written as shrines to him after his death at once acknowledges the elements of fragility in their subject and seeks to eradicate it through the perpetuation of the poet in rooms and buildings and grave-sites and those 'little rooms' that are sonnets; all simplify the poem and its maker into an unambiguous perpetuated value of projected well-being. After having just visited the major Keats shrines and read and reread the dozens of poems to Keats, I confess to the pleasure of submission to the enshrining temperament for, as the nineteenth-century English poet Alice Meynell put it, 'my ended poet.' They seem to bring me 'closer' to the actual Keats, which is apparently where I would like, on occasion, to be. Recently I noted that in a very successful retail bookstore there were 13 different editions of Keats's poetry for sale, only one of which made any pretension of being complete or accurate; the rest were all selections clearly aimed at the 'general' reader of poems, which of course means that person who probably reads very little poetry at all. They were in some cases quite beautiful, well-designed volumes, in their own way further shrines to the poet. I thought, while staring at them, of my visits to Harvard, Hampstead, and Rome and my sense of the lived life in small, dull rooms, that emptiness and greyness that accompanies the summer and autumn ripeness of his famous poems ('the wealth of the globed peonies'), and the connection between these two facts of Keats's afterlife seemed very intimate. But then my awareness of and interest in showing the ideology of canonizing a poet through these facts erupts with equal intensity and I am left believing that both sides of my response to 'Keats' are true and somehow to the point, and both together are what I want to acknowledge. Criticism these days tends to obliterate those compelling things that draw us as critics to literature as being irrelevant to the algebra of literary engagement. It's all too easy to measure the weight of our literary attachments in strictly demystifying and historicizing terms and deny as important the various 'pleasures of the text' including the overtly mystifying ones produced by the relentless and popular procedures to enshrine the poet and his/her work. Yet my curiosity about these phenomena may stem from my own history or from my own period of growing up, in the period following the Second World War in a suburban city – Denver – physically far from the lands of holocausts and yet undoubtedly shadowed by the grey emptinesses they produced. Literature became for me early in life a not-so-transitory bright-ness in this world, along with the need to find strength in and through the poem, an ancillary presence, an accompaniment. Unlike the period during and following the Vietnam War, that fol-lowing the Second World War, at least for most teenagers, did not bring with it much criticism of society or demystification of its values (except in the powerful fiction, poetry, and sociology of those older than ourselves). The process of surviving with holo-caust in the collective unconscious involved discovering images of beauty that I could associate with permanence which for me meant literature. The arduous process of melting this powerful but frozen source of value into something to which the critical mind had greater access has been the story of my relationship to literature over that past 15 or so years, but presently I am just as much com-pelled by the kinds of attraction that literature originally held for me. Or rather, I am interested, and have been for at least ten years, in finding a vital place for the aesthetic in our society. I see myself, or I make myself into, a kind of representative figure (representa-tive of one? of a few? of many?) for whom the aesthetic functions as a primary experience of social and cultural, as well as intensely personal (emotional and intellectual) life. Previously (in *The Current of Romantic Passion*) I have remarked on Herbert Marcuse's arduous efforts over a lifetime to find a place for the aesthetic amidst a critical consciousness, efforts that I find admirable and important. The aesthetic response does not have to be 'merely' consoling and escapist, positing a frozen world of illusion to be preferred to social reality – 'utopian' can include the consciousness of ideological limitations; but, to shift the language, art and approaches to art that encourage forms of regression do not have to reify consciousness in a retrograde state: all is fluid; we live in *moods* that build and contribute to the uses we put them to; moods and the objects or occasions that stimulate and specify them com-plicate our experience in ways that only enhance being. So – Keats enshrined, fetishized, reduced to banalities? Let us, to be sure, dis-cover (the familiar expectation of the today's critical narratives) what has been left out and distorted; but let us also find out what remains, what has been garnered and brought forward for our attention; what did those hungry generations of the nineteenth and early twentieth centuries think about Keats's art, and what did they give to a public that has clearly been feeding (if at times in an after-dinner way) on Keats's life and poetry for over a century.

In the last few years I have returned to Harvard, where I went to college and where I immediately identified with the enshrined Keats, in order to visit the Houghton Library and its Keats Room with its heavy walnut paneling and glass cases. With my last trip (1993) I determined to visit (or revisit) the Keats shrines in England and Italy, intuiting that they too spoke and projected a special language of enshrinement that fixed our way of reading the poet's works.

23 October 1992: A large room, a huge, pale oriental rug in the middle with nothing on it except two comfortable chairs and a little table with several *Keats-Shelley Journals* on it, a vast space with glassed cases (packed with books, manuscripts, memorabilia) against all four walls beneath which are locked cabinets with overflow materials: *heavy walnut paneling everywhere*. An explanatory note on a mantle at the far wall says that the room is 'presided over by the calm and confident life mask of the poet.'

Keats *contained*. Very different from the death room in Rome where, oddly, Keats seems more alive. The books, manuscripts, and artefacts here result from the voracious collecting of Arthur Houghton, Jr, with Amy Lowell's collection in the background – where, so to speak, is she? – the paneling is oppressive. I feel in this room a half-virtuous imperialism; it is an aspect of bourgeois art, the containment – not the suppression – of the erotic life (in this instance, in poetry). Two Oscar Wilde poems on display. Here is one: very beautiful and, particularly in this room, moving:

Sonnet
on the sale by auction of Keats
love-letters

These are the letters which Endymion wrote
    To one he loved in secret and apart,
    And now the brawlers of the auction-mart
Bargain and bid for each poor blotted note,
Ay! for each separate pulse of passion quote

The merchants' price! I think they love not art
Who break the crystal of a poet's heart
That small and sickly eyes may glare and gloat.

Is it not said, that many years ago
    In a far eastern town some soldiers ran
    With torches through the midnight, and began
To wrangle for mean raiment, and to throw
    Dice for the garments of a wretched man,
Not knowing the God's wonder, or his woe?

Oscar Wilde
'86

Fanny Brawne created a serious problem for Victorian readers of Keats (see below). The publication of his letters to her conjoined two trouble-spots in the current image and value of Keats: erotic passion and commercialism. How curious, then, to find a poem condemning the commercial and acquisitive spirit here, in the heavily walnut-paneled room at Harvard! But what legitimates its presence in this room is the interpretation of the letters in relationship to the divinity of the poet and his poetry: the letters do not belong to his divinely creative work which stands above and beyond the 'mean raiment' passion, the crazy absorption in the image and body of Fanny Brawne and in the anticipation of death that passion started. Wilde's poem supersedes and interprets for us the letters themselves (many of which reside in the darkness of heavy bindings behind the wire-mesh cabinets). That's in keeping with the Keats Room, ideology. Perhaps ten Keats manuscripts on display. What touches me the most is one of the early sonnet 'To my brothers' beginning 'Small busy flames,' written on a little piece of paper – the size of the paper, with the writing all crowded together suggests the original fraternal intimacy – it, the intimacy, comes back! shocking and vital in this room. It has a few headnotes by Charles Ollier, the publisher of *Poems* (1817):

[in upper left]
1817
This was copy
for the press

[in upper right]
Sonnet by John
Keats in his own
hand-writing. Chas.
Ollier
his first publisher

Small, busy flames play through the fresh laid coals;
   And their light <whisp> crackling o'er our silence creep
   Like whispers of the household gods that keep
A gentle Empire o'er fraternal souls.
And while I search for Rhyme around the Poles,
   Your eyes are fix'd, as in poetic sleep,
   Upon the Lore so voluble, and deep,
Which aye at fall of night our ease condoles.
This is your birthday Tom, and I rejoice,
   That thus it passes smoothly, quietly:
Many such eves of gentle whispring noise
   May we together pass, and calmly try
What are the worlds true joys – <the> ere the great Voice
From its fair face shall bid our spirits fly –

How often, I wonder, did Keats write, happily, with another male in the room (cf. Charles Brown)? Closing my eyes in the Keats room, with the life mask behind me (does it turn its head at all to look at me?), I see the two brothers sitting together in their (inevitably smaller, barer, duller, hotter) room, Keats at his desk, Tom, like myself at the moment, with eyes gently shut, breathing regularly; is he – like Rilke's Eurydice relinquishing the light and the body after the feverish glance back – *schon Wurzel*, already a root? the silent Tom. I hear the faint crackling in the fireplace. Or maybe it wasn't quite *this* good, but Keats made it so in the sonnet, itself a 'pretty room' to contain the peace desired in the other pretty room. The poem is just another gentle whisper in the room, an apostrophe to the young, soon-feverish brother sunk in poetic sleep, a prayer that the spirit of this room may carry the brothers into the larger room of the world (that the world remain a room). The sonnet is written as if it should have a magical potency to place and keep them forever in it – wonderful paradox! – a gentle Empire. Tom occasions the prayer but also his poetry asleep with him like a ripe apple full of sugar is the presiding genius of the room.

It may be useful to consider Keats's and Wilde's sonnets together: after all, on this day in 1992 the artists of the Houghton Library chose to do so. They raise a concern about secrecy and intimacy in poetry. Wilde, and the many outraged lovers of Keats, wanted the young poet's passion for the younger Fanny to remain secret, to stay unpublished so that the figure of Keats (and his poetry) could soar unstained. This leaves a space for a notion of

Keats as a *contemplative* poet, contemplation being perceived as a form of mental innocence and spiritual power. 'To my brothers' is clearly a poem of intimate, non-sexual contemplation, a breath of poetic innocence. Thus the two poems in the Houghton reinforce the desired view of Keats. But good poems often refuse to obey the outlines of value that people sometimes ascribe to them; they don't settle down. It is impossible for me to read Keats's sonnet without seeing in it a plan, not at all innocent, that will place the poet in a troubling but stimulating relationship to that which lies *beyond the human scale*. The 'gently whispring noise' belongs not to strictly human discourse but to a wilder, uncontained source of poetic possibility, the ur-language that poets have often engaged in order to make sense of their social selves; the smooth, quiet state lies close to an eruptive, boundariless lake of language to be tried; Tom, a sleeping homoerotic muse, enters the room to sunder the room of the poet's tender and easy contemplation. 'Spirits fly' – the poem ends but without saying where or how or with what consequence. There is a freedom here that the museum cannot acknowledge.

The Keats Room at Harvard reminds me of the first serious American edition of Keats edited and introduced by an earlier member of Harvard nobility, James Russell Lowell (1854). I have in my hands my own copy of this edition; it is in terrible shape, with a cracked spine severing the book, at the gatherings, into two parts (between, as it happens, stanzas XXIX and XXX of *The Eve of St. Agnes*: 'And still she slept an azure-lidded sleep'). My grandfather, the poet Melville Cane, received it on his eighty-fourth birthday in April 1963 and wrote in it: 'a gift, from Hiram Haydn, of the family heirloom.' Hiram Haydn was, for many years, a distinguished editor-in-chief of *The American Scholar*. My grandfather gave the book to me sometime in the late 1970s. I must get it rebound. (Is this literary history? – that my present reading of Keats has found a path from Lowell, Emerson, Harvard, *The American Scholar* ('the American Scholar'), into the poetry side of my family?)

Since school I, like most students of British Romanticism in their forties and fifties, assume that the origins of our formative perceptions of a poet like Keats come from the likes of Matthew Arnold and Pater, the Pre-Raphaelites, and the early British biographers Milnes (Lord Houghton) and Sidney Colvin. But that British tradition does not embody the harsh rigidity of twentieth-century readings of Keats in North American universities. Perhaps, in the United States, we labor under the powerful critical collective unconscious of James Russell Lowell's 1854 'Life' (the 36-page introduction to his edition of Keats's *Poetical Works of John Keats*. For nowhere in British criticism does the adulation of Keats register such a systematic denial or rationalization of the social, political, and sexual or passional feature of his work. Without discussing a single poem Lowell erects the scaffolding that will support the majority of our readings of Keats's poems, readings the idea of which I have 'known' and accepted since I first read Keats in 1958 at age 15 in the Oxford Standard Authors volume (1955, ed. Garrod) before I had seen a word of criticism.

The essence of Lowell's 'Life' is that everything good in Keats's life-and-works does successful battle with, by overcoming, 'the world.' The essay swells with three landmark phenomena of the poet's life: his lower-middle-class origins, the devastating reviews of *Endymion*, and his death around which Lowell organizes a Keats of transcendent energies, convictions, and tendencies. Having come from a nearly anonymous family without cultural pretension, Keats nonetheless is validated by a separate, parallel ancestry – that of the great poets and the gods of poetry. Although Lowell says that he 'left school in 1810 with little Latin and no Greek,' the allusion to Shakespeare's education gives him membership in the family of the immortal bard.[1] (This is a conclusion precisely opposite to that arrived at by Marjorie Levinson, who describes Keats's career as guided by a consciousness of *never* having direct access to that family of immortal poets.[2]) Keats struggles, says Lowell, to cultivate this second, Orphic family. It follows that his energies are directed towards discovering the sources of his life not in society but in the eternal commune of the muses and the poets: 'Keats learned at once the secret of his birth, and henceforward his indentures ran to Apollo instead of Mr. Hammond [the master surgeon to whom Keats was apprenticed]. Thus did the Muse defend her son.'

The reviewers' attacks on *Endymion*, says Lowell, were systematic and devastating: 'there is no solace [for such attacks] but the consciousness of suffering in a great cause. This solace, to a certain extent, Keats had; for his ambition was noble, and he hoped not to make a great reputation, but to be a great poet.'[3] Not engaged, in other words, with a readership (or with competing readerships), Keats looked towards the 'eternal reader,' dwelling beyond interest in critical and social response. Lowell declares that the 1817 volume of *Poems* 'attracted little attention.' Perhaps, but what attention was given revealed what critics did not like about his poetry – its self-absorbed, regressive sensuality in theme and imagery, adversarial writing that shows Keats's acute understanding of prudish contemporary literary trends and preferences and his rejection of them; and his 'Cockney couplets,' those equally, flagrantly excessive, loose, recklessly and indolently enjambed lines that flaunted, according to William Keach,[4] the controlled and controlling aesthetic and political vision of Pope and his followers. Lowell, on the other hand, would mean by 'adversarial' the ability, of a strongly spiritual person, to withstand and transcend the buffets of the commercial world.

A common view of Keats, urged by Lowell, is that he represents a perfect, startling, and exemplary fusion of opposites: the bodily and the spiritual, the masculine and the feminine, and – most grandly – the life and the work (or the 'man' and the poet): 'energy and sensibility were remarkably mixed up'; '… the moral seems to have so perfectly interfused the physical man, that you might almost say he could feel sorrow with his hands, so truly did his body, like that of Donne's mistress, think and remember and forbode.' Although the fusion seems balanced, in fact the work and spirit take precedent over, absorb, the life, the body, and implicitly the social world which the life and the body engage. A recent feminist reader of Keats's ambiguous sexuality might appreciate the analogy to Donne's mistress, but would have to recognize that for Lowell any such fullness of sexual identity would create not confusion or contradiction but would merely occasion Keats's heroic spiritualization of sexuality altogether.

Only once does Lowell open a vein of the worth of Keats's poetry – when he addresses the power of Keats's language: 'veiled in the old legends which make the invisible powers the servants of some word. As soon as we have discovered the word for our joy or sorrow we are no longer its serfs, but its lords.' Again, success in poetry is expressed as a hierarchy of transcendence and control, but there is here an acute statement at least about Keats's intention: to recover a particularly mythic power that only poetic language gives. Lowell may be alluding to a power of ritual, a sacred power of a scope far greater than that afforded to an individual, social consciousness. That is, Keats's poetic language is qualitatively different from and not merely an extension of his ordinary social discourse.

The most recent complete editions of Keats's poetry, those of Stillinger (Harvard) and Allott (Longman), present the poetry in chronological order. Lowell presents a rough amalgam of Keats's lifetime editions – (a) *Endymion* (1818), (b) *1820*, (c) *1817*, and (d) posthumously published poems. He doesn't include the late poems to Fanny Brawne except 'To – –,' tucked unceremoniously between 'Fingal's Cave' and 'Hymn to Apollo,' hardly a way of calling attention to it. The Keats of 1854 more easily fits Lowell's essay than does the Keats of 1994, or even 1966 in Paul de Man's excellent Signet selection, which includes a 'late period' of largely the passionate poems to his beloved. Lowell says, near the end of his essay, that Keats's poetic gift 'is a repose always lofty and clear-aired, like that of an eagle balanced in incommunicable sunshine.' The Fanny Brawne poems reject repose as, alas, a fiction of an earlier, uninvolved life. The edges here are jagged, cries of passion strain against the sonnet form, thoughts refuse to 'flow' or come 'like leaves to a tree,' but continually drive against limits and abruptly change direction. The poem of contemplation (if it ever existed), a pure serene of poetic thought, has disappeared; in its place is the confused cry of the lover, wanting and yet fearing to be heard. Lowell, I believe, must have had access to Lord Houghton's *Life* ... (1848) but left out these poems, including the now canonical sonnet 'Bright Star.' The American selection (i.e. vision) of Keats could not apparently tolerate this poem of passionate excess in a poet whose gift was poetic repose, but such a poet fits securely into the paneled cabinets of the Keats Room at Harvard.

THE KEATS HOUSE, HAMPSTEAD, ENGLAND

6 May 1994. After landing in Heathrow early in the morning, taking the underground to east London where we crash in a friend's house for several hours, my wife and I head out on the underground again to Hampstead, walk to the Spaniards Inn for a ploughman's lunch and ale, flirt with the edges of Hampstead Heath down and around to Keats Grove and the Keats House. It's late now, they're closing the house to tourists shortly and won't budge, not even for an American scholar with notepad ready. After 45 minutes, we're on the underground once more, back to Hackney.

8 May. It's Sunday in Rome. We wake up near the Spanish Steps; the Keats-Shelley Memorial House is closed, but the steps themselves are packed with Romans. We manage to find a taxi driver who, through our broken Italian, learns that we are asking to be taken to the English, or Protestant, Cemetery. It's an hour before a mid-day closing but enough time to sink into the atmosphere of the young English poet whose gravestone says: 'Here lies one whose name is writ in water.' Roman cats (who, we are cautioned, may have rabies) rub against my leg. After 45 minutes, we cross the Tiber to the Church of Saint Cecilia and *her* remains and then walk on this sparkling Roman morning, recrossing the Tiber, watching a large wedding party disgorge from another church, to our favorite restaurant, Piperno, in the Piazza di Cenci where my wife spots the Italian movie star Roberto Benigni (*Down by Law*) and we surprise him happily with our praise of his film. Later in the day the train is taking us to Bologna.

11 May. This morning at the University of Bologna I teach a class on 'sight' in Romantic poetry, drawing my examples carefully from Mary Robinson, William Wordsworth, and Charlotte Smith. One can hear a new conversation in the voices of English Romanticism, now that the women poets are speaking up. But my lecture is cut short when the taxi arrives to take me to the station for a train back to Rome and a very quick visit to the Keats-Shelley Memorial House by the Spanish Steps. Three-and-a-half hours later and I'm in a Roman taxi to Keats's House. After an hour-and-a-half in his death rooms and a hurried dinner near the train station, again, I'm on the 'Pendalino' back to Bologna. We are nearly flying on the ground through Tuscan hills as the sun sets. Everything that draws my eyes outside – the fields, the hills, the sky – becomes a cooler and deeper blue. *Dov'è Keats adesso?*

14 May. Piazza Maggiore, Bologna. A small, neat street-sweeping *macchina* driven by a young woman cleans the gutter on the piazza where last night the communists (accompanied by rousing music piped from loudspeakers) worked a crowd of hundreds. The space is full of shoppers and other living citizens of the bright eye who walk at moderate pace: the 'heart-of-the-day ballet' (Jane Jacobs). The cappuccino is perfect and I have sweetened it. Do the citizens of Bologna notice that with each step and gestured speech they release the rare perfume of civility? For a week I have been teaching Romantic poems to young people from the region. I have cared to insist that verse be known by its perfume rising in ineffable clouds at the turn of the line.

Yesterday I picked up a book (in German and in Italian translation) I didn't know existed: poems by Robert Walser, master of miniature fictions that catch micromoments in the author's life, prose moments inviting one to protect or reveal the spark known only in writing over it in the script of the thankfully too brief. The piazzas of Bologna find the human scale. My German is fair, my Italian weaker; I read back and forth across the poems, Walser and the translation, picking up bits on each side of the page to make something I know – an ant building a little pile of sand. Do I find, here, in Bologna, between the two texts, a perfume of, as Walter Benjamin says, a pure language?

Two hours later the taxi to the airport, the flight back to London where it's grey and raining. A major football championship has quieted London streets, but it's late in the day and, with the sun and civility of Bologna still pressed at the forefront of my brain, I grab a taxi to take me once again to the Keats House, Hampstead, before it closes. This time, in the bad weather, I'm particularly irritated with the rule-bound guards of Keats's home who make me leave, in the rain, exactly at five o'clock. *Behungen* with luggage, I trudge up Hampstead High Street, stopping at a little French bistro for coffee ice cream and tea, with very soothing Edith Piaf as accompaniment, and back on the underground.

15 May. A drive to Heathrow (it's Sunday again), and home.

On this trip Keats kept appearing for brief moments and then disappearing, tenuous, dying and dying again, bright or somber, always quickly swamped by a necessary taxi ride, a closing time, a train to catch, and by brilliant impressions of other things. But the parentheses of my journey – Hampstead and Rome – were Keats's, a spiritual geography the significance of which has only sharpened with time. The dominant nineteenth-century linkage – Keats-and-death, Keats-and-brevity – was recovered through my late twentieth-century speed-up. Not only in my head, however; the linkage is declared as one walks into the Hampstead house, where the poet lived in 1819 and wrote most of his most famous poems, and one sees first of all in the entry way a picture of the Spanish Steps in Rome: Hampstead is proleptic of Rome and early death, like Coleridge's memory of shaking Keats's hand in April 1819 and imagining that he found 'death' in it. Conversely, in Rome, in the death-house, one sees in the entry way Severn's portrait of Keats sitting in his Hampstead study thinking about poetry. Poetry and death and contemplation.

Weeks after making these two trips to Hampstead, I realize that I have not had anything particularly like, presumably, the feelings expected from visiting the home of a famous poet. I realize that I was not moved, that I did not encounter his spirit, his presence, or even his absence in these rooms, which have 'museumed' the poet out of existence! I suspect that this happens often in such shrines, but why did I notice it so strongly here? The most important months of his brief life were spent here in Hampstead, most of his best poetry written here, his passion for Fanny Brawne loomed here, his friendship with Charles Brown, his meeting with Coleridge, the writing of his stupendous journal letter to George and Georgiana Keats, his recovery (if that is what it was) from the death of his brother, his questioning of career, his writing plays; all happened here at Wentworth Place. It was the locus of extraordinary activity, both outer and inner. I suspect that a psychological revolution of major proportions was occurring (see my discussion of the February–May 1819 journal letter below): for not only was he engaged in events and writing at his highest level but he also, from a different angle, seems (like the silent but efficient energies of his 'Autumn') to be waiting while inchoate forms of griefwork and choice-of-life-work and, I believe, work on his relationship to poetic language are grinding out some sort of reconfiguring of his drives and intentions. And yet there are indications of a vacancy, which may or may not belong to inner realignments. One of the explanatory signs on the wall outside his bedroom claims that Keats found his room dark and 'dull.' The long journal letter (February–May 1819) speaks of 'a dull day,' while in memorable passages he describes his 'indolence.' One could, reading these words as keys to the whole, choose to call this a time of emptiness and non-fulfillment, and thus see Wentworth Place as a cipher or merely an anticipation of the great, tragic death in Rome, with the wonderful poetry of the spring a mystery.

Part of the sense of emptiness (though the House, of course, is crammed with interesting artefacts) may come from Keats himself who eschews the domestic life. ('There is a Sublimity to welcome me home – The roaring of the wind is my wife and the Stars through the window pane are my Children.') On the first visit my wife, who did not know Brown's account of the composition of the 'Ode to a Nightingale' in the front yard, remarked that she assumed from the imagery of the poem that it had been written in a forest or woods, that is, Hampstead Heath, and concluded, after hearing of the poem's reputed origins, that Keats seemed to avoid domesticity – that is, he displaced the physical reality in which the poem was produced onto a wilder, non-domestic scene. Keats, in this regard, differs greatly from Wordsworth, who finds plenty of poetry in his garden and house and whose Dove Cottage today immediately evokes a sense of an inhabitant called Wordsworth. Thus the museum has itself picked up on these cues of emptiness and inanition from Keats. But more is at work.

The house, to begin with, has been altered since Keats lived there. A very large room on the main floor was added, which throws the balance off, increases the sense of indoor space far beyond that which Keats would have known. Display cases of arte-facts and manuscripts and publications travel around all the walls, each case being covered with a cloth (presumably to minimize light damage) which one removes to look at the exhibits; but the cloths make one think of a funeral parlor with the body and its effects on display. Then the staircase, which for Keats more or less went up to his bedroom, has been moved away from the landing, a change that once more opens the space; where now one can project onto it the possibility of serene privacy, perfect for the 'contemplative' poet, in the past it might have been stifling, or, as Keats complained, 'dark' and 'dull.' His study on the main floor has very large windows which seems more to let the inside out than the outside in, as if there were a kind of osmotic release of interiority into the backyard. As a living space, the house lacks a clear sense of inte-rior/exterior boundaries and offers odd proportions *vis-à-vis* its human inhabitants. Brown had the front room, spacious and looking onto the front lawn; the Brawnes lived in a suite off to one side. A tiny hallway currently leads from the front door to a point where one goes off to the right and the Brawnes, straight ahead to the back of the house, or left to Brown's room and Keats's study. Keats's rooms were in the back, the bedroom upstairs and the study downstairs. In a less bright and cheery version of the house, it must have been oppressive in these back rooms, particularly on rainy days. But for this reason one can more appreciate the final paragraph of his three-month journal letter, or journey letter, which announces spring breaking the dullness: 'this is the 3rd of May & every thing is in delightful forwardness; the violets are not with-ered, before the peeping of the first rose ....'

His small bedroom has been made more airy, as I said, by the removal of the staircase, but also by the opening up of the doorway so that there is almost no interior wall between the room and the hallway. At present there is a small canopy bed, a small table and two chairs (the table originally owned by Brown) and a fireplace on the wall opposite the bed. Above the fireplace is a reproduction of Severn's death-bed drawing, but it has been drawn *larger* than the original, which strikes me as significant. Not only is this bedroom of Keats-very-much-alive channeled into the visitor's eye through that other bed, but the drawing's exaggerated size calls attention not to the human Keats but to the one appropriated by myth: this is a mythic not a human scale. On the wall outside the bedroom is an explanatory plaque that identifies this bedroom with that moment in February 1820 when Keats came home shivering and flushed and spit up arterial blood, 'my death warrant,' on his pillow. There is a radical collapse of time here: 1819–1820–1821; the bedroom belongs not to the poet's quotidian wakings and sleepings and dreamings but to the end of the world, the drama of extinction, which the curators subvert with the mythicized version of Severn's sketch.

The sitting room is dominated less by death and more by the privileging of contemplation as the state in which great poetry is produced. On the wall is a reproduction by Edward Dyer (1933) after Joseph Severn's posthumous portrait of Keats in this very sitting room at Wentworth Place. Keats is sitting on a chair, with his elbow, supporting his thinking head, resting on the back of another chair. Outdoors, presumably replete with 'the song of night's sweet bird,' feeds the serene intensity of the poet's mind. On the floor of the room, precisely where the portrait indicates the location of the chairs, *are* two chairs. All that's missing here is Keats, which the imagination attempts to supply. If the bedroom tries to pitch Keats into eternity by catapulting life into death and into the myth of his eternal life, the study seeks to accomplish a similar thing by freezing the moment of poetic inspiration, giving it a permanent material existence. It is precisely the remove from life that becomes the strategy of capturing inspiration in an eternal instant. It is the act and presence of reproduction that fosters the sense of presence and authenticity: the chairs reproduce the image in the painting which is a reproduction of another painting which in turn is a memory of the poet in the privileged moment. The insistant materialism of the display (culminating in the slightly absurd-looking chairs) becomes the instrument for honoring the pure serene of spirituality in the poet's activity.

The linkage of death and poetry and contemplation is reinforced by an explanatory plaque in the room that sutures two unrelated events into immediate and permanent proximity: the death of the poet's brother Tom in December 1818 and the composition of the 'Ode to a Nightingale' five months later. The first association is not particularly relevant to this room, and the second one is only secondarily since Keats and Brown, according to the latter, put together here the scraps of paper on which the 'Ode' had already been set down.

The Keats House presents the poet's life between and centering upon two poles in the narrative: his death, anticipated, and the composition of the 'Ode to a Nightingale.'

The Nightingale: To the left of the House and to the front is a small garden plot in the midst of which is growing a very young plum tree that has replaced the original tree under which, said Charles Brown, Keats wrote the original draft of the 'Ode to a Nightingale' on scraps of paper. These scraps later were placed silently and unobtrusively by in Keats's study; and when Brown came upon them, he joined with the poet in putting them into their present order – sibylline leaves, descended from some Orphic source to the young, vulnerable poet shaded by the plum tree absorbed in the nightingale's song itself funnelling to this moment from world collective experience. The planting of the replacement tree extends the moment of creative genius into the present and future: the composition of the 'Ode to a Nightingale' will never cease; here on the front lawn it remains 'forever young.' The act of writing the lyrical poem about the deathless bird, like the poetic contemplation rendered by the two chairs in the study, belongs not to the world of social persons and to the production of poems but to the aura of poetry hurled into a world beyond death. The presence of the nightingale is powerful in Hampstead, linked as it is to the references to death and its transformations. The lines from *The Fall of Hyperion* describing Moneta's face indicate the thrust of the Keats museum:

> ... bright blanch'd
> By an immortal sickness which kills not;
> It works a constant change, which happy death
> Can put no end to; deathwards progressing
> To no death was that visage; it had pass'd
> The lily and the snow; ...

The nightingale joins together the world of death, myth, and poetry in a manner that obliviates the world.

Adding to the mythical level of Keats, the nightingale, and the poem's composition is a problem of locating the song and the event. Brown, of course, says that Keats wrote the 'Ode' under the plum tree in the front of the house, the tree where the nightingale was supposedly singing. But Severn declared that the singer was pouring forth 'in a tree *behind* Wentworth Place.' And in *The Keats House: An Historical and Descriptive Guide* (n.d.) there is internal contradiction. On p. 30 we learn that the plum-tree '*may* have been the tree under which the famous *Ode* was written.' But the author says on p. 11: 'On the lawn, immediately in front of the house is the venerable mulberry tree, – still fruitful and still flourishing despite its 300 years of growth, beneath whose branches the *Ode to a Nightingale* may have been written.' So the two songs, bird's and poet's, refuse to settle conveniently in one spot but circle the house forever, forever swirl among the trees.

The study, presumably foregrounding Keats-as-poet (with the chairs as the focus of the room), is filled on the walls with drawings of many of Keats's friends, most of them as older people: Charles Cowden Clarke (e.g. 1872), Fanny Keats (as an old woman), Shelley, Leight Hunt, Hazlitt, Haydon, James and Horace Smith, Wordsworth, Lamb. These portraits, in other words, extend past Keats's life into the mid-nineteenth century, suggesting by the correspondence of them with Keats's presence here that the room places him in an after-life. There is also a drawing of Keats's grave in Rome from the 1830s. Having noticed this after I had made the trip to the Protestant Cemetery, I was shocked to see it in a state before Severn's body had been laid to rest next to it. It seemed desolate, truly the way Keats imagined his afterlife, obscure and writ in water. It made *this* room more desolate, too, Keats tucked away in the back of someone else's house, a cipher of a person, dwindling ever towards that death marked throughout this house.

In the added room, with the display cases, there is a letter, to Mrs Samuel Brawne, Fanny's mother, from 24 October 1820, written in the Naples Harbour while the *Maria Crowther*, Keats's transport to Italy, was docked in quarantine. The letter, like many other artefacts and signs at Hampstead, sends the interest forward to Rome and death.

Give my Love to Fanny and tell her, if I were well there is enough
in this Port of Naples to fill a quire of Paper – but it looks like a
dream – every man who can row his boat and walk and talk
seems a different being from myself – I do not feel in the world –

The passage isolates an appealing feature of the posthumous Keats,
at once fully alive to the details of the world around him and yet
elevated, through the approach of death, to another order of being.
Later he almost repeats himself: 'O what an account I could give
you of the Bay of Naples if I could once more feel myself a Citizen
of this world.' In this same dream-letter, he speaks of the pretty
Miss Cottrell, at a more advanced stage of tubercular wasting than
himself, whose 'bad symptoms have preyed upon' him, and then of
Fanny: 'I dare not fix my mind upon Fanny, I have not dared to
think of her.' He feels better when the first 'Lady vanishes' and
cannot stand to commit emotions to the second. On the other hand,
'the only comfort I have had that way has been in thinking for
hours together of having the knife she gave me put in a silver-case
– the hair in a Locket – and the Pocket Book in a gold net –' The
objects fill with passion and stay filled into the afterlife, for us. But
we don't see what Amy Clampitt calls the 'starved stare before the
actual, / so long imagined Bay of Naples.' Or, his plan, as Tom
Clark describes it

> ... to kill the monotony
> of his agony during the days of the quarantine
> when his final formal love cry to Fanny Brawne
> was sent from the hideous closed cabin
> with laudanum, but Severn kept the bottle from his hands.

In the same room are two tiny, lovely watercolors by Severn
done on the journey to Italy: the first of the *Maria Crowther* and the
second, called 'Moonlight at Sea,' about which Severn said: 'After
this I drew a Moonlight scene from the Sea which took until 12
(middle watch) [after] 'the house had gone to rest' – Keats was in a
sound sleep.' The moon is full in the sky, gleaming on the waters;
all else is dark. These bring one closer to Keats than most anything
else in the room, to know what the sky was like that night while
Keats slept. But it projects its own allegory in the received tradition: the poet, in his posthumous fame, glows amid the darkness of
the rest of the world.

Oh yes, and there are the two Brawne rooms, off to the right of the rest of the house as you enter. These moderately spacious and airy rooms give little sense of the people who inhabited them in 1819. Just cases of *objets*, bits of this and that the most interesting of which is a sampler by Fanny Brawne, with lines on it sewn in from Thomson's *The Seasons* ('Autumn,' ll. 177–92), beginning 'The lovely young Lavinia once had friends' and ending 'Her form was fresher than the morning rose,' not particularly distinguished but calling to my mind Wordsworth's Lucy, 'fresh as a rose in June,' Fanny – as powerful and as ephemeral as Lucy, making all the difference to Keats, in life and to his readers afterwards when (see below) she enters the late nineteenth-century debate about her commercial versus her spiritual value to the poet.

Six small turn-of-the-century illustrations of Wentworth Place hung together in a corner of the back room make the house look larger, more elegant than it actually is. An original marble bust of Keats by an American, Anne Whitney, worked in 1873 and based on the life mask renders him in baby-smooth features, with thick, well-combed hair, still unravished.

But … there are those thin walls. Fanny, the beloved, is just feet away. Can a young man fantasize love and then enact it when she and her mother can be heard tramping about, at times perhaps quarrelling, interrupting thought (even poetry) in the next room? Mustn't one associate the beloved with distance from home? As painful and fateful as the voyage to Italy was, it may have been ('had Keats lived') a necessary physical separation from her to make her more real along with his feelings for her and the possibility of a more mature life of love. One stares at the walls between the two quarters – Keats/Brown and the Brawnes – and wonders about the contradictions and constraints of love in Hampstead, the claustral effects of such relentless proximity, and then recalls the more dominant message of the museum: Keats is the poet of Rome and death, of unfulfilled loved for a young woman, living just a few breaths away from the 'current of [his] heart.'

The basement, along with the bare kitchen areas, one for Brown/Keats and one for the Brawnes, offers a gift shop full of many items including tapes of the poems, gift books of poems, the life mask (which I purchased for the third time – mine keep breaking), notepads, bookmarks, and many postcards including:

- two different nightingales (one from a 1st century AD fresco at Pompeii);
- Keats's drawing or tracing of the Sosibos Vase;
- 'Isabella,' by Joseph Severn (1877);
- 'Isabella,' by Averil Burleigh (1911) ('Hung over her sweet basil evermore');
- 'Isabella,' by William Holman Hunt (1866–68);
- 'Isabella,' by J. E. Millais (1849);
- 'La Belle Dame,' by John Waterhouse;
- 'La Belle Dame,' by Sir Frank Dicksee;
- 'Eve of St. Agnes' (Madeline after Prayer), by Daniel Maclise (19th c.);
- 'Eve of St. Agnes,' by William Holman Hunt;
- a painting and an ambrotype (*c.* 1850) of Fanny Brawne;
- a photo of the study with the two chairs.

Almost every one of these postcards features a woman (even including the urn as unravished bride with its maidens over-wrought), and most of the women exude female desire or the woman as object of desire. Three of the Isabellas show her cheek pressed – simultaneously in longing and fulfillment – against her pot of basil. The knight-in-arms and the beautiful lady hunger towards each other, lips apart. Madeline undressing. Eros. Erotic confusion. Rich, dark colors. I've spread out all these cards on the table and think: this is what they've taken from the Keats House and exiled to the basement!

But the nightingale – twittering on a twig, perched on a pole thick-set among leaves: where is the sexuality here? And in Fanny Brawne, demure, composed. Where is the erotic confusion of Keats's life?

The stability of Wentworth Place after Keats's death was not always secure; or, to put it in terms of the fever caught by his elegists, destruction, death, and oblivion haunted the house for a century. Fanny Brawne's mother continued to live here in the 1820s; as she was saying goodnight to some party guests in 1830, her dress caught fire and she burned to death. In 1921 a drought caused the old plum tree (the Nightingale's) to 'perish.' A year earlier Wentworth Place was almost torn down as an 'eligible building site' for an enormous block of flats. Having heard about it by accident, the Mayor of Hampstead, calling on Sir Sidney Colvin and Amy Lowell from Boston, formed a National Committee to preserve the house of Keats.

DYING – PIAZZA DI SPAGNA, ROME

Two illustrations of Keats-in-Rome have shocked me: one, already mentioned, shows Keats's grave without Severn's next to it (and Severn's young son between and slightly behind the two). How much do we associate the death of Keats with Severn? – Severn's unfailing friendship and aid during Keats's last months and Severn's lifelong preoccupation with Keats, in his own paintings and drawings and in his later life in Rome. For us, because of this history and because of the image of the two graves together, Keats is not alone in death. Yet before Severn's death in 1879 Keats's grave, alone only with flowers and with no name on the stone, bespoke the desolate anonymity which he projected onto his future. When she refers to the poet sailing to Rome as 'tattered cargo' and to the Keats of the Spanish Steps as 'the mind's extinction,' Amy Clampitt acknowledges the trajectory of anonymity, the trans-formation of a consciousness into an object (as in the death of the Homeric hero who exchanges his *psyche* for a mere thud of tumbling flesh in the dust of Troy).

We associate the dying of Keats with the apartments on the side of the Spanish Steps, a beautiful slope of wide stairs sweeping upward to the Church of San Trinitá del Monte, almost always swarming with people moving either towards or from business or just gathering for the 'heart-of-the-day ballet.' So it is also a shock to see, as one does in the Keats-Shelley Memorial House, illustra-tions of the same site before the construction of these steps or even of the apartments in which Keats lived. In one picture there is simply a gentle slope of land upward, with a tree on it and a man walking down the grassy incline. The presence of the pastoral where one expects to find the urban is unsettling: it seems like a gaping wound.

Bathsheba Abse, former curator of the Keats-Shelley Memorial House, said she was planning to put a bed in Keats's bedroom, to make it look more like it did in 1820–21. 'Everyone walks in expect-ing to see a bed,' she said. It will be very simple, given that Keats and Severn had very little money, just an iron frame. As with the Hampstead House, little here remains of the original contents of the rooms, but one feels nonetheless closer to the poet and his experi-ence. This, after all, *is* the house of dying and death. In his bedroom are the 48 painted flowers (apparently roses) on the ceiling, which Keats stared at for several months. And here is the chimney piece, 'original to the house, which dates from 1725, and was preserved when the furniture in the room was burned, and the room was redecorated after Keats's death. In this fireplace Severn sometimes cooked for Keats or heated up their food which was sent in to them from a small Eating-House, La Trattoria del Lepre ("of the Hare") in Via Condotti facing Caffe Greco.'

The room thus radiates experience out and back, connects to other points in space and time. And looking up at the Keats-Shelley Memorial House from the Piazza di Spagna with a late afternoon sun shining brilliantly on its warm pink stone, I lose the depth of death interior to these walls; the house, with its cheery exterior beauty, commands that one view it. The secret, which I believe I hold above what this swarm of Romans know, of poetry and death, remains far, far within. I carry the secret down the Via Condotti and stand with it across from a building, now an expensive jewelry store, from which Severn would bring Keats his food. Back in the room I look out on the Steps through windows in Keats's bedroom that bring good daylight into the dark corner. You open onto the noise of the Steps – hear the 'busy hum' now of people on this warm May day – up and down the steps, walking, sitting, talking, shouting, calling. So much life, so close to the dying one. A flower stall, shirts and other souvenirs, *motorini*, horse-drawn carriages, cars at the other end of the square – tall palms and brilliant red roses. Maybe 200 people, most under 25, just hanging out. Pigeons. Someone long-haired takes off his coat, finds an empty spot, and settles in. (In the 1960s the Spanish Steps were the place to get drugs in Rome.) *I* can go out there whenever I wish. Here Keats was, thoroughly confined, growing more and more entwined with his ceiling-flowers – did he see them wave and tremble? Did he feel the sun on them? Did he, like Van Gogh, that other death-steeped artist, live in sunflowers?

The tiny bedroom is full of Keats associations – at one end a glassed-in case where the head of his bed probably was, many items on the walls. I like the weird mix of items – there is not a lugubrious cast to the room, nor is it particularly *tasteful*. There is a picture of Enfield School. Drawings of people like Cowden Clarke, Carlino Brown (son of Charles), painting of a middle-aged Fanny Keats, the haunting silhouette of Fanny Brawne – quite beautiful, really, she holds herself high and, in fact, she is about the highest thing in the room and next to the open window. They've placed her next to Fanny Keats, who in turn is next to Keats painted among the trees near the shore of the wide world, one leg characteristically crossed over the other. From Keats we go down to a painting of the English Cemetery and under that is a copy of the 'To Autumn' manuscript at Harvard. Keats-in-contemplation, to death, to the most telling of seasons and problematic for the history of his readers: the season of fulfillment but also anticipating the season of death.

I am not surprised to find 'To Autumn' here, but the other manuscripts in the room are startling since they swerve back to life, to beginnings, to love. Over the fireplace are manuscripts of the opening lines of *Endymion* and the opening lines of *Lamia*. One needs to be reminded of them to imagine their effect in this pinched room of tattered cargo:

> A thing of beauty is a joy for ever:
> Its loveliness increases; it will never
> Pass into nothingness; but still will keep
> A bower quiet for us, and a sleep
> Full of sweet dreams, and health, and quiet breathing.

> Upon a time, before the faery broods
> Drove Nymph and Satyr from the prosperous woods,
> Before King Oberon's bright diadem,
> Sceptre, and mantle, clasp'd with dewy gem,
> Frighted away the Dryads and the Fauns
> From rushes green, and brakes, and cowslip'd lawns …

Both poems speak of the warmth and brightness of spring and summer and most of all of the life-in-things, the principle of animation that Keats's poetry acknowledges from the beginning and to which it is arguably dedicated, the dreams of sleep, the Dryads and Fauns of the natural world.

Next to the fireplace (and therefore close to the above manuscripts) is a small display case with first of all a manuscript of *Lamia*, Part I, ll. 185–90:

> … for she was a Maid
> More beautiful than ever twisted braid,
> Or sigh'd, or blush'd, or on spring-flowered lea
> Spread a green kirtle to the minstrelsy.
> A Virgin, purest lipp'd, yet in the lore
> Of love deep-learned to the red-heart's core.

So death is only one of the markers on the walls here – there is school, family, *the lover in her haunting, thin blackness, the profile which gives all but eyes and lips* – but the lips are across the room (just a few feet) in the lines from *Lamia*, who the poet asserts, has the sexuality of a virgin – still unravished ('I should have had her in health I would have remained well'). Like 23-year-old John Keats, Lamia is new to love but learned in the lore of love, knowing perhaps too much for what has been experienced. Red-heart's core: sexual, to be sure, but lugubrious in this room, Pre-Raphaelite, anatomized, ghoulish. The lines, however, make an odd kind of sense when we return to the display case to notice the two, crude drawings by Tom Keats of, supposedly and probably, his older brother John. In the first he is sitting open-legged, head-up; it's a poor drawing, the proportions are wrong making the poet look outsized and monstrous. In the second he is sitting cross-legged with book resting on knee, looking down at the book, arm on the pages. The display case reveals Keats's confused, unworked-out relationship to love and sex. The full, overripe imagery assigned to Lamia exists alongside the as yet more natural intimacy and relaxedness of brothers. The case also reminds me that the eroticism of *Lamia* belonged to a *scheme* for earning money, for becoming a popular poet.

In this room all is collapsed: sexual love, brotherly love, death, and poetry. Poetry, here, is the thing he did, his craft or hobby or ambition, not transcendent but connected to the rest of the room by a parataxis of objects.

Diary entry from eighteen months later, 30 November 1995, 26 Piazza di Spagna: Keats's bedroom where he lay dying seems to me smaller than it did on my last visit – more prosaic, more confining. If in 1994 I found each picture on the walls a vortex of possibility and richness, if I found the room *lyric*, today it seems bare and dull, a place that a poor, unknown, very young poet far from home, on the far shore of a miserably exhausting sea-journey, who at one moment threw his rotten food out of this window onto the Steps below, might die ....

Walking above and beyond the Spanish Steps on the Pincio, where Keats briefly walked and rode horseback, I now see the roofs of Rome, blurred images in the dusk, more like ocean waves seen from the air. The moon follows. From here, Keats is insignificant in

Rome, far from that desperate, blank, airless room with mortality like a fist in his throat.

Perhaps the lovely warm burnt red-pink colors of surrounding buildings, the softness of Roman air and mingling voices would flush the greyness of dying and give it occasionally the color of wonderment, poetry perhaps the soft undersong, the image of a ten-syllable line (he imagined a new poem in late November). Indeed, according to Robert Gittings's biography Keats was in good spirits from 29 November to 10 December ('an Indian summer of self-renewal'). But all this would occur – as is typical of the late stages of tuberculosis – in the interval between blood-spitting and blank, starved enervation and the incommunicable inwardness – or is it emptiness – that dying can produce: maybe the warmth of the colors of the buildings with a late-afternoon sun warms only the living who stroll, who *fanno la passeggiata*.

A lovely pair of sonnets by Karl Shapiro (1984) catches our inevitable 'mortal' poet and his absorption into the collective, while he lay in the small room at 26 Piazza di Spagna. The first begins:

> The water-poet lay down with flowers above
> And the half-sunken boat below his head.
> Bitter with young and unrespondent love
> Poetry lay foundering on the Italian bed.
> Vision and terror held him while he bled
> Himself of character and identity.
> Upon the coffered ceiling his soul fed
> Festoons of roses to his fevered eye.

The roses, noticed by every visitor and written about by many, are now part of an eternal nature yoked to his feverish entropy. In the third quatrain of the second sonnet his transformation into the collective seems complete:

> Now he's a library and a sacred name,
> Voices take off their shoes when here they tread,
> And quite a few remember the belle dame
> Who sidewise leant beside his glowing head.... .

But the final couplet recovers the voice of the living person:

> When to his healthy friend he turned and said,
> *Severn, please don't be frightened*, and was dead.

Metonymy: the trope in this instance for the *translation* of the poet into his poetry, the dying person into his living name: the crossing over, however, followed by the crossing back ('he turned').

Staring at the walls, the fireplace, the portraits and manuscripts and memorabilia, the rosette patterns on the ceiling, hearing amid the internal silence of the room the sounds from the Piazza and the Steps, one needs the letters of Keats and Severn of the last months to recall the wasting body, the flarings up of dying rage, and the presence of Joseph Severn with a terminal patient. Reading the physician Lord Brock's pamphlet, 'John Keats and Joseph Severn: The Tragedy of the Last Illness,'[5] one realizes that Keats's dying was handled consistently with bad judgment and medical incompetence. Partly, of course, this resulted from general ignorance about the nature and treatment of tuberculosis. Severn's letters report not only his own views but those of Dr James Clarke (Keats's physician in Italy) and Keats himself in a way that applies, to the medical situation, Keats's existential and epistemological self-observation of two years earlier about straining at particles of light amid great darkness. Keats probably should not have gone to Italy at all, the disease having progressed too far for a change of climate to benefit him and the sea voyage being thoroughly debilitating. (Severn called the ship the *Maria Crowther* a 'black hole.') He should have been given less strenuous exercise and more rest and more fresh air. He certainly should not have been bled as a response to his own vomiting of blood. And as for Dr Clarke's diagnosis, that Keats's illness was primarily in his stomach and not in his lungs, Lord Brock observes: 'It is difficult to criticise doctors in the generally backward state of medical knowledge then, but even in the absence of the stethoscope it is difficult to condone such a rubbishy assessment.'[6]

In contrast to the vision of Keats-in-eternity given by the poets of the nineteenth and early twentieth centuries, to be discussed shortly, the poet as a source of energy and well-being for others, a site of calm beauty and power, the actual process of the final weeks exhibited the chaotic dissolution – accompanied by rage and discouragement and grief and occasional wellings up of resistance in the form of pleasure or humor or expressions of concern for his caretaker – that is dying, a process exacerbated by medical ignorance and bad decisions.

Like the passengers on the *Maria Crowther*, tossed helplessly about the English Channel, Severn and Keats seem to have been mentally and physically at sea in their small rooms, locked in the condition of the dying patient. No moment, to me, more exemplifies the state of their isolation than that around what Severn called 'that cursed bottle of Opium,' which Keats, having bought before leaving England, wanted to drink in order to end his miserable days and which Severn, under the influence of Dr Clarke, kept from him. In the letter of 25 January 1821, Severn wrote to John Taylor about this monumental struggle:

> The hardest point between us is that cursed bottle of Opium – he had determined on taking this the instant his recovery should stop – he says to save him the extended misery of a long illness – in his own mind he saw this fatal prospect – the dismal nights – the impossibility of receiving any sort of comfort – and above all the wasting of his body and helplessness – these he had determined on escaping – and but for me – he would have swallowed this draught 3 Months since – in the ship – he says 3 wretched months I have kept him alive – and for it – no name – no treatment – no privations can be too bad for me – I cannot reason him out of this even on his own ground – [7]

Gittings and Clarke assume that Severn was firm and fixed in his position. But the passage goes on to register Severn's genuine ambivalence:

> but now I fall into his views on every point – before I made every sacrifice for his personal comfort in his own way – trying every manner to satisfy him – now I must do the same mentally – I even say he should have this bottle – but I have given it to Dr Clarke – the fact is I dare not trust myself with it – so anxious I was to satisfy him in every thing – [8]

He listened to Keats, he seems to have changed, and absorbed the latter's longing for death as right for him, but was caught by the equally strong drive, supported by Clarke, to preserve life no matter what the cost. Severn was fully identified with Keats and swayed with him like a ship amid high waves. (Back in September Severn had written to William Haslam: 'I have the vanity to think that Keats and myself would continue our harmony even in sleep.'[9]) He at least *thought* the unpopular view that the dying person should have the right to put an end, under such hopeless and uncomfortable conditions, to his own life.

How different dying was then from what it has currently been made into! It occurred in medical ignorance and amid no serious technology. The energies brought to the denial of death in today's hospital world were unknown, and yet it is moving to observe Severn writing to friends about his expectation for Keats's imminent death while he keeps it from the subject himself. Even though medical knowledge abounds and teams of researchers fill the sites of dying with hope and possibility, there is still – in, for example, many cancer and AIDS patients – the expectation of certain death. Many AIDS patients, as the disease progresses, reveal within themselves the presence of tuberculosis, an eerie archaism from the nineteenth century. And while opera has insisted that tuberculosis could be a 'beautiful' death, Keats's seems to have more resembled that of AIDS – ugly and terrifying. What remains in both instances is the opportunity for a connection between the living and the dying, a loving attention. This Keats received from Clarke as well as Severn, and this he gave back in kind. But in this regard Keats's dying was no different from his living: his capacity to give and receive affection was high and continual.

On 28 January 1821 at 3 a.m., in the little room Severn completed his famous death-bed drawing of Keats under which he wrote: 'Drawn to keep me awake, a deadly sweat was on him all this night.' I am aware of two wonderful poems about this drawing, one by Rilke and the other by the Australian poet Dennis Haskell, who – like many poets writing about Keats – are intent on knowing, or representing, the *countenance* of the beloved person, whose pain and life (like that of Eurydice) are lost to us. Gittings – in the role of biographer – moves the drawing back into the life: 'Keats's head, the hair matted with sweat, cast a shadow on the wall in the light that flickered from the little fireplace with its decoration of marble lions. Immense exhaustion filled his weary sleeping features.'[10] The poets turn to the crisis of poetry, which is the problem of response to death: the vanishing of the person into oblivion and meaninglessness or the conservation of the image of the person in meaning and in terms of the larger structures that include but are not determined by death.

According to Rilke (in J. B. Leishman's translation) and Haskell, Severns tells only part of the story of his sketch. The pain, says Rilke, 'falls back again upon its dark possessor.' The eye and the mouth ('Song's open door') will never see or sing again; we grieve the ceasing of all change. Yet the countenance is altered in the drawing: 'Not that of features still combined / with the same understanding as before.' By the close of the third stanza, the transformation of death seems complete. But the fourth and final stanza offers, through the forehead

> A lasting bridge across those liquefying
> relationships, as though it were belying
> the locks that cling about it, gently grieving.

Haskell is absorbed in the shadows behind the head:

> ... haloes of shadow
> surround his sunken face,
> hair or mystery in shadow
> circular and grotesque ... future.

The shadows have a content that shifts the balance from the 'exhausted player' (Tom Clark) to an extended world of meaning and value and connection, crossing the barrier of an 1821 death into the world of his fame and his influence. To give to shadows such substance is a kind of creation, a making new that sets this revised version of the poet and his work on an *open* trajectory of possibility and chance. Neither poem seems to me temperamentally elegiac although both register the sadness of the poet's end. Both call the dying forward, out of the little room, and into the world of new deaths and new poems.

The Keats-Shelley Memorial House, of course, is much more than the death-bed room. The next room belonged to Severn, now a library of primary but mostly secondary materials of Keats and Shelley. Bathsheba Abse recently added a large display case which includes among many items an absurd collection of *hair*, preserved by Leigh Hunt of Keats, Shelley, and himself. This, to me, concretizes the tinge of homosexuality that touches the life of Keats.

The remaining rooms on this floor were originally a separate apartment; in 1906 the Keats-Shelley Association purchased all of them and created the shrine to the three second-generation Romantic poets Byron, Shelley, and Keats. Walking out of the Keats rooms into the larger ones devoted to Shelley and Byron, one cannot help but notice in the pictures and artefacts the representation of wealth and women and travel and connections. Suddenly one is mingling with the English poetic aristocracy. (On one wall portraits of Lord Byron and Keats are practically side by side.) By comparison Keats seems a poor cousin indeed. Yet how easily, in this setting, one forgets Keats's lowly origins and meager supports. The iron bedframe, to be added, one hopes, will help remind the tourist of the differences among the three. The poetic aristocracy towards which Keats seems to have yearned must come from sources other than inherited wealth and position; I believe that the many poems written over the century after his death bent their energies to ensure that end. Here by the Spanish Steps it is more complicated. First of all, the house really belongs, as it were, to Keats: *he* actually lived and died here. He brought Shelley and Byron, nearly a century after his death, to be celebrated here with him. By yoking the three together, the Keats-Shelley Memorial Association violated some of the uniqueness of Keats, the complexities of his life and his poetry, his social as well as poetic situatedness. His death and his poetry appear as part of an institution, which focuses on an afterlife to the detriment of the history of his lived life. The Keats-Shelley Memorial House and the nineteenth-century reading of Keats's significance and influential power include him in the aristocracy of poets by deflecting him from history and into an Orphic community of great world poets.

Signora Vera Cacciatore, an earlier curator of the Keats-Shelley Memorial House, wrote a pamphlet that is sold, in several languages, at the House: 'A Room in Rome.' She moves back and forth between giving a brief history of the House with testimony from persons who have visited over the years, always moving or at least about being moved, to recording the poet's own testimony in prose and poetry of his experience there and of his positions on poetry and on his life found in his letters. The book is a good companion to the tourist. But it has as well a subliminal plan, to embroider the room of death with a vision of the poet's principles and of images that characterize this vision during his final months in Rome. He is first of all a poet of contemplation and, by extension, a poet of Negative Capability, who by striving to overcome his ego streams into the collective life of the culture.

In every way it is an impressive house, belonging to Piazza di Spagna, that very Roman piazza, but, because of Keats, belonging to the world. He bought it – to quote Shelley's words – *He bought it with price of purest breath,* to give room to poetry and poetry is the voice of mankind; it is Man's voice, freed at last. When this abstract voice gets the chance of finding a body again, then the miracle is accomplished. This chance is given daily, in Rome, in the small room where John Keats lived, as the lines of *Endymion* or *Lamia* or the *Ode to Autumn* are whispered or recited. It is the New Zealander and the Australian on his way back home; it is the passer-by who happens upon the plaque outside the house; it is the Oxford or Harvard student, the old lady from Glasgow, the young girl from old Calabria. Negative Capability, which allows the poet to be content with half knowledge, allows 'Keats' to mingle with the spirits of people as various as the workings of his own brain. Cacciatore specifically links Keats's formulation to the universality of his appeal. She also associates the importance of 'flowers' (as in the 'festoons of flowers' on the ceiling over his bed) and 'water' (as in 'Here lies one ...') with this appeal and with the essence of his appeal deriving from his ties to nature and to the sources of consolation in our lives. She directs the tourist to 'read' Keats as a poet not for *his* but for *all* time because he has, as Shelley said (quoted in the pamphlet) been 'made one with Nature.'

Travelling from Hampstead to Rome and back to Hampstead, I experience images of Keats floating free of history, free from their moorings in place. Partly this results from my activity, my moving and thinking and imagining and taking in imagination the sights previously moored. But this is a function of the houses in Hampstead and Rome, as well, which offer in the entry way of each a picture that rightly belongs to the other place: the Piazza di Spagna in Hampstead, Keats in his Hampstead study at the Piazza di Spagna. An engraving of the gravestone in the Hampstead study, sketches done in Hampstead by Tom in a display case in Rome, the original death-bed sketch by Severn in Rome, a reproduction in the Hampstead bedroom. These crossings – like my travel-crossings described earlier – have what feels like an intentional result, to lift the poet and his images out of their history into a transcendent ether that insists upon his being a poet 'for all time.'

Reproductions of documents and paintings, even in the postcards, similarly affect the poet's and the poems' historicity. 'Mechanical reproduction,' rather than reducing the 'aura' around the original, may actually extend or isolate the aura away from its origins, as if the reproduced pieces circled like satellites around a no-longer existent sun.

THE GRAVE – PROTESTANT CEMETERY, ROME

Heap turfs of daisies on my
pretty pagan grave,
beneath the pyramid's
restless eye –
and say if with thy
crystal conscience thou
wouldst not wish thine
own heart dry
of blood – so in my
veins red life
might stream again –

Tom Clark

Outside the cemetery the cars and trucks of Rome honk and screech around curves and accelerate and jam to a halt; 'there' the noise is endless and pressing but 'here,' inside, it seems far away. Umbrella pines rise over the gravestones shielding from this world the world of the dead – lacing the sky with their green. The pyramid of the consul Cestius (as Samuel Johnson said of the Egyptian pyramids, a monument of the insufficiency of human enjoyments) dominates eccentrically, incongruously over the cemetery; but it *is* there, so what can one do but accept it as incongruous but part of the reality of the place. Keats's stone stands, a burning speck beneath the trees, across the graveyard, in the corner, as the eye turns from the pyramid. His plot is paired with Joseph Severn's (added 1879), behind and between the two being that of Severn's infant son. It's shocking to see that one of the great poets of the modern Western world has a grave so small, so simple, and so (apparently) shunted to the periphery of the property. Yet as I stand there, now having walked over to it, or sit on the bench by it, the perspective shifts and the margin, as it were, becomes the center. The thin stone slabs making a nearly square rectangle contain the plot easily, like a sonnet. (His poems, however, of visionary playfulness push against forms.)

The grave, unlike many graves of famous figures, startles one by its more-or-less human dimensions: its size does not correspond to the mythic stature of the poet; I feel the presence of an actual person; it makes one weep, but this also may explain how one can sit next to it on the bench in great calm.

Keats wanted daisies to grow over his grave. Daisies are so common, almost weedy! This does seem to fit with the grave's dimensions. One must recall, however, that Wordsworth called the daisy 'the Poet's darling':

> A hundred times, by rock or bower,
> Ere thus I have lain couched an hour,
> Have I derived from thy sweet power
>   Some apprehension;
> Some steady love; some brief delight;
> Some memory that had taken flight;
> Some chime of fancy wrong or right;
>   Or stray invention.

And in the daisy's presence: 'Oft on the dappled turf at ease / I sit, and play with similes.' In this constellation of graveside elements and associations, the fusion of Keats as poet and Keats as person is apparent.

Today the sky is absolutely blue, the temperature about 40°. A small woman of perhaps fifty-five bends over, stationed, to read the epitaph on the gravestone. Her husband seems restless and wanders among the other tombs. Both visitors are small, perhaps Keats's height. A cat (one of dozens roaming the cemetery or basking in its sun) sits on the warm stone, stares at me, licks the dirt away from its paws. His eulogists urge Keats to *sleep on*, like his Endymion: one feels sleepy here, a drowsy numbness. I feel on the edge of Keats's oblivion, or that Keats's fame settles, by definition, so close to his vanishing.

At the bottom of the gravestone a dirty postcard is stuffed behind the leaves:

> Such water that can
>   nourish a parched intellect
>   my friend
> Sleep well
>   Ramon

The sense of the history of pilgrimages to this spot, recorded in many poems and some prose, overwhelms me. The diminutive, marginal grave-plot suggests, along with anonymity, an intimacy, recalling those elegies to recently dead brothers: for example,

Catullus's *carmen 101* ('multas per gentes et multa per aequora vectus') with its tortured line-opening, 'nunc tamen interea,' now nevertheless meanwhile, which expresses (along with 'nequiquam,' in vain) the sense of urgency, skepticism, impotence, and hope; the simultaneous uselessness and necessity of the task of speaking to the dead ('mutam cinerem,' mute ash) in their permanent silence; the juxtaposition of the eternity of death with the utter immediacy of speech (Catullus, in his hasty journey to his brother's grave, saying that his poem is wet with his tears). This poem gets adumbrated by the early-Romantic Italian Ugo Foscolo's sonnet 'In Morte del Fratello Giovanni' (1803).

To the side of the plot and on the wall of the cemetery is a plaque: under a laurel wreath in stone is Keats's profile and then the following:

> K-eats! if thy cherished name be 'writ in water'
> E-ach drop has fallen from some mourner's cheek;
> A-sacred tribute; such as heroes seek.
> T-hought oft in vain – for dazzling deeds of slaught
> S-leep on! Not honored less for Epitaph so meek!

The perfusion of eulogy poems from the decades since 1821 (which I will consider later) and of the many sentiments cannot mask the simple power of the grave – its location, the transparent, limpid power of the stone, 'all that is mortal of,' the violets and green covering the grave. 'Here lies one whose name was writ in water' conveys obscurity, absence in the corner of the English Cemetery. But in the above acrostic, as typically happens with poems written to or about Keats, 'water' becomes the sign of grief given to persons who acknowledge the sacred privilege of the heroic in the young, sleeping poet. This tempers and shifts the obscurity of the gravesite into its opposite, fame, and attention turns from the abode of the obscure to 'the abode of the eternals.' Wild rose vines fall along the plaque.

The history of the grave marks this shift: in the years after Severn is buried next to Keats, and Severn's infant is buried behind and between them, Keats becomes part of an institution. Whereas Keats has the *broken* lyre on his stone, Severn has a *full* palate and five strong brushes on his; whereas Keats has no name on his stone, Severn has his own name and also Keats's on his. Keats's short, broken, assaulted yet anonymous career is absorbed into Severn's long and relatively serene one. Tradition's obsession with the purity of Keats is reinforced, only a few feet away from the poet's grave, by the gravestone of Severn's son:

> Here also are interred
> the remains of
> Arthur Severn
> the infant son of
> Joseph Severn
> Who was born 22 Nov 1836
> and accidently [*sic*] killed
> 15 July 1837
> The poet Wordsworth
> was present at his baptism
> in Rome

The association of the death of a young child with the poet who wrote most eloquently upon the innocence of young children (and the death of his own daughter in 'Surprised by Joy') establishes the circuitry of innocent youth cut short with Keats's life and further propagates here in the grave-plots an aristocratic family of poet-artists whose work is validated through the Wordsworthian eye of youthful genius and wisdom. (In a different aristocracy, etched into the back of Severn's gravestone are the names of nearly four dozen contributors to this monument for Severn, including several poets who wrote poems to or about Keats: J. W. Fields, D. G. Rossetti, H. W. Longfellow and the famous editor of Keats's works, H. Buxton Forman.)

4

Keats Enshrined in Poems:
the Nineteenth-Century and Traditional Poetics

In the past 13 years there have been two major sequences of poems about Keats in English – one by Amy Clampitt (*Voyages: A Homage to John Keats*) and another, book-length, one by Tom Clark (*Junkets on a Sad Planet*). Individual poems have also recently appeared – including those by Jorie Graham, Jane Kenyon, Galway Kinnell, Stanley Plumly and Mark Halliday. Surrounding the year of the 200th anniversary of his birth (1795), poets seem to want to give voice to or about Keats; they want him to keep on living, or to bring him back to life. But the phenomenon of poems about Keats is not new; indeed I suspect that no English poet except Shakespeare has occasioned as many celebratory and evocative poems as has Keats.

The first striking thing to observe is that most of these roughly one hundred poems written from 1823 (not counting Shelley's magnificent *Adonais*) to the present are driven less by Keats's life or by his poems and more by his death; Keats is that poet who by definition died young. He wrote beautiful poems in all too brief a span – and died. After reading through these many eulogies, I can go further and say that, for the tradition of poet-readers, Keats has become the poet of death. Now, other poets have died young, like Shelley himself; and other poets have died fairly young – Byron, Dylan Thomas; and others – well – how old is 'too young?' But only Keats seems entwined in death. Alice Meynell, as I said earlier, called him 'my ended poet.' Let me propose that this fact turns out to be, no matter what else it may be, a comment on his poetry, a comment on what it is and on what readers would like it to be. Keats-in-his-death has substantially contributed to his *canonical* status among poets and moreover, to a canonical – that is particular, biased, and rather limited – way of reading his poems. These tribute poems probably fed significantly the shape that the Keats shrines at Harvard, Hampstead, and Rome finally took.

Keats-in-his-death first of all means 'Rome.' Towards the end of his life Keats remarked that he seemed to be living a 'posthumous existence.' The American poet Stanley Plumly, ascribes to Italy in the final months of Keats's life the posthumous landscape of Keats's mind. Italy isn't really Italy but a kind of coldly golden reverie of memory and anticipation. Riding in a carriage on the road from Naples to Rome, Keats – according to Plumly –

> is alone,
> among color and a long memory.
>
> In his head he is writing a letter
> about failure and money and the ten-
> thousand lines that could not save his brother.
> But he might as well be back at Gravesend
> with the smell of the sea and the cold sea rain.
> waiting out the weather and the tide –
> he might as well be lying in a room,
> in Rome, staring at a ceiling stylized
> with roses or watching outside right now
> a cardinal with two footmen shooting birds.

Plumly distinguishes this state from the quotidian facts of history that typically are called the poet's life:

> The biographer sees no glory in this,
> how the living, by increments, are dead,
> how they celebrate their passing half in love.

Italy for Keats is a gentle slope towards death such that one asks in vain: where does life end and death begin? Or, where does death begin and poetry end? The last line quoted from Plumly – 'how they celebrate their passing half in love' – quotes Keats himself: 'And many a time have I been *half in love* with easeful death, / Called him soft names in many a mused rhyme.' Death is embedded in Keats's poetry, Italy in England. Italy, then, becomes the land where Keats, as Tom Clark suggests in *Junkets on a Sad Planet*, enters a kind of delirium in which he 'is unable to differentiate the objects of his vision from purely subjective phenomena,' where he begins to identify with death.

The poets say that in Italy he drifted upward into a dreamscape of easeful death, a place of ripeness, a place from which he is not to be pitied but praised and rejoiced in. The place of this Elysium is Rome, specifically the Protestant Cemetery. Rome, in these poems, is not the irritating and crude city that his friend Joseph Severn, laboring on Keats's behalf in his dying days, describes negotiating with great difficulty.

Nor is it, precisely, the gentle, late-autumn pleasure that Keats knew for about 25 brief days (15 November to 10 December 1820). As Gittings sketches it:

> The view from the windows, as he rested in the little bedroom, was a constant delight. The piazza was full of small workshops, mosaic-makers, engravers, sculptors and plaster-moulders. On the Steps lounged a continual crowd of artist's models in local costumes, waiting for hire; their bright colours mingled with those of huge stalls of flowers, brought in for sale from the Campagna, whose scent floated up to Keats. By day, the Steps were alive with song, conversation, and the shuffle of innumerable sandals. By night, when the thronging people and the flocks of goats or cattle had departed, the fountain in the piazza came into its own, Pietro Bernini's broken marble boat, the Barcaccia, with lion heads at prow and stern. Its quiet music sent Keats to sleep, until the early morning voices of the passers-by woke him gently again.[1]

Keats also often climbed the Spanish Steps to the Pincio, the spacious hill of tree-lined walks and the Villa Borghese, overlooking Rome and St Peter's dome, 'a dark grape colour in the lemon-tinted dusk.'[2] Or, he would walk through the city among the shops and banks to the Corso. Inside the apartment at 26 Piazza di Spagna he listened to Severn play Haydn who Keats said was like a child, 'for there is no knowing what he will do next.'

Nor is the Rome of the poets the Imperial City with its layered acknowledgments of conquests and defeats, of deaths and imprisonments, instead rather the Eternal City, absorbing in pastoral comfort the history of civilization that now includes the spirit and poetry of John Keats. Untouched by the vicious early nineteenth-century politics of culture (the *ad hominem* attacks on his long poem

Endymion, which, the myth went, weakened his sensitive poet's nature to the point of death), invulnerable to the eroding flush caused by the tubercle bacillus, 'Rome' bespeaks the brotherhood of poets, the poem as flower of Elysium, the tear as the rounded liquid speech of unequivocal love and adoration: 'I love my poet.' Wrote Shelley in *Adonais*, his elegy on Keats:

> To that high Capital, where kingly Death
> Keeps his pale court in beauty and decay,
> He came; and bought, with price of purest breath,
> A grave among the eternal. – Come away!
> Haste, while the vault of blue Italian day
> Is yet his fitting charnel-roof! while still
> He lies, as if in dewy sleep he lay;
> Awake him not! surely he takes his fill
> Of deep and liquid rest, forgetful of all ill.

To praise Keats gravely is to go to Rome, quickly, with a sense of urgency, and, like Keats sunk in his own lake of death, forgetfully, to recover a time before experience. The poem-to-Keats enacts the *nostos*, or return, finding Keats in his true home, a bit like Aeneas enshrined in Rome, the place of his origins as well as of his destination. But, like the returns in the epics, this one is not a regression to a place and time of greater simplicity; rather – in wish, at least – it carries with it the self-consciousness, the historical entanglements, the 'erring' paths taken by real persons and societies, towards a new synthesis. Keats's (or the poets') 'Rome' is congruent with Schiller's Elysium as the manifestation of art's gathering and utopian reworking of history; it is precisely not the crude elementary Arcadia of traditional pastoral. I say 'wish' because the poets, in wishing synthesis, often produce the Arcadian reduction. In this century of Romantic, Hegelian, and Marxian syntheses, these poets perhaps compose with not enough attention to the difficulties of embodying or predicting utopias, they take too literally Shelley's command to 'Come away! Haste' to Rome. Shelley himself, on the other hand, acknowledges magnificently the losses and gains of urging Keats into the abode of the eternals. Whereas many of the poets praising Keats see a simple economics of gain – Keats as an eternal assures, by the nature of his vast empathetic genius, that the gentle rain of universal consolation will pour upon the living – Shelley perceives that Keats's afterlife of fame, his metamorphosis into the *ground* of poetry, will allure captivated living poets into spectral, isolate existence:

> The breath whose might I have invoked in song
> Descends on me; my spirit's bark is driven,
> Far from the shore, far from the trembling throng
> Whose sails were never to the tempest given;
> The massy earth and sphered skies are riven!
> I am borne darkly, fearfully, afar;
> Whilst, burning through the inmost veil of Heaven,
> The soul of Adonais, like a star,
> Beacons from the abode where the Eternal are.

Shelley's poem, of course, stimulated Keats's canonization. *Adonais* voices the general nineteenth-century view of Keats's death: emotionally sensitive to malicious public criticism of his work, he was weakened to the point of death physically. Triumph, which Shelley's poem promises, can only occur in 'the abode where the Eternal are.' In many later poems praising Keats one hears echoes of Shelley's original. As Susan Wolfson has suggested, the death-centered view of Keats begins with his life and poetry, is immediately taken up, translated, by Shelley in *Adonais*, and thereafter is a feature of 'Keats' for the rest of the century. 'Dying,' she quips, 'it turns out for Keats's fame, was a good career move.'[3] But it is the later poets who have given Keats his home in eternity with an intensity and a specificity and a commitment that is unusual for the praised poets of the past. I am asking here if these poems written over a century and a half have significantly contributed to how we have read Keats. Having recently discovered a cache of such poems at Harvard University's Houghton Library, published not as a collection but simply found singly in 50 or 60 books of poems by various hands, I have begun to meditate on the complex exchange that has occurred over time among Keats's poems, these tribute poems, and the history of Keats-interpretation that together begin to dream a dream of a poet who died too soon and long ago in Rome.

The canonization of Keats begins with the perceived tragedy of Keats's life, the vicious mishandling of his poetry by his contemporaries, and by Keats's own sorrowful self-evaluation in his proposed epitaph: 'Here lies one whose name was writ in water.' His worth for posterity seems inversely proportional to the degree of personal and institutional animus directed at him along with the striking brevity of his life.

Some of the poems take the position of defending a person wrongly accused of a crime. Indeed they become in the nineteenth and early twentieth centuries a courtroom full of indignant lawyers who accuse the accusers – the critics of Keats – of maliciousness and wrongheadedness and praise the defendant for his greatness but greatness as innocence and purity; his moral grandeur stands in stark contrast to the willful, mean-spirited egotism of his detractors. A sonnet by S. Laman Blanchard published only two years after Shelley's *Adonais* in 1823 inaugurates the tribute poems with what will become a characteristic outrage:

> ... I did think
> That moment on the cold and shadowing shame
> With which thy starry spirit hath been crowned.
> How vain their torturings were! for thou didst sink
> With the first stone cast at thy martyred fame;
> How like the snow that's ruined by a sound!

Keats had not yet established, by the writing of this poem, and would not for another two decades, his fame as a poet, so that Blanchard cannot easily refer to the clear success and quality of Keats's art and craft. The poem occasions the assumed antagonism between the poet and the hostility of society as embodied in the critic. Both this and *Adonais* pitch the dead poet into a field of fame through his apparent martyrdom, a fame that precedes any posthumous assessment of his actual worth as a poet. In this narrative of Keats, the critic is completely the villain, characterized not only as unfeeling but myopic. Nearly 100 years later Perry Marshall can write of the evil critic:

> His pin-point eyes detect the fine defects,
> His ready pen is much a microscope,
> The dotless 'i' this organ quick detects,
> Though in the dark its guardian had to grope.

The critic thrives on *the gaze*, which – like Apollonius's in *Lamia* – withers its object; in this regard Keats's poetry (and character) are raped by criticism, a feature of the myth that confirms the tendency to see him, sympathetically, as feminine.

Genius is risk-taking and exploration. The critic, by contrast, is confident in his superficiality. Says W. C. Bennett in 1860:

> Even as a saint,
>   Ere he be crown'd with heaven, devils abuse,
> So bat-eyed critics as a devil paint
>   Genius, to hail whose greatness they refuse.

A second phase of attack, this time less on critics and more on commercial publishing, occurred late in the nineteenth century when Keats's love letters to Fanny Brawne were first published. At this time his fame as a poet was secure; but equally secure was the association of his fame with a kind of divine innocence that nonetheless retained a radical vulnerability to criticism of his personal life. This his wild and wonderfully articulate passion for Fanny Brawne was thought to be. Matthew Arnold, in his famous essay on Keats, shows dismay at these letters, and more to the point at their publication, arguing by implication that they were proof that Keats could never achieve the stature of true poetic greatness, such as that possessed by Shakespeare and Aeschylus.

> ... a merely sensuous man cannot either by promise or by performance be a very great poet, because poetry interprets life, and so large and noble a part of life is outside of such a man's ken, ...

But the poets continued to defend him against those who wished to find fault with his passions. Curiously none of his Victorian adherents supported or praised him *for* his intensities; none found that these love letters might have been a measure of his greatness as a poet, although Arnold's preoccupation with sensuousness in the essay suggests that he knew he was onto something very telling about Keats but saw it in a negative light.

Swinburne, for example, referred to the occasion for these letters as a 'loathsome love,' which should have remained with Keats in the grave. They sought to separate his personal life from his poetic afterlife, insisting upon his eternal innocence. Moreover, they were outraged that people should wish to *buy* this book or these letters, that the poet's fine soul should be sullied by the commercialization of his private, in their view, failings. A sonnet by John Albee, published in 1883, expresses the fury at the publication of the letters:

Rest, hunted spirit! Canst thou never sleep?
Ah, when the ghouls and vampires of the Press
Vex thy all tender soul in wantonness
Canst thou know aught of peace, but still must weep!
… My curse upon this prying, prurient age!
And curst the eyes not closed in angry shame!
For him whom English air and critic pen
Twice baffled ere his splendid, youthful gage
Had measured half the heaven of love and fame,
This shameless book has murdered once again!

The spirit of these retorts is that given at Hamlet's death: Vex not his ghost, except that it is said of a journalistic avidity for sensational feature stories. Swinburne, in the following year 1884, wrote four 'Post Mortem' sonnets full of scorn and rage and putting on a mock-helpless rage. Here is the fourth:

Shame, such as never yet dealt heavier stroke
On heads more shameful, fall on theirs through whom
Dead men may keep inviolate not their tomb,
But all its depths these ravenous grave-worms choke –
And yet what waste of wrath is mine, to invoke
Shame on the shameless. Even their natural doom,
The native air such carrion breaths perfume,
The nursing darkness whence the vermin broke,
The cloud that wraps them of adulterate ink,
Hath no sign else about it, wears no name,
As they no record in the world, but shame.
If thankfulness nor pity bids them think
What work is this of theirs, and pause betimes,
Not Shakespeare's grave would scare them off with rhymes.

At times the phenomenon of Keats's posthumous existence reminds me of the moment in the *Iliad* when the Achaians and Trojans are fighting over the body of the dead Patroclus. Keats is fetishized, both by those trying to save his soul from commerce and criticism and by those who wish to sell it to the highest bidder. A lock of Keats's hair, a page from a book, a sight on Hampstead Heath, the Roman grave itself all are worshipped as signs that bring the poet closer to the present. Or there is the following:

So, you have been with Severn, and have heard
The tongue that spoke to Keats the last farewell,
His on whose breast our darling's dear head fell,
When his great life sank from his latest word.

In a 1920 sonnet by Christopher Morley, written on the occasion of the auctioning of a letter by Keats to Fanny Brawne, there are two fetishized objects that compete with each other for attention and value: the first is the letter itself against which Morley protests its sale, and second are two allusions – one to Keats's sonnet, 'Bright Star, would I were steadfast as thou art,' and one to Shelley's *Adonais*, which after a century had become almost as much a venerated touchstone as any line from Keats. The sonnet is addressed to the purchaser of the letter, a Dr Rosenbach:

How about this lot? said the auctioneer;
One hundred, may I say, just for a start?
Between the plum-red curtains, drawn apart,
A written sheet was held.... And strange to hear
(Dealer, would I were steadfast as thou art)
The cold quick bids. (*Against you in the rear!*)
The crimson salon, in a glow more clear
Burned bloodlike purple as the poet's heart.

Song that outgrew the singer! Bitter Love
That broke the proud hot heart it held in thrall –
Poor script, where still those tragic passions move –
Eight hundred bid: fair warning: the last call:
The soul of Adonais, like a star.....
Sold for eight hundred dollars – Doctor R!

The sonnet reveals a kind of competition between the fetish as object of commercial use and the fetish as quotation and allusion. Morley, of course, would rather have the reader see quotation and allusion as triumphing over the cold quick bids of the auction, and in a sense, through this poem, they do. But from another point of view he is deftly telling the tale of the afterlife of a famous poet in a capitalist society. The letter becomes emphatically material, a script, the writing itself as well as a tattered sheet for a play of tattered if tragic passions.

But Keats's passions, even, or particularly, for Fanny Brawne, cannot solely be described as tragic. They were – as is much of Keats's poetry – also labile, inchoate, playful. In Morley's caustic response to the auction-of-passion, however, tragedy reigns – the 'bloodlike purple' recalls to me, outrageously, the genuine tragic passions of Aeschylus's Cassandra, the lyric nearly indecipherable cry of desire and death and admonition, the cry of the nightingale. But is this distortion of the emotions at the auction itself? Do those buyers sense the erotic play between the young poet and his beloved? And do they wish, so to speak, to bottle it in the commercial, largely male, world?

After reading a dozen poems written in this spirit, one forms a picture of the history of a poet whose audience wanted to find him or place him outside of our world, untouched by criticism and commerce, untouched – one might say – by a social existence. And yet their attitude often makes him strangely susceptible to commerce, to having a relentlessly material, fetishized value. One even begins to suspect the sonnet form itself, in which many of these poems occur, as being fetishized, not so much a poem that elegizes the poet or a poem reaching out across the blank space of isolation or a poem of celebration and conservation of the image of the great poet, but a poem become a token, a sacred object that, in the act of composing it, surrounds the poet and Keats in a magic circle of eternal mutual possession. The posthumous figure of Keats, when prayed to and praised, when defended against evil persons and social practices, assures the writer that poetry affirms the existence of a place of no corruption, a place that, in Keats's phrase, pours a balm upon the world.

Such a view drives the common response to Keats's self-inflicted epitaph – 'Here lies one whose name was writ in water' – and organizes an astonishing number of tribute poems arguing against the obvious implication of Keats's judgment, that his poetry and the name of the author behind it are headed for oblivion. Working from the language of the epitaph itself, these poets assert that Keats was thoroughly wrong about his fame; they recast his suggestive imagery towards an affirmation of being, power, and healthful influence:

> Art thou aware
> Thy name in every singer's orison
> Is writ in stars, not water?
>
> Elsa Barker

Thou whom the daisies glory in growing o'er, –
Their fragrance clings around thy name, not writ
But rumor'd in water, while the fame of it
Along Time's flood goes echoing evermore.

D. G. Rossetti

'Here lieth One whose name was writ on water.'
But, ere the breath that could erase it blew,
Death, in remorse for that fell slaughter
Death, the immortalizing winter, flew
Athwart the stream, – and time's printless torrent
grew
A scroll of crystal, blazoning the name
Of Adonais!

P. B. Shelley

What was his record of himself, ere he
Went from us? 'Here lies one whose name was writ
In water.' While the chilly shadows flit
Of sweet St. Agnes' Eve, while basil springs –
His name, in every humble heart that sings,
Shall be a fountain of love, verily.

Christina Rossetti

Thy name was writ in water – it shall stand:
And tears like mine will keep thy memory green,
As Isabella did her Basil-tree.

Oscar Wilde

With these passages (and others like them) we need to shift the focus from the defense of Keats's spirituality in the face of the perceived inroads made by criticism and commerce to what we might call the mythic or collective content of his afterlife in poetry. With his death, according to the tradition we are evoking here, Keats leaves the realm of actual poetry – its passions, its politics, its religion, and above all its poetics and vocabularies – for the *ground* of poetry, its mythic substrate. Poetry has its origins and its destinations; it speaks in a language of social persons but it can be said to hearken to its

origins in the historical and mythic waters of the past of its civilization. Those who praise Keats do so by registering the high degree of
his absorption into the *waters* of poetry, the fount from which all
poetry springs and which great poets continually replenish.

The fragment from Shelley (third in the previous list) elegantly
charts the mobilization, after the death of the poet, of the non-
human sources of life that turn Keats into Adonais and water into a
scroll of crystal, an ur-language of permanent resource. Death
releases energies that transform, renew, and establish a presence (if
not a text) new to the world and rejoicing in it, and a name.

In this regard I suspect that Keats's sad judgment had its ambigui-
ties, that for a poet to be associated with water after his death, with
the stream of Orphic music, was not such a bad thing, and that it
reflected his opposite drive and self-estimate: to be among the great
English poets. But it is the drive of many of his poems, to reach out to
sources of benign energy beyond the ordinary capacities of persons,
to engage – often through prayer and petition – the foreignness of the
collective energies of civilization and anchor them to our isolateness
in order to let us become familiar, or known, to ourselves: 'Already
with thee!' The tributes of later poets merely follow out the optimistic
trajectory of Keats's allusive epitaph. The tributes themselves, this
snowfall of modest, worshipful poems, *are* the announcements of
Keats's fame, the *rumor* of it, in the sense of a soft, insistent, spiritualized noise or hum. Wrote Richard Watson Gilder in 1887:

> Many the songs of power the poet wrought
> To shake the hearts of men. Yea, he had caught
> The inarticulate and murmuring sound
> That comes at midnight from the darkened ground
> Where the earth sleeps; for this he framed a word
> Of human speech, and hearts were strangely stirred
> That listened.

Many images in these poems encourage the identification of the
dead Keats with the collectivity and the ground of poetry. They cast
an Ovidean atmosphere over him, a sense of metamorphosis of the
harried, passion-burdened person, swamped by financial worries,
disease and death, troubled love, hostile reviews, and, thankfully,
the love of beauty in all things, into, with his own wasted death,
one of nature's things, a nightingale, a hyacinth. His grave provides
fertile soil for the flowers which are both his own poems and those
that come after him. At night the moon-goddess spreads her mild

beams over the Roman grave, as she did to her favorite Endymion who was granted not death but eternal sleep and whose spirit thus sweetly permeates the air of those who love him. And by association, Keats the poet becomes the pastoral singer 'mid sylvan glades where ran Bacchantic revelers.' Death transforms Keats from a poet who writes poetry into the ground of poetry itself, the source and end, outsized, smaller and larger than human but benign and therefore granting to us our sense of human scale.

Shelley, in a passage from *Adonais* that reminds one of Wordsworth's Lucy as an evocation of the ground of poetry and its power, says of Keats:

> He is made one with Nature; there is heard
>   His voice in all her music, from the moan
> Of thunder, to the song of night's sweet bird;
>   He is a presence to be felt and known
>   In darkness and in light, from herb and stone,
> Spreading itself where'er that Power may move
>   Which has withdrawn his being to its own; ...

Compare this with lines from Wordsworth's 'Three years she grew in sun and shower':

> Myself [says Nature of Lucy] will to my darling be
> Both law and impulse; ...
> And hers shall be the breathing balm,
> And hers the silence and the calm
> Of mute insensate things.... .
> The stars of midnight shall be dear
> To her; and she shall lean her ear
> In many a secret place
> Where rivulets dance their wayward round,
> And beauty born of murmuring sound
> Shall pass into her face.

Keats becomes a 'Lucy,' a source of light and motion unseen but felt, to be praised because it grants health to others. This association with a feminine figure corroborates the view of scholars like Susan Wolfson and Margaret Homans who have documented the issue and the presence of feminine characteristics and temperament – perhaps including the veiled rape allusions that reinforce the violence done to him by his critics – imputed to Keats during the building of his reputation.

The Lucy-effect seems even more important than the poems he wrote:

> And yet we know his spirit never dies,
>   Sweeter than all the songs he ever sang,
>   Soothed in the languor of eternal Sleep,
> Like his beloved Endymion he lies,
>   Forever beautiful, forever young!

The poets typically address him as Endymion, Adonais, Hyacinth, Sebastian, and most of all the nightingale, absorbing him into the mythology of Greece and Europe so that he participates in the westering movement of soul that was thought to authenticate the spiritual life of England in the eighteenth and nineteenth centuries. These figures take up marginal positions in human stories – caressed by women, fought over by goddesses, kept childlike, beautiful in both masculine and feminine ways, beloved by women but also by men, brought to early and in some cases violent deaths. Yet the problematics that these figures imply are kept low: the nightingale's iron time is invisible, and only its song, 'liquid and musical,' remains.

The same transformation of the passional, political rough edges of these images into images of serenity apply to the view of his life. The broken reed of his short life in time seems paradoxically to ensure the completeness or perfection, the roundedness of his life for later generations. Thus Elizabeth Barrett Browning in *Aurora Leigh* sums up his life and fame with a beautiful transmutation of a life lived for oblivion with a name writ in water:

> By Keats's soul, the man who never stepped
> In gradual progress like another man,
> But, turning on his central self,
> Ensphered himself in twenty perfect years,
> And died, not young (the life of a long life
> Distilled to a mere drop, falling like a tear
> Upon the world's cold cheek to make it burn
> Forever).

This extraordinarily dense passage works upon an infelt understanding of the tradition of Keats tributes and perhaps of the tradition of poetic genius compelled to early death. The waters of oblivion have become the tear, not sorrowful but nourishing, of fame acting sharply upon the survivors. This has occurred by a refiguring of the operative metaphor of life: if life is ordinarily a journey (stepping in gradual progress), life for Keats has been a distillation; if the journey ordinarily is mapped upon a path, here it is mapped on a sphere; if the journey implies an outwardness with experience as a form of encounter, here the distillation implies an inwardness, an ensphering of self to its essence. Miraculously the completeness of the poet's life (whose life can be said to be complete?) has been with it from the start, during twenty perfect years. The process works, paradoxically, to expand its influence – the hero-poet becoming the tear that weeps for its own loss and the inevitable losses of persons but also the tears of those persons falling in acknowledgment of their grief at the loss of the poet: a universe of falling tears created. To anticipate the later part of this essay, we can associate such completeness ascribed to the life with a poetry of closure that assigns all representations of experience to the past; the soul presents itself as tear-like in its efficiency because it celebrates elegiacally the end of experience. Like Keats on his death-bed, the tear embodies the same acutely precious moment: all essence, and then nothingness. The distilled 'mere drop' that is now Keats – his central self writ in water – comes from afar, from the abode of the eternals, to console but also to revivify a disheartened world.

With reference to the concept of the afterlife, Hannah Arendt (in *The Human Condition*) distinguishes usefully between immortality and eternity, the former – derived from Homer and the pre-Socratics – refers specifically to our humanity: we have an individual consciousness and an individual profile of living and in this sense do not conform to cyclical or static accounts of existence assigned to the rest of natural creation. Immortality is the proposed extension of this human life along its linear and singular path beyond death, in terms of its *productions, such as poetry*. Eternity, a largely Christian construction, describes a state of being, a change of state such that one's productions as a mortal are no longer relevant. We assume that a poem written in tribute to another poet refers to the latter's immortality, the power of his or her poems to then survive the poet's death in the lives of readers, so that the naming of a poet is a metonymy for poems written. Yet the poets who wrote to or about Keats often imagine him in a new state, an Elysian fields of comfort and peace, and, because of this radical translocation, he beams his concern for distraught humanity. From the 'abode of the eternals' Keats's poems no longer command attention since they have been superseded by his radiant spirit. It's a matter of place: if Keats in life and his poems were and are 'here,' he now resides 'there.'

We do, of course, continue to read his poems; indeed, Keats's poems, particularly his Odes, have assumed a place at the top of perennial interest among the canonical lyrics of the British tradition. How, then, does the fact that the nineteenth and early twentieth centuries have created an 'eternal' rather than an 'immortal' poet affect the way we read him?

His lyrics (just as, in E. B. Browning's and others' poems and in the biographies, his life, though cut off, is miraculously complete, like Shakespeare's) are evaluated through the category of completeness. His last great poem, 'To Autumn,' for example, continues to receive the ultimate praise, his most 'perfect' poem and one of the most 'perfect' short poems in English, the poem closest to that *easeful death* praised in the 'Ode to a Nightingale,' where it is *rich to die*. Autumn: the season of perfection, completion, maturity, the season that grants to its poets a vision of life as comedy written under the category of death. In a poem of autumn, and Keats's is the prime specimen, the parts submit graciously before the whole. The value of maturity or perfection stands outside, surrounds, the poem's craft, its moment-to-moment discoveries.

The 'Ode on a Grecian Urn,' which may be the poem that stands for all Romantic poems, adds another important dimension to the feature of perfection: it is about a work of art, moreover, a Grecian work of art. A poem about a modern person looking at an ancient artefact, the 'Ode' dramatizes the coming-into-being of ancient Greek culture as history's and art's golden age, characterized by its *serenity*, gained by appreciation after its historical moment. It has, as Lionel Trilling long ago said, pastness as one of its attributes. Yet the urn itself contains images of actions of great moment – high passions and ritual sacrifice; the observer does not simply acknowledge the passions of lovers, for example, but transposes them into an eternity of stasis; the lovers, he assures them, will be 'Forever warm and still to be enjoyed, / Forever panting and forever young.' Or, they will *be forever*. It is, I believe, no accident that in the tribute poems Keats himself is often 'forever young' and, like his urn, a 'friend to man' who equates beauty and truth. Love, death, religious and civic ceremonies, all acknowledged on the urn, are finally absorbed into or swallowed up by the serene benignity of a

Grecian forever. The urn, one might say, normalizes or subdues the intensities depicted on it, and the poet/observer/speaker normalizes the intensities of the urn as it existed in time – where the beauty of narrative and decoration merged in significance with its use, as a container of ashes. Modern criticism has by and large affirmed this value of the Ode, that art transcends the experience represented within it, subdues that experience, freezes it, and prefers the fact of its agelessness to the fact of its recalling and perhaps recreating a series of passionally and socially alive occurrences. Similarly in the 'Ode to a Nightingale' the 'here' of the poem is defined by weariness, fever, and fret where men sit and hear each other groan, and 'there' is the place of the nightingale, distanced from the world, a mythical creature of the collectivity who, says Keats, was not born for death.

The place in which we find art stamped as 'forever young,' where we admire art for beauty and tend to minimize its potentially disruptive forces, is the museum. Indeed, the critic Philip Fisher has called the 'Ode on a Grecian Urn' 'a museum with one work inside.' The museum is a kind of eternity, an elsewhere, a 'there.' The museum director tends to collect works that contribute to that sense of 'there'ness. In Keats's opus the museum is that selection of poems that over the years become honored for their projection of the value of art over experience, and the other poems are denied inclusion or devalued. The tribute poems have helped to turn Keats into a museum, the anthologies and selections that make up what we call the canonical works of a poet and, in the reading of him, the canonical interpretations, which emphasize – just like the subsequent tribute poems – the elegiac, death, and the artistic *unity* that death, or rather the afterlife of fame, imposes upon the disparateness and variety, the raggedness of the historical and erotic moments that comprise poems as originally functional entities.

5

Readings

'ON KEATS'S GRAVE,' ALICE MEYNELL

He said that the greatest delight of his life had been to watch the growth of flowers. And when dying 'I feel them growing over me'.

> They waited not for showers
> But made a garden in the dark above him,
> – Stayed not for summer, growing things that love him.
> Beyond the light, beyond the hours,
> Behind the wind, where Nature thinks the flowers,
> He entered in his dying wandering.
> And daisies infantine were thoughts of his,
> And different grasses solved his mysteries.
> He lived in flowers a snatch of spring,
> And had a dying longing that uncloses
> In wild white roses.

This poem by Alice Meynell (1869) is one of the most serious of nineteenth-century poems about Keats. The rambling length, both of the poem and of the shifting feet of lines, attests to the entwining of the poet in her subject, which is the spirit of poetry operating currently in the dead Keats and the living Meynell. The opening paragraph ascribes to death the unnatural attention accorded Keats by those who buried him, unable as they were to let the season, in its own time, acknowledge his cathexis to flowers. Yet death, in February, does not preclude his absorption in flowers because, in his case, the home of this poet is the home of the growth of all things.

> Down from the low hills dark with pines
> Into the fields at rest, the summer done,
> I went by pensive ways of tombs and vines
> To where the place I dream of is;
> And in a stretch of meditative sun

69

Cloven by the dark flames of the cypresses
Came to the small grave of my ended poet.
– I had felt the wild things many a dreamy hour
Pushing above him from beyond the sea,
But when I saw it
It chanced there was no flower;
And that was, too, a silent time for me.

Many poems recount the pilgrimage of a living poet to the grave of Keats in Rome, but this one retraces the psychic connection and impulse as well. The world-attraction to Keats is literal, drawing the poet to Keats as if the grave were in some sense one of the sources of life. The journey is not through cities but through the signs of death-and-afterlife and through vegetation; the state of mind is dream, even the sun is meditative. The urgency of the living poet, her poetic silence, pushes her towards Keats: it's November, with no flowers and no poems.

O life of blossoms – Proserpine!
O time of flowers where art thou now,
And in what darkness movest thou?
In the lost heart of this quiet poet of mine
So well-contented with his growth of flowers?
Beyond the suns and showers
Stirrest thou in a silence that begets
The exquisite thought, the tuneful rhyme –
The first intention of the violets,
and the beginnings of the warm wild-thyme?
Indeed the poets do know
A place of thoughts where no winds blow,
And not a breath is sighing,
Beyond the light, beyond the hours,
Where all a summer of enchanted flowers
Do mark his place, his dying.
Sweet life, and is it there thy sceptre passes
On long arrays of flowering grasses
And rows of crimson clover?
Are these the shades thou reignest over?

Come ere the year forgets
The summer her long lover.
O Proserpine, November violets!

As with Keats's and Shelley's odes, this one turns to the invocation of a deity, this one flourishing the purple sex behind all flowerings. Proserpine's rape (corresponding to Keats's death at the hand of violating critics?) lurks obscurely behind the reference, perhaps signalling the woman poet's intimate relationship to the lyric voice of pain, a voice hinted at throughout Keats, with the association to Proserpine and to the nightingale. The source of this poetry dwells 'beyond' and 'behind' the visible world; the poet journeys in the vicinity of that collective power of inspiration and fruition.

> – Where art thou now?
> And in what darkness movest thou
> Who art in life the life of melodies?
> Within the silent living poet's heart
> Where no song is,
> Where, every one apart,
> Arrays of the morn fancies err
> Vaguer than pain in sleep, vaguer than pain,
> and no winds stir; –
> Over these shadows dost thou reign?

The flowers gone back to darkness, the poet opens, in their absence, to the world of dream hoping to find the goddess there. She also hungers for authenticity of voice, for a goddess who rules a land in which she can thrive. The death of Keats does not overwhelm her; rather she welcomes the possibility of entwining herself with his and Proserpine's size beyond the human scale since it is only in a place of such outsized and still geography that the voice for her poetry will be found.

> See now, in this still day
> All winds are strayed and lost, wandered away,
> Everywhere from Soracte to the sea.
> All singing things muse in the sun,
> And trees of fragrant leaves do happily
> Meditate in their sweet scents every one,
> The paeans done.
> All olives turn and dream in grey at ease,
> Left by the silver breeze.
> Long smiles have followed the peal of mirth.
> – But silence has no place for me,
> A silent singer on earth.

Although it is November, the day emerges serene, the imagination of the poet, her previously outlined paradise of poetic origins, seems here to equivalate to the natural day. This Wordsworthian at-onement ought to open the way for Proserpine in her life, but it hasn't yet.

> Awake!
> And thro' the sleeping season break,
> With young new shoots for this young poet's sake,
> With singing lives for all these dreams of mine,
> O darkened Proserpine!
> Out of the small grave and the thoughts I love
> Stir thou in me and move,
> If haply a song of mine may seem a dim
> Sweet flower grown over him.
> Oh come from underground and be
> Flowers for my young dead poet and songs for me.

> November 1869

Meynell tries to establish the relationship between the death of the poet, the life or sources of poetry, and the making of new poems. Keats being 'her' poet, she prays not in the general case, to all poets, but only to her ended one whose peculiar power stems from his proximity – by virtue of youth and innocent strength and by his genial wisdom about flowers – to the sources of life. Proserpine, Psyche, Mnemosyne, Diana, all feed him in vibrant waking dreams; the living poet needs to know that in order, through poetic prayer, to postpone the oblivion of the dark months.

'JOHN KEATS,' DANTE GABRIEL ROSSETTI

> The weltering London ways where children weep
>   And girls whom none call maidens laugh, – strange
> road
>   Miring his outward steps, who inly trode
> The bright Castalian brink and Latmos' steep: –
> Even such his life's cross-paths; till deathly deep
>   He toiled through sands of Lethe; and long pain,
>   Weary with labor spurned and love found vain,
> In dead Rome's sheltering shadow wrapped his sleep.

O pang-dowered Poet, whose reverberant lips
And heart-strung lyre awoke the Moon's eclipse, –
   Thou whom the daisies glory in growing o'er, –
Their fragrance clings around thy name, not writ
But rumor'd in water, while the fame of it
   Along Time's flood goes echoing evermore.

Rossetti defines Keats's life as a crossroads – one road the outward life of London, undistinguished, run-down, the place of the novels of Dickens, Gissing as well as the place of hostile readers wishing oblivion upon him, and the other road the *inward* life of poetry marked as Greek and mythological, a place of muses and divinely engendered sleep. Death is the point of the crossing of paths and the transportation into the lap of the present poet not of words but of fragrance of daisies, 'rumor' or the hum of mighty workings (in Keats's phrase) and the echo of fame. This and many other Keats tributes crystallize his poetry through certain characteristic poetic gestures such as hums and fragrance and shadows. In this regard their interpretation of the poet is not inaccurate. But they often abstract this ephemera from its erotic basis in Keats and therefore read him as a poet whose effect confirms the separation of soul from history and the body and from language itself.

'THE POETRY OF KEATS,' GEORGE MEREDITH

The song of a nightingale sent thro' a slumbrous
valley,
Low-lidded with twilight, and tranced with the dolorous
   sound,
Tranced with a tender enchantment; the yearning of
   passion
That wins immortality even while panting delirious with
   death.

Keats's bird is not the skylark (of Shelley, Blake, Clare, even Wordsworth) who *greets the day*, whose song follows the brilliant, sudden trajectory of its flight, upward to near vanishing and back down plunging towards its nest. If the skylark heralds life, the nightingale fills the earth with easeful death, enchantment, an enchaining and delirious passion of song to the other side of the barrier, sleep as well as death, orgasm-as-immortality. The nightingale, indeed, in its song lubricates the transformation of death into sleep, the sleep of the hero Endymion which has become the sleep of Keats from which fragrance and low sounds arise.

'THE GRAVE OF KEATS,' OSCAR WILDE

Rid of the world's injustice, and his pain,
   He rests at last beneath God's veil of blue:
   Taken from life when life and love were new
The youngest of the martyrs here is lain,
Fair as Sebastian, and as early slain.
   No cypress shades his grave, no funeral yew,
   But gentle violets weeping with the dew
Weave on his bones an ever-blossoming chain.
O proudest heart that broke for misery!
   O sweetest lips since those of Mitylene!
   O poet-painter of our English Land!
Thy name was writ in water – it shall stand:
   And tears like mine will keep thy memory green,
   As Isabella did her Basil-tree.

Rome

Wilde does make the death seem recent, almost contemporary. Keep green, reads the penultimate line. Then, Wilde through his tears repeats the actions of Keats's Isabella and ritual collapses the time of then and now. But to invoke Keats's lips turns the poem itself into a kiss; the distance of the years, the barrier between life and death and between poetry written aye long ago and that being written now collapses in this most intimate and sensuous of connections. ('Fold / A rose leaf round thy finger's taperness / And soothe thy lips' – *Endymion*.) The poet enters the vicinity of Keats-as-living-man: the homosexual references – Sebastian and Sappho, the kiss implied between poet and poet, the tears that make the flower of memory grow, the identification with the poet's heroine, all act to return us to the poet in his greenness. Cut off in death, Keats returns – through the poem – to that moment of early, rapid sexual-and-poetic growing. The sonnet works like a spring ritual, a spell cast over the poet-in-winter to make him start to live, visibly, again.

6

Flowers, Keats, and Death

Just as hair grows for a while past death, flowers growing over the grave prolong the life of that person or, more accurately, convert that life into a new one. Behind the new life, of course, is the loss of the old, a sacrifice or exchange woven with the continuity. Proserpine, goddess of flowers, recalls pain as well as new life. And as in Ovid the principle of continuity demands an adjustment downward on the evolutionary scale: person back to flowers. But in some of the preceding poems the proximity of flower to dead body and the grave's earth is very great; fragrance hovers around the name, violets around the bone. Violets themselves grow close to the ground. Violets that *weep* become violets that *weave*. Meynell beautifully makes the flowers one with Keats's thoughts and feelings:

> And daisies infantine were thoughts of his,
> And different grasses solved his mysteries.
> He lived in flowers a snatch of spring,
> And had a dying longing that uncloses
> In wild white roses.

It is a short leap from this passage to the late-Victorian representations of Keats's pot of basil: Severn's 1877 painting of Isabella resting dreamily upon the fecund fragrant herb that was once her lover, or Averil Burleigh's illustration for a 1911 edition of Keats's poetry, showing a richly draped, long- and fair-necked Isabella embracing the pot and, with eyes closed, smelling the plant's compelling fragrance.

Analogies of human life to plants have always accentuated the tragic distance of the unrenewable life of persons in contrast to the renewable one of flowers. Thus the erotic love of Isabella for her pot of basil can't help but have a necrophiliac tinge. But all that changes when the flower becomes the next poem, and in turn the next flower over him: 'With young shoots for this young poet's sake.' The new poem, like the flower, extends the poet's life but

75

now as an expression of the gratification of her new love, a new fecundity of shoots/poems, or, as Wilde says, 'gentle violets weeping with the dew/Weave on his bones an ever-blossoming chain.' The frozen 'forever *young*' of the lovers on the Grecian urn now becomes perpetual creation, a 'forever young' forever animated and creating, like Keats's gardener Fancy 'who breeding flowers, will never breed the same.'

The haunting image of flowers growing on Keats's grave, so preoccupying the Victorians and still compelling today, may prompt the critical question: does this comment on Keats's poetry? Perhaps this transformation of person into flower into new poem is an observation about a potentially open-form poetry, in which attention is paid less to the preservation of the image of the poet and more to the poet's dissolution into the life of the world itself.

7
Quoting the Nightingale

The nightingale's song, the self-same song that found a path through the sad heart of Ruth, the eternally present, eternally vanishing song, is continually being quoted, by Coleridge, by Wordsworth, by Clare, by Keats, and again and again by the praisers of Keats. It no longer has a body and rarely has a pain, but it lodges itself in bodies and sonnets. Fragments of the lyric voice that the praise poets implicitly invoke are caught in order to grant their work its authenticity and in order to link them with the source of poetry that precedes them. Keats has become a nightingale whose pathos and tragedy is waded through by later poets in order to catch some lines of his song as well as his remarks. 'Here lies one whose name was writ in water' is only the most famous – most are small phrases, even single words: darkling, covert, hoodwinking, living hand, forever young, bright star, melancholy storm, warm, cold, kisses four. Allusions work similarly: Endymion, nightingale, urn, Hyperion, Isabella, autumn.

The quotation, in this case, removes the original from its poetic context, its original 'warmth,' in order to join it to the modern source of poetry which is Keats, the stream or fount of poetry. Quotation often fetishizes the original, metonymically: to quote a phrase of Keats is to possess by reclaiming a part of Keats himself, his body become his spirit. To quote is also to write a fragment of biography; the lines of poetry are subdued by the story of the life. This strikes me as having limited value for the project of keeping the poet among the living.

> – ...sometimes, when you're entranced, you forget what
> entranced you, the entrancement alone is enough –
>
> Yannis Ritsos, from 'Moonlight Sonata'

Keats's readers have been entranced. They write of an air filled with streams, tears, nightingales, flowers, and darkness. Only a person entranced could attended to all these elements of earth and

77

water and air. And death as an element – entranced with death in Keats, they insist upon death's sweetness and its trailings that never truly vanish. Enchanted they forget the words, the discourse the poet sought to establish, the cadences and measures, the precise renderings of confusion and how confusion is filled with streams, tears, nightingales, flowers, and darkness. And death. In such for-gettings, they forget themselves, their own words and cadences, and their own confusions. As a result, Keats-the-poet has appeared to leave to us hungry generations a vocabulary darker, more liquid and death-filled, more – tonally – a viola or clarinet of the middle and low register, than his actual poems show. The point is the con-fusions. For all that darkness and liquidity is there but in the form of risk and extremity. Instead, the poems praising Keats predict consolation in the reading, an anchoring in eternity. But Keats, in his confusions, wrote to free these images and his language from all moorings, which, as a disciple of Milton and Wordsworth, would have been taboo. The image of the poet in his dream whirling through a wintry atmosphere kissing a Francesca catches precisely the sense of intensity and extremity unmoored.

8
Biography and the Poet

'Shakespeare led a life of allegory; his works are a commentary upon it.' When he said this, Keats was, I believe, trying to imagine a life *of* poetry, a true autumnal ripeness:

> Ripeness is
> what falls away with ease.

Jane Hirshfield

Poetry is not simply what is left or what comments upon a life, but it is life freed of fiction and report; it is language-on-the-wing. But biographies of poets usually give life precedence over poetry or make poetry fit into the contours of the poet's living. It has been a commonplace of Keats since F. R. Leavis and Lionel Trilling (and by implication Matthew Arnold) that we need to remind ourselves that we are interested in Keats because of his poetry and not because of his luminous and inspiriting correspondence; we are drawn to the life because he is a poet and not the other way around. But the history of Keats's biographies, of which there have been many, would suggest the opposite: it is Keats's life that fits our needs, that in itself has a *shape* of importance, perhaps of mythic importance. Consider the two most popular biographies of the twentieth century: Aileen Ward's *John Keats: The Making of a Poet* and Walter Jackson Bate's *John Keats*. Bate introduces his subject by offering the analogy to a Dickensian hero:

> ... the life of Keats – even at first reading – has always seemed haunted by a feeling of familiarity. It reads like something we have read before, and are eager to hear again. At least one explanation is not far to seek. Of no major writer, in any language, have the early years more closely paralleled the traditional folktales of the orphan forced to seek his own fortune. No self-conscious fear of sentimentality, no uneasy wriggle backward into the sophistications or

timidities of detachment, can minimize this moving and unex-
pected beginning.... Lincoln offers a parallel: we wonder how
someone who subsumes, with large honesty, so many of our
modern aspirations – who attained so much more than most other
statesmen (or, in the case of Keats, than most other writers) –
should have begun life as characters in an older allegory do.[1]

Bate makes it very clear that Keats did not fall eventually into the
welcoming arms of a benefactor to usher him into a full-blown life
of comfort, happiness, and longevity, but that fact only adds to his
participation in a myth then colored by tragedy: the myth of
fulfillment and completion cut short.

We learn from the early pages of this monumental volume a
motive for a biography told on this scale and in this mode:

> Whatever our usual preoccupations, in approaching such figures
> we become more open to what Johnson thought the first aim of
> biography – to find what can be 'put to use.' That direct interest,
> so broad in its appeal, continues just as strongly for the profes-
> sional writer who, like the poets of Keats's own day, has wrestled
> darkly with the fear that there is little left for the poet to do –
> little that will permit the large scope or power of the poetry of
> more confident, less self-conscious eras in the past .... Hence,
> despite the most radical changes in taste during the last hundred
> years, no English or American poet (however widely he may
> swing away from any of his other predecessors since the death of
> Shakespeare) fails to drop the usual querulousness over poetic
> idiom or other details when he comes to Keats, and to look
> quietly, closely, and perhaps with a suspended, secret hope.
>
> (p. 2)

It is clear to me that this 'anxiety of influence' (and Bate was the first
to address this subject systematically for English literature) about the
decline of poetic vitality, purpose, and function in the post-Romantic
periods has driven Bate's interest in the mythic proportions of the
life of Keats. Since, goes the argument, poetry is declining in
significance and power and since we presumably don't want that
to happen, we had better look *uncritically* and in wonderment at a
poet who lived, as Trilling remarked, during the period of the last
vestige of health in Western civilization. If one, as I do, rejects
emphatically the view that poetry has been steadily weakening

and that poets constantly look back in dismay at the gigantic older poets in successful competition with their later brothers and sisters, then one must call into question the rationale for the mythologization of Keats.

Aileen Ward has no interest in seeing poetry on the decline and her book reads the better for it. Nonetheless she too shapes Keats's life within larger paradigms of personal tragic heroism. It begins with the threat of Napoleonic invasion of England in 1803 which Keats, as a young boy, would have sensed all around him and perhaps played out as the wargames of youth. Ward then claims that:

> ... years later, when he faced the last separation of his life – leaving the country and the girl he loved, to die in a foreign land – these days stirred in his memory. With the thought of the journey waking him up each morning at dawn, he nerved himself to leave England, he wrote, 'as a soldier marches up to a battery.' The image is significant. From the time of his first encounter with the world, life was to seem a test of whatever fortitude he could bring to it.
>
> (p. 3)[2]

While both Ward and Bate, in spite of individual differences, appear to rely upon the monomythic journey of the hero, Ward further situates her life of Keats in a paradigm which can be abbreviated with a memorable phrase of Keats: 'beauty that must die.' She speaks of the happiness of his life until age eight when his father was killed by a horse. But her account, for example, of his life at Enfield School focuses that early happiness with a particular, sensuous ('Keatsian') intensity:

> A fine pear tree stood in the playground, and a morello cherry grew against the courtyard wall; strawberry beds were planted beside the pond, and the boys who watered them were given the berries when they were ripe. Here Keats must have sampled his first 'antiquated cherries full of sugar cracks' and acquired the weakness for 'pear-tasting – plum-judging – apricot nibbling – peach-scrunching – Nectarine-sucking and Melon-carving' to which he later confessed. Probably he too had his garden plot to tend, for he developed a close and loving knowledge of flowers, to judge from the drawings of pinks and violets scattered up and

down the margins of one of his lecture notebooks. Beyond the school the meadows stretched away to the dark edges of the forest, from which the song of nightingales unfurled endlessly in the still May nights.

(p. 8)

Three paragraphs later she begins: 'The family's future looked bright; then disaster struck out of a clear sky' (p. 9). Or, to paraphrase the 'Ode on Melancholy,' the beauty of this sensuous enjoyment turns to poison while the bee-mouth sips. All pleasure follows an inevitable trajectory into pain, loss, or death.

to do so — Let us leave him to his misery alone
except when we can throw in a little more —
The fifth canto of Dante pleases me more and
more — it is that one in which he meets with
Paulo and Francesca — I had passed many
days in rather a low state of mind and in the
midst of them I dreamt of being in that region
of Hell. The dream was one of the most delightful enjoyments I ever had in my life — I floated
about the whirling atmosphere as it is described
with a beautiful figure to whose lips mine
were joined at it seem'd for an age — and in
the midst of all this cold and darkness I was
warm — even flowery tree tops sprung up
and we rested on them sometimes with the
lightness of a cloud till the wind blew us
away again — I tried a Sonnet upon it —
there are fourteen lines but nothing of what
I felt in it — o that I could dream it every
night —

As Hermes once took to his feathers light
. When lulled Argus, baffled, swoon'd and slept
. So on a delphic reed my idle spright
. So play'd, so charm'd so conquer'd so bereft
. The dragon world of all its hundred eyes
. And seeing it asleep so fled away;
. Not to pure Ida with its snow cold skies
. Nor unto Tempe where Jove grieved that day;
. But to that second circle of sad hell
. Where in the gust the whirlwind and the flaw
. Of Rain and hailstones lovers need not tell
. Their sorrows. Pale were the sweet lips I saw

= Pale were the lips I kiss'd and fair the form
I floated with about that melancholy storm

1. MS of 'As Hermes once' in a letter from Keats to George and Georgiana
Keats, February–May 1819

2. *La Belle Dame sans Merci*, by Sir Frank Dicksee

3. Keats on his death-bed, by Joseph Severn

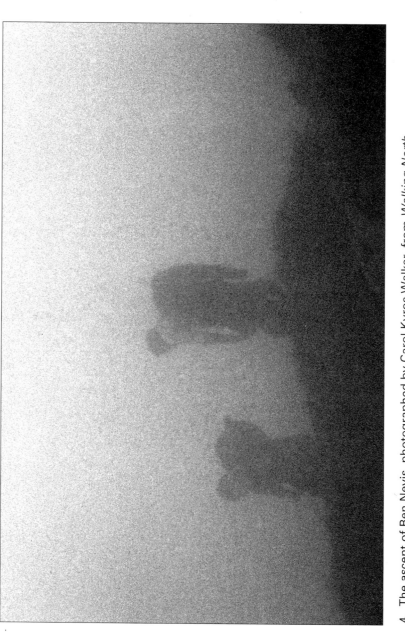

4. The ascent of Ben Nevis, photographed by Carol Kyros Walker, from *Walking North with Keats* by Carol Kyros Walker

9

Poetry and/as Biography:
Amy Clampitt's
A Homage to John Keats

These mythic patterns of organizing Keats's life are so strong that it has become nearly impossible to think of his life *or* his poetry in any other terms. Put slightly differently, it is difficult to disentangle the poetry from the life, to do anything but find it in some sense an epiphenomenon of these molds into which his life has been placed. To turn from prose biographies to poetic sequences is to be faced with the same issue. In Amy Clampitt's *A Homage to John Keats* (1986) – a 22-page, eight-poem sequence – that draws primarily upon the poet's career from 1816 when he had written 'On First Looking into Chapman's Homer' through the *annus mirabilis* of 1818–19, it is the telling of the story of his life, largely as a matter of imagination and inner experience, that gives significance to the poems and not the other way around. We recognize familiar patterns in the narrative. In Keats's life, and therefore in his poetry that follows predictably in its wake, beauty leads to tragedy, sadness, and death; imagination and hope lead to tragedy; books lead to 'reality,' and pleasure turns to pain and self-consciousness. One could ascribe an implicit organic analogue to this account: the root leads to the flower, the flower to the fruit, and the fruit to the plant's and the season's at least temporary end. Elegy seeps through all; all is always already finished and complete. Death resides within and defines all experience. Referring to Keats's Paolo and Francesca dream, Clampitt says:

> Dream of being warm, farewell.
> Exposure on a cold hillside,
> good morning.

The penultimate poem, 'Winchester: The Autumn Equinox,' begins with the references in Keats's letters to autumn's warmth during the writing of his final ode –

> … how beautiful
> the season was – ay, better than
> the chilly green of spring, the warmed hue
> of grainfields' harsh stubs turned pictorial
> with equinoctial bloom, the tincture of
> the actual, the mellow aftermath of fever:
> purgatorial winnowings, the harvest over.

And it ends, inevitably, with a quick slide from autumn 1819, with the failed second effort at epic, to the very end:

> Hampstead: Fever
> and passion. A comedy. A sonnet. In letters,
> now and then a cry of protest. The rest
> is posthumous.

With the structure of death's retrograde influence on life comes another familiar pattern in the making of Keats's life: poetry as a necessary fiction, an illusion, a defense against suffering leads to the abandonment of illusions for the direct and heroic encounters with reality (what Lionel Trilling referred to as Keats's 'mature masculinity'). Tragedy and death are reality which, upon Keats's embrace of them, means perforce the end of poetry anticipated in prescient and confrontative bits of wisdom seeded in poems, such as 'beauty-that-must-die.' Poems radiate the end of poetry. Curiously, this conforms to what I previously described as the modern academic Romanticist (e.g. Bate, Harold Bloom, and Paul de Man) penchant for assuming that great poetry belongs to the past, that poetry recognized as important for the empowering of persons has happened and is not now happening, that poetry is dying, just as Keats's poetry died as he 'was reaching maturity.' (But Keats – wise and more truly prophetic than his twentieth-century critics – had a very different vision of his making of poems, anticipating a future of fecundity and variety:

> A rosy sanctuary will I dress
> With the wreathed trellis of a working brain,
>   With buds, and bells, and stars without a name,

With all the gardener Fancy e'er could feign,
    Who breeding flowers will never breed the same ...)

Perhaps the most interesting observation that Clampitt makes concerns Keats's problems with domesticity: she repeatedly draws attention to his shifting residences; like Hazlitt he has no fixed home, no
place of assured return. Keats, she suggests, may have fantasized a
'home' in poetry itself, yet poetry like the permanent home he longed
for was an illusion. But what does this say about the poetry that he
wrote? – that it most likely is a form of defense or, more radically, a
form of regression to a conditon of familiarity. The strenuousness of
poetry would emerge in the recovery of the familiar (like Odysseus).
But it also would preclude much occasion for visionary efforts in
language, which, in traditional as well as modern poetry, usually
demands a poetics of the strange as well as of the rich, a poetics
which in criticism is typically not granted to Keats.

It follows from this paradigm that as Keats matures as a poet, he
becomes less, in Clampitt's word, 'bookish.' (Paul de Man, in his
well-wrought Introduction to the Signet Keats (1966) sketches the
same program for Keats's career.) Thus the early 'Chapman's
Homer' sonnet is bookish while the late *Lamia* is described as an
experience, and a negative one at that:

    Illusion, snared in a brisk running couplet,
      was his new preoccupation ....

The passionate Fanny Brawne poems, relieved of any bookishness,
enter the current of his tragic life, instanced here in the loss of his
brother and sister-in-law to America:

    The opening of the West: what Miltonic
    rocketry of epithet, what paradigm
    of splendor in decline, could travel,
    and survive, the monstrous region (as he'd
    later depict it) of dull rivers poured
    from sordid urns, rank tracts unowned
    by any weed-haired god he'd ever heard of,
    that had fleeced his brother George?

One sees, even in this poem of postmodern times, the insistence
upon poetry, referenced under death, as the occasion of its own
undoing. Bookishness and literariness are a sign of weakness or at

least of immaturity. It is a prop from which a greater poet can release himself. But for Keats to face reality is to face imminent death, which is in a sense to dispose of poetry as mere illusion. Some of the nineteenth-century tribute poets thus preferred the comforting yet energizing spirit emanating from him and his work to the actual poems themselves. It is as if his authenticity as a lyric poet were proven by the ease with which his poetry is fitted to the angles of his too-brief life.

This – even though Keats would say (thinking of the poetry of Shakespeare's plays and *Paradise Lost*) with passionate certainty: 'I look upon fine Phrases like a Lover,' and even though he can wrestle with himself over the relative usefulness, for his future poetry, of Milton, Dante, and the 'English' Chatterton. Why, I ask, is it bad for a poet to be bookish? To be bookish, in a positive sense, would imply that the poem does not necessarily conform to the pattern taken (or assumed to be taken) by the life, that it follows the logic and the sensations set out for it by other poems and others' fine phrases. And to insist that 'reality' should replace books as a sign of a poet's maturity does not consider the complex and permanent, seductive necessity (possibly excluding of others) of books and language for a poet. Death, as Hélène Cixous beautifully outlines in *Three Steps on the Ladder of Writing*,[1] greets the serious writer on the first step. I think that those readers who would (in some fundamental way) find Keats successfully abandoning bookishness for reality want to account for his early death in which he abandoned writing forever and too soon: to face reality and life (e.g. 'what shall I do with my life?') is in his case to face the sure imminence of his death; part of his genius, then, is his refusal to be stuck in books and, implicitly, his own poetry. In this sense, he makes a graceful, not an 'awkward,' 'bow' out of life. From this perspective his later, greater poetry, holding more of 'reality' (the tragic outlook) within it, contains the germ of the end of poetry altogether.

10

Cosmic Biography:
Tom Clark's
Junkets on a Sad Planet

Tom Clark's superb book[1] raises the possibility, unsettling for academic critics, that poems may make the best criticism. Harold Bloom and others unearthed this spectre of professional obsolescence twenty years ago, but the more recent excitement over historical research and over the use of highly technological languages brought to bear upon the act of reading has conveniently allowed the earlier possibility to be forgotten. Actually the critical potential of poetry ought to release us from the other bondage, that criticism cannot tap into the liberties afforded so-called 'creative' writing, in, for example, the simple use of association and metaphor, to say nothing of more elaborate commitments to changes in style and genre. After all, how do we know clearly what answers, explanations, and information criticism is supposed to produce? Isn't the relationship between poet and reader far more vulnerable and open? And, if, as Allen Grossman beautifully says, 'poems are traces of the love of the human world for itself,' and 'the will that drives such love intends the continuation of that world as a whole',[2] then poems – as least as much as criticism but in a different idiom and perhaps with different priorities – ought to be driven by love to recuperate understanding. Who knows what 'knowledge' will emerge or be created by such writing?

In the history of Keats reception, the rigidities of response have taken a form peculiar to this instance: the work, as I have said, is typically read in terms of the compelling life. What makes *Junkets on a Sad Planet* more or less unique is that here the genius of Keats shows in the way his eye and temperament were continually defined outside of death and therefore outside the biography, not – by any means – without reference to the story of the life but not bent or subdued to it: this books inverts the notion that the language of ordinary consciousness (biography) and social identity

87

drives the poems to the known horizons and that poetry may in fact access a language from beyond those horizons.

'Outside of death': by which I do not mean denying death, avoiding it. Indeed, Clark gives *poetic* seriousness to Keats's relationship to death, and this intensity, this giving over, becomes an ecstasy – 'now more than ever seems it rich to die.' What happens is that for the great, inspiring, uplifting, generous writer like Keats, death, while having permeated the life, having annihilated occasions of love (his mother, his younger brother), cannot imaginatively victimize the heroic poet who, instead, demands that death go free, mingling deeply with the poetic self and then with the reader. It is, of course, a commonplace to associate Keats's most productive months of writing – the winter and spring of 1819 which yielded *The Eve of St. Agnes* and the odes and other small poems as well as the magnificent February to May journal letter to his brother and sister-in-law – with the death of his brother Tom in December 1818. From the point of view of poetry this is not an event to mourn and keep mourning, to nurture the death in death. It, after all, has given a flowering. This is the view of Hélène Cixous:

> Each of us, individually and freely, must do the work that consists of rethinking what is your death and my death, which are inseparable. Writing originates in this relationship. In what is often inadmissible, contrary, terribly dangerous, and risks turning into complacency – which is the worst of all crimes: it originates here. Yes, it is mortal, it is bad, but it is also good; this depends on us. We can be the killers of the dead, that's the worst of all, because when we kill a dead person, we kill ourselves. But we can also, on the contrary, be the guardian, the friend, the regenerator of the dead.
>
> Writing is this complex activity, 'this learning to die,' that is, not to kill, knowing there is death, not denying it and not proclaiming it.[3]

She further observes that to write in this second, positive relationship to death places one on the extremity, for it means that one empathizes with death and therefore must be very near it, in fact on the border between life and death. One loses the ordinary social identity, becoming a person of the book, a voice from death and collective consciousness. The biography, as usually constituted, reduces this extreme condition to the normative one, and Keats's

poetry – its 'improvement' and 'maturation' – reinforces the devel-
opmental achievement of the life. Clark has returned the life into
the poetry as a commitment to a vision beyond that of social discourse and tragedy. For Clark, Keats's is primarily a language of
'the book.'

To pose the problem of *Junkets on a Sad Planet* in Keatsian language, how would 'Keats' (the life and the poetry) look if one
pushed the concept of the Negatively Capable and 'camelion' poet
to its logical extreme? Clark traverses Keats's life and career and
poems in 188 pages of verse and prose lyrics, utilizing biographical
detail but constantly leaping out from it. For example, here is Keats
recalling the visit to Windermere and Wordsworth's home in the
summer of 1818:

> I went out in a boat, caught two trapped
> Trout which were cooked for our dinner.
> The waiter gossiped to us about Wordsworth's
> Pathetic electioneering, but the sun
>
> Going down shot through the clouds all the gold
> Nature normally holds off from us
> As time washes round these human shores,
> And I had two views of the lake that won't fade:
>
> The moving waters at their priestlike task
> Of pure ablution, patient, watchful
> Like a sort of north star which in shining can
> Not cease to be steadfast and open-lidded
>
> Over the wonders of the great power;
> And diamonds sparkling on the oars, full night still
> Far off, but already at this latitude
> Polaris growing bright against the sky.
>
> (pp. 66–7)

The diarist here records the *labor* of catching and preparing the
meal, and local political news, both reflecting an immersion in the
life of the moment and of the people and of the body. But this con-
creteness and fullness of the life does not stop there, turning in mid
line and around only a comma to engage, quite literally, the skies
and the stars in their astrological dimension. At this point the

poetry becomes embedded with Keatsian reference from the sonnet 'Bright Star' and the letter from Scotland to Tom (25 June 1818):

> There are many disfigurements to this Lake – not in the way of land or water. No; the two views we have had of it are of the most noble tenderness – they can never fade away – they make one forget the divisions of life; age, youth, poverty and riches; and refine one's sensual vision into a sort of north star which can never cease to be open lidded and stedfast over the wonders of the great Power.

The letter, rising out of the world of 'divisions of life,' into the eternal, soon sinks back again, but Clark sustains the pitch towards the collective, making the biographic seem eccentric, partly by letting Keats's epistolary as well as poetic language swim in the pure serene of his (Clark's) own verse.

Clark begins his book, before the Table of Contents, with a page of two epigrams from Keats and from Adorno and a 'notice' by himself, all of which addresses the divesting of ego from poetry for the sake of the world that poetry intends. First from Keats's 'camelion Poet' letter to Richard Woodhouse, 27 October 1818: 'A Poet is the most unpoetical of any thing in existence; because he has no Identity – he is continually in…and filling some other Body…' Then from Theodor Adorno's *Aesthetic Theory*: 'Mimesis, understood as the non-conceptual affinity of a subjective creation with its objective unposited other… What the artist contributes to expression is his ability to mimic, which sets free in him the expressed substance.' Clark writes of Keats as Adorno's mimetic poet, one whose ego is continually diminished before the 'expressed substance' of the world. His book, in this way, is anti-biographical, its voices speak from different corners of the cosmos: 'The book may be read by turns as a poetic novel, biography in verse, allegorical masque, historical oratorio for several voices' (including those of Keats, Fanny Brawne, Charles Brown, and Keats-after-death).

The biographies (and the criticism that barters poetry for life and poetry for history) assume that Keats speaks in the social/historical voice in his poetry. Clark believes that poets can speak in their own voice – extraordinary, transpersonal, mythic, of death – and that Keats is such a poet. In this sense the tradition is right that wants to identify Keats with the nightingale ('the voice I heard this passing night was heard / In ancient days...'), and it is why Clark privileges the nightingale in his sequence.

Section 5 is called 'Phosphorescence,' 'the glow that comes / Up like stardust from the things growing there.' The nightingale, in the 11 poems and prose poems of this section, sings through the coming and fading of havens of intenseness, genuinely, authentically outliving the poet and the reader, but noncompetitively, offering the poet an alternative to oblivion, to that 'Mortality like a fist closed in Keats' throat.' Its song also becomes the ur-poetry of the West, the 'vowelled undersong' of pain upon which the modern poet strangely, at times anxiously, inscribes his words necessarily recovered in the human scale.

Dying
Back into ambient underground rustling, then rising,
Birdsong continued to flow from the covert glade,
Drowning Brown's garden in a grief-drenched shade.
Mortality like a fist closed in Keats' throat

While the golden lyre lying at his side,
Touched by no one, tuned to no human register,
Poured out liquid notes to the unwearied underground
Ear of the alert listening forest, smooth,

Clear as claret cool out of a cell a mile
Deep. All through that aching starlit spring
In Hampstead the god kept being born
As the stunned, exhausted player was abandoned.

The nightingale's song seems to part or open a space between fist-like mortality and Apollo's golden lyre that sings and rearranges the materials of grief and limitation, helping to define 'poetry' as expansive, phosphorescent, entering through human agency the expressed subjects of things, yet admitting that the player is exhausted, that death and the ego and the body are there, to be discarded when the poem survives. Put differently, Clark finds the world of nature and myth fully animate and personified, *the* subject, while the 'mortal body of a thousand days' is just that, secondary, a vanishing.

What Keats 'hears,' however, and sees is something not defined by person or poem but what works closer to the energy or spirit, a quickening, in all things. In this sense he joins, according to Clark, the visionary company. Phosphorescence is the sign of the visionary, at once fragile like the dew and yet when snared in a poem strong and lasting.

The nightingale's song, in Clark's book, spreads itself throughout May 1819 (the month of the ode's composition), its fragile sound growing in tenacity and influence as it flows into poem after poem, extending past the month of the poem's flowering into the summer and autumn and following summer and fall when death is at hand, just as phrases and words of Keats's poems keep seeding and flowering in Clark's poems:

> Concealed in the glade, the bird opened up again into pure, tireless sounding – a quick series of low fluty notes, a clear long note on one pitch then spiraling up the scale, becoming fainter until the last long drawn out notes fade – time passing, the brevity of life, its tenuousness, its fragility – it begins to grow dark, today also is over –
>
> (p. 106)

There is the biological bird, the physiological sound; yet the words carry the song into a poetic read-out of the birdsong: 'pure,' 'tireless,' even 'sound*ing*' in its present participial form, projecting the notes into an endlessness, but registering the arc of human time in the Keats story, with a quote from the 'Ode to a Nightingale': 'fade.' Eternity is an eternity of fading. Here the fading song becomes a condition of the Keatsian *Gestalt*, like the phrase he uses in his near delirious vision of Fanny: I eternally see her eternally vanishing. The fading song is matched but complicated in the person of the poet listening 'to that which is without language / a place in the realm of sound / spirit...':

> the
> poet as silent witness over there
> under his plum tree bower – his whole
> being going out into the song, leaving
> him reported among the missing
>
> (p. 105)

The poet veers off, in the presence of the nightingale, in two directions: into, proleptically, the wasting away of the body and into the 'there' of nightingales. This double vanishing is the correspondence that Clark seems to want to cultivate – that 'Keats' is a double-threaded braid of history and the collective, of the personal and the transpersonal, of prose and poetry. And while 'Keats' requires both threads, emphasis needs to be placed on the collective and poetic as separate from and more persistant than the biographical and physiological one.

In the voicing that he gives to Charles Brown over the famous account of composing the 'Ode,' Clark recasts the prosaic Brown into an oxymoron of a practical, down-to-earth visionary, adding a Chaucerian *primavera* energy to frame it: 'In that pleasant forward spring [contrast this with Brown's 'In the spring of 1819'] when everything living quickleapt into sudden bloom, some bird – a thrush, or early nightingale – set up its nest in a covert of my garden, keeping Keats up late those fine nights with its tranquil and continual joy of song.'

There are, as I see it, two purposes to Clark's belaboring the nightingale episode and its diffusion into the 'Ode' and then the history of Keats-poems. The first is to envision the song itself as having entered the stream or ground of poetry which becomes, in time, Keats himself. The second is to focus the poet's encounter with the bird as a 'going out of one's own nature,' an ecstasy of attraction to the quickening of the birdsong, a locus of spirit. The result becomes, for Clark, the moment of poetic affirmation, of the 'world's love for itself,' or, as Adorno says, it 'sets free in him the expressed substance' that poems agree to represent.

Late in the sequence the nightingale – amazingly still singing when Keats has stopped – marking the dying of Keats, (1820) embraces its ancient, tragic terror and pain, and Keats begins to go through the Ovidian changes from mortal to mythic bird. Clark, in this sense, takes seriously the transformation that the tradition of Keats eulogies has proposed: what does it mean for a poet to be transformed into 'the' nightingale? The nightingale is a mix of history and song, of experience and language, overlapping, each feeding and making the other. It lives only in an afterlife and as such is marked by a further mix, that of the experience, song, and language of the poets of the afterlife and is thus constantly vulnerable to renewal. Every new recovery is a thorn plunged again into the breast of the bird that cries out in the latest language its pain:

Teru, teru. Mimetic – liquid and musical as the words
Well Walk, where he wandered with Hunt, saw
Poor Tom's ghost, broke down, that last awful
Suffocating August – it is the wounding of Philomel
That produced the lyric, a wild quiet echoing
Of mortal tribulation that drowns in
The singer's voice, as the singer dies and
The pain that drives expression is extinguished
With the sudden curtailing of the song.

That the poem, with its Philomel references, lights upon a
moment in Keats's life when death was not far off and when poetry
had ceased, attests to the focus upon the afterlife. Indeed, this
period of blankness in poetry is heavily represented in Clark's
book; moment after moment, scene and phrase in letters, go
through the *torque* of Clark's contemporary discourse built up with
phrases and allusions from Keats to produce the life freed of the
limiting discourse of death and tragedy which, so to speak, is given
wing. A later poem, 'Percipience (Late 1820),' demonstrates even
more dramatically the torque of the poet's metmorphosis into a
modern living language and vision, beginning:

The last chapter starts that March, with the
    palpitations
That usher the naked heartache, the wound grief
Into the increasingly complex song – elegiac,
Then lyric, this liquid wounding rising in the voice
As it issues out of the quiet covert of the glade

Like bubbles rising in some clear sparkling wine
Shot through with morphine, shading violet to green,
Cool slipstream currents – Styx, Lethe – the *Maria
Crowther* becalmed in Portsmouth Roads, where
He writes of a sense of darkness coming over him –

The complexity of the nightingale's song increases as death
approaches and poetry has ceased; but the pressures of mortality,
the complications of feelings and gestures and miscommunications,
and the 'spell' under which his friends were cast even though none
of them but Severn could get it together for travelling with him to
Italy, and of course the intensities of leaving Fanny Brawne behind,

all these increase. But, Clark insists, 'Keats continued to woo / The immortals though his own mortality closed, / Torn by this unfortunate commitment / To song... .' He compares the young poet to Orpheus and 'the love of one lost girl,' when he 'didn't look back with sufficient / Alacrity at the dead mythology gaining on him' (p. 158). The test of the contemporary praiser of Keats is to give life to that dead mythology, which means to cast the poet in a new language that, in this case, translates the 'Teru, teru' into our own words and, by association, weds Keats's words to the 'deep song,' in Lorca's phrase, of the nightingale.

And how does Clark's reversal of mythic and biographical priorities affect his reading of Keats's famed but uncertain relationship to women? Clark handles that not by resorting to categories of psychopathology but by proposing (as he has his character Keats say) that he has two 'I's, his habitual self and then that self that ever communicates with collective images, the skies, the constellations, the self that already is the nightingale. The first self recognizes that women irritate him, that he will never marry because of this and because he hasn't enough money or good prospects. The second self invents or, perhaps, traces the likes of Cynthia, Madeline, La Belle Dame, the Francesca figure, the goddess Psyche, Lamia, Moneta. But of course he cannot always tell which 'I' is dominant at any one moment, particularly with women who stimulate such a range of needs and drives and desires. I think this is probably true for Keats who eventually, however, would have had to revise the rigid distinction.

Fanny Brawne, who might have become the key to such revision, concentrates (for Clark) both selves, creating such an agony that only on his death-bed can he say (quoting from the Letters): 'I should have had her in health I would have remained well' (p. 170). This, I believe, is the general position taken by Dorothy Van Ghent in *Keats: The Myth of the Hero*,[4] who clearly associates Fanny Brawne with the heroines of Keats's romances and who also situates Keats squarely in the matrices of mythology. For her as for Clark he lives as a poet 'upon the night's starred face,' tracing the shadows of 'Huge cloudy symbols of a high romance.' One wishes that Clark would have incorporated and complicated his view with that of Marjorie Levinson in *Keats's Life of Allegory*, who proposes that the significant sexuality Keats played out in his poetry was autoeroticism becoming more and more a conscious feature of his representation. As such the female 'other' becomes flattened, purposively emptied of its subjecthood but also freed – in the language of poetry – to become more playful signs of cultural preferences and less constrained to old cultural expectations.

At the same time to imply that Fanny Brawne and the heroines of lyric and romance are not as real as his autoerotic vision seems to belie the meaning of myth (few modern workers in myth and legend are not to some extent absorbed in the content) and the meaning of his letters and poems to Fanny Brawne. Coming to terms with both positions would be truly liberating for our readings of Keats and 'Keats.' Both Clark and Levinson, however, have attempted to liberate Keats's language from its early nineteenth-century contexts. Levinson, perhaps more than Clark, has observed Keats doing that himself. Both take seriously, in another aspect of the same gesture, the belief, which comes down from Keats's time, that he led (as he said Shakespeare led) a 'life of allegory.'

11

More Readings:
Towards an Open Poetics in Keats – Countee Cullen, Mae Cowdery, Galway Kinnell, Robert Browning

'… maybe there is no sublime; only the shining of the amnion's tatters.' This line near the end of Galway Kinnell's poem 'Oatmeal,' about the poet's having breakfasted with his imaginary friend John Keats, catches a change – a complication – in the most interesting rereadings of Keats among twentieth-century poets. The inadequacy of the notion of the sublime is that it stands in for 'the divine' and for a version of 'Keats' *sans* body and social self and even poetics. Take, for example, Countee Cullen's quatrain from the 1920s, 'For John Keats, Apostle of Beauty':

> Not writ in water, nor in mist,
>   Sweet lyric throat, thy name;
> Thy singing lips that cold death kissed
>   Have seared his own with flame.

Stopping at the end of line 1, I judge the poem as simply a Harlem Renaissance version of the many nineteenth-century protests against Keats's epitaph and am consequently nearly anaesthetized against it, assuming it will celebrate the disembodied spirit of Keats. But the strong accents launching line 2 proclaim a more sensually infelt definition of Keats than one would predict from the tradition: 'sweet lyric throat.' The reversal of the oblivious tendencies of the epitaph and of time takes the poem into a homoerotic doubling with death (kissing and searing and singing) made more dizzying by its containment in the cleanly chiseled quatrain. In this sense the poem does not stabilize Keats in the empyrean but

97

inaugurates something new, unpredictable, powerful. ('Fame,' for example, is cradled by 'flame,' a release of energy.) 'To John Keats, Poet. at Spring Time' begins by more fully urging the renewal of Keats with the congruent renewal of spring and Cullen's own poems:

> I cannot hold my peace, John Keats;
> There never was a spring like this;
> It is an echo, that repeats
> My last year's song and next year's bliss.
> I know, in spite of all men say
> Of Beauty, you have felt her most.
> Yea, even in your grave her way
> Is laid. Poor, troubled, lyric ghost,
> Spring never was so fair and dear
> As Beauty makes her seem this year.

And it concludes:

> 'John Keats is dead,' they say, but I
> Who hear your full insistent cry
> In bud and blossom, leaf and tree,
> Know John Keats still writes poetry.
> And while my head is earthward bowed
> To read new life sprung from your shroud,
> Folks seeing me must think it strange
> That merely spring should so derange
> My mind. They do not know that you,
> John Keats, keep revel with me, too.

The convergence of Cullen, Keats, and spring recalls a similar convergence of Keats, Psyche, and spring in the 'Ode to Psyche' as well as the tradition of the Epithalamion, a spring wedding poem: 'And you and I, shall we lie still, / John Keats, while Beauty summons us?' Cullen summons Keats the way the latter summons Psyche, over the abyss of a wintry forgetfulness of years, into the acknowledgment of a forgotten value for the spiritual life, the sexual awakening of spring. In both poems Keats is less a personality, a history, and more an energy-of-poetry invoked in the second poem as a pulse of nature (one that reverses the prison-house trajectory of Wordsworth's 'Vision Splendid' in his 'Immortality Ode'). And like Keats's encounter with Psyche, Cullen's with Keats is a secret, the announcement of which signals the event as 'strange,' as a defamiliarized condition of both spring and poetry. Folk-inspired 'black' poets like Langston Hughes criticized Cullen as having abandoned his African American heritage for a white poetic tradition that, in the early twentieth century, could not be better embodied than in the figure of Keats, the 'true poet' untainted by politics and social history, the poet of the aesthetic of Beauty. But Cullen's relationship to Keats seems to me quite subversive both of white poetics and of the standard reading of Keats: what does it mean for the black North American poet to 'keep revel' with the nearly archaic sexually ambiguous 'lyric ghost' late of Hampstead and Rome?

Mae Cowdery's 'A Brown Aesthete Speaks' (1928), another poem from the Harlem Renaissance, similarly tenses the political energies of aesthetic beauty by marking the moment when she 'met Keats and Poe' as a turning point in her art's sources of inspiration: from African American to European. It is a protest poem addressed, presumably, to a white establishment critic who wants her to keep her 'brown' poetry tied to her African American topics and atmospheres. Having supported the white artist's wish to gain from African American culture, she insists that she conversely has the right to absorb European culture since in both cases the point is 'questing Beauty.' She ends (alluding to the European Matthew Arnold, to European as well as to popular American culture):

> Oh friend, let's be kind to one another!
> Let us be mutual teachers,
> Mutually questing El Dorado;
> Lovely Arcady;
> Those are wonderful Hands that fashioned us!
> Handle those cosmetics softly;
> I would more beautify these curls,
> This skin,
> Would refine this brain.
> Oh chide me not if I met Keats and Poe,
> If I met Keats and Poe –
> And love them!

Beauty, supposedly neutral, is exposed here as universal, but in this poem 'universal' is a provocative concept since what is traditionally taken as the province of white European high art is claimed for the aesthetic spirituality of African Americans. Thus Keats's pure poetry becomes part of political controversy.

Just as Cullen's glorying in Keats does not thrust him into a vacant sublimity, similarly Galway Kinnell's 'Oatmeal' does not reduce him to a prosaic trafficker in craft and grain. To be sure, Kinnell's Keats is a materialist one who said to the modern poet that in 'To Autumn'

> ... two of the lines, 'For Summer has o'er-brimmed their
>   clammy
> cells' and 'Thou watchest the last oozings hours by hours,'
>   came
> to him while eating oatmeal alone.

And he can see Keats 'drawing a spoon through the stuff, gazing into the / glimmering furrows, muttering,' thus suggesting that a 'furrow' of oatmeal roughly equals a line of poetry. Kinnell delights in retelling Brown's story of Keats writing the 'Ode to a Nightingale' 'quickly, on scraps of paper, which he then stuck in his pocket' and then, with a friend, tried later on to order them, 'but he isn't sure to this day if they got it right.' That last phrase, 'got it right,' has a Writing Program ring to it, which he counters with this soaring cadenza:

> He still wonders about the occasional sense of drift between
>   stanzas,
> and the way here and there a line will go into the
>   configuration of a
>   Moslem at prayer, then raise itself up and peer about,
>   and then lay
>   itself down slightly off the mark, causing the poem
>   to move
>   forward with God's reckless wobble.

This is the part of Keats's poetry driven by something other than craft or 'getting it right'; it is the shining of the amnion's tatters. But the sentence clearly refers to a quality of the verse itself, that the sentences don't fit neatly, submissively into the metrics and stanzas, that the 'feet' wobble through the 'passages' instead of stepping smartly through them, in perfect time. That a line can 'raise itself up' suggests its operation in a vertical as well as horizontal coordinate; perhaps Kinnell reads the 'Ode' as groping or inclined towards a more open form (as in the sonnet on the sonnet). Perhaps, as the personifications hint, the vertical coordinate refers to a spoken element ('Moslem at prayer'), one which the poet Cid Corman finds in Keats. Of the opening passage from *Endymion*, he thinks that the iambic pentameter line is effectively broken according to *melody* and breath. 'I find that these lines hang on triple-phrasing':

> A thing of beauty   is a joy   forever
> Its loveliness   increases;   it will never
> Pass   into nothingness;   but still will keep
> A bower   quiet for us,   and a sleep
> Full of sweet dreams,   and health,   and quiet
>   breathing.

'As is evident, Keats wrote this poem using the "line" as his basic unit of structure, his conscious unit of structure; but his ear, his voice, combine to assert a strong melodic structure that sustains the much-modulated base rhythm.'[1]

Kinnell underscores his concern with poetics by following up the previously quoted passage with the following contrast:

> He said someone told him that later in life Wordsworth heard about
>   the scraps of paper on the table, and tried reshuffling some stanzas
>   of his own, but only made matters worse.

Wordsworth: *not* a poet truly interested in spoken speech, but a poet committed to the logic of sequence and transition and to the authority of the stanza, the line. Moreover, Kinnell seems to associate Keats's wobbly line and shuffled stanzas with his Cockney class:

> He had a heck of a time finishing it ['Nightingale'] – those were his words – 'Oi'ad
>   a 'eck of a toime,' he said, more or less, speaking through
>   his
>   porridge.

A poem about Keats raises the question: who was this poet? As with Tom Clark's book, the biographical answer does not address the experience of the reader far down the avenue of time who, like Kinnell, knows him- or herself to be 'face to face' with a presence that is at once a life, poems, and a history of reading them. 'Oatmeal' beautifully proposes a greeting of the spirit that accounts for life, poems, and history but does not settle for the traditional views (encountering Keats at breakfast is a bit like encountering Cupid and Psyche, again, in the grass); it draws the reader closer to the phenomenon of 'Keats' without reducing him; he gets more familiar and simultaneously more ineffable, more an idiosyncratic poet/eater-of-oatmeal and more – like his nightingale – joined to a collectivity that includes Spenser, Milton, Wordsworth, himself, and Kinnell.

And Browning, who asks at the end of his appreciation, apparently but not at all certainly about Keats, 'Popularity,' 'What porridge had John Keats?' 'Oatmeal' is a modern-day translation of 'porridge,' what becomes both in Kinnell and earlier in Browning something of a labor-class designation. Browning's Keats is compared to an anonymous fisherman from 'Tyre the old' who nets the murex with its treasured Tyrian purple; the work of the fisherman touches the lives of the well-to-do everywhere (silk manufacturers and merchants, society painters, monarchs) but remains himself unknown. Even to Browning the 'true poet' flickers in the midst of the great darkness; his task is to name the poet as an immortal, to 'draw' him:

> Stand still, true poet that you are!
>   I know you; let me try and draw you.
> Some night you'll fail us: when afar
>   You rise, remember one man saw you,
>   Knew you, and named a star! ...

Anonymous because his work and his presence don't enter the market economy or the circulation of persons in 'society' except at the extreme edges, if at all, he can only be known, it seems, negatively, by what he is not. Yet to know him would be to establish a marker by which significance is measured: he's at once absorbed in the material world yet outside it (more fit for assessment by – echoing Milton – the 'earth's feast-master'), defined yet not defined by society's standards of achievement. Others have identities, such as society painters who utilize the 'blue' paint from the Tyrian dye in their acceptable works that feed them well. Where and how are we to know him? –

> Hobbs hints blue, – straight he turtle eats:
> Nobbs prints blue, – claret crowns his cup:
> Nokes outdares Stokes in azure feats, –
> Both gorge. Who fished the murex up?
> What porridge had John Keats?

Browning asks: what is a Keatsian artist, and what is his art? Society *extracts* the Tyrian dye from its origins and *distills* or *refines* it into an essence, a 'blue,' a heavenly blue of unalloyed color and content; it is this distilled, purified substance that becomes currency for silk manufacturers and merchants and for the toady painters. Seen as a narrative of the capitalist civilizing process, the dye merely begins with the fisherman and comes into its own after being distilled, marketed in various forms, and absorbed into the objects of culture that bring glory to their owners. Like Yeats's golden bird of Byzantium, they exist out of nature to keep a drowsy emperor awake. The fisher-Keats, however, works at the origins, *in* nature:

> Yet there's the dye, in that rough mesh,
> The sea has only just o'er-whispered!
> Live whelks, each lip's beard dripping fresh,
> As if they still the water's lisp heard
> Through foam the rock-weeds thresh.

In this poem the fisherman is the poet with no visible identity but fully present in the 'world' he has brought up from the sea. The analogy of the poet to a fisherman and the words-of-poems to fish in the sea is old, at least as old as Lu Chi's *Wen Fu, The Art of Writing*. But the poems of Browning's Keats, and – like Kinnell – by implication the relationship between sentences and lines is not 'pure,' fitting and fitted (as Blake derisively said of Wordsworth), but are richly impure, the way the world really is. Suppose one looks at the vision of this stanza, in which the dye is only part of the sea's fecund profusion, not as the first prosaic step of Tyrian purple into the market economy of drowsy emperors but as the only moment of 'true' poetry, the Keatsian moment, then one has a definition of 'Keats' and of his poetics, in which labor, beauty, and nature are one and one with poetic language: no 'popularity' here but a poetry that deserves the dense, breathless language of Browning to fashion a definition of a restless, continually active art of sea's whisperings and water's lispings. To conserve the image of this poet, to make him stand still for a moment, is a major task since 'high Victorian' society prefers the reduced, the distilled, to the 'real of beauty,' with each beard dripping fresh. Moreover, it, by definition, prefers the stable, closed forms (remember that Keats's Tory reviewers hated his loose couplets), the congruence of content and form, a heaven's blue of the harmonious, to a poetics of motion, of moving from perception to perception, of the sexual energies of life. This is the real meaning of the characteristic Keatsian 'sensuousness'; it is part of a poetics of nature and the body, or correspondence and cosmic confusion.

12

Mark Halliday's
'There: For Keats' and Keats's
'Epistle to J. H. Reynolds, Esq.':
Against Monumental Poetry

The final piece for review is a short poem, published in *Poetry* in 1992, by Mark Halliday, called 'There: For Keats.' Like many of the tribute poems, this one quotes from Keats himself but not from the typically referenced poems, the odes and some of the sonnets and the letters. This plays upon one of his most interesting works, the so-called 'Epistle to J. H. Reynolds, Esq.,' a rambling poem of heroic couplets that saunters through the telling of a nightmarish dream, imagines its opposite in a serene painting by Claude, philosophizes on the relationship between imagination and truth, and recounts his own unease facing the 'core / Of an eternal fierce destruction,' all in the service of granting his friend Reynolds improvement in health. It moves, in other words, in and out of certain generic expectations, passing through what Keats calls 'moods.' It is, compared to his odes and sonnets, shapeless and unpredictable but very much grounded in the world of 'here,' his phenomenal life, never seriously entering the image-world of mythology and the collectivity. Moreover, Halliday's poem rhymes every line the same, and the rhyme itself comes from the 'Epistle.' The effect of this poem is, as with Clark's book, to free Keatsian language from the traditions of curtailing it in the expectations of tragedy, but in this case it also returns the reader to Keats's poem to show that he too was both capable of and interested in a gaming with language.

Once again, the 'Ode to a Nightingale' silently offers the source of this poem's geography. 'Here' is the place where the poet resides as a biographical person, albeit in the 'Ode' the version of 'Here' is somewhat hysterical: 'The weariness, the fever, and the fret / *Here*, where men sit and hear each other groan; ...' 'There' belongs to the nightingale and the Queen Moon on her throne: 'Away! Away! For I will fly to thee, …' 'Already with thee! Tender is the night, …' – the residence of song and the sources of poetry and the civiliza-tion's most valued signs. The tribute poets repeatedly note the degree of Keats's fame by locating him in the 'there' of immortality, an Elysium for poets marked by peace, love, mutualities of giving and receiving, and the place where a 25-year-old poet recently dead can instantly metamorphose into the fully realized maturity of one who lived a much longer and more complex life. Mark Halliday comments on (deconstructs) the 'there':

> Peace is where the body finally goes
> after trying all the moves its fever knows;
> asylum where your debt for what you chose
> need not be paid and the interest never grows;
> bower where no one's lips look like a rose
> and no one hopes you'll take off all your clothes.
> Preferment's not an issue there, you strike no pose:
> tenure is freely granted though you're off your toes.
> It's where the river Lethe darkly flows
> (except it doesn't). No one comes to blows.
> The lover there lies safe in perpetual doze –
> woman who has no dreams of lusty beaus
> and thro' whose curtains peeps no hellish nose;
> man unthinkably unworried by his foes.
> All sound there would be blank as endless oh's;
> no messy voice can say 'here follows prose.'

Whether or not Halliday had seen the same cache of tribute poems, many of which seriously celebrate a 'there' of peacefulness, I don't know. Whether it's through scholarship or intuition, he has delightfully caught the worshippers in their own trap, by giving some concrete for-instances of the realm of 'there.' It all amounts to a summary of that blissful, semi-erotic state that Keats liked to cul-tivate: 'delicious, diligent indolence,' except that 'there' is not dili-gent nor particularly delicious; it has no reality at all and as such is not worth the time it takes to formulate its apparent utopian value. Most important, poetry does not partake directly of the world of 'there' since 'All sound there would be blank as endless oh's.' In 'there' poetry is finished, has been completed and, by a kind of metonymy, if poetry is finished, so is the experience that produced it. Halliday, by playfully exposing the silly fantasy, suggests something about not only his but Keats's poetry, that they belong not to an otherworldly serenity but to what Keats called the world of pains and troubles and also the world of confusions, pleasures, and wordplay. If most of the tribute poems imply that Keats wrote a poetry of closure, 'There' produces, and by the allusions to the 'Epistle' argues that Keats produced, at times a poetry of aperture, of ongoing process in which the poem itself resides. Halliday's poem works by a list of correspondences; for example, we learn what preferment, tenure, Lethe, lovers, and sound mean in the domain of 'there.' The elements of the poem create together a coherent universe even though it turns out to be an empty one for poetry. The structure of this poem projects the possibility of an infinitely expanding list that leaps from association to association.

Before looking at the 'Epistle' as the source for 'There,' I will digress to explore the presence of this kind of poetry in Keats's work. Even in the familiar, closed forms, one can see alive the deep interest in not so much the conclusions but the energies of poetry. Take, for example, 'To Autumn,' which, instead of portending the end of the season, passing through ripeness into the completeness of death, the sense of maturation and its inevitable decline or emptying out, and – more than anything – standing for this movement as a symbol of Keats's career, might be seen as working relentlessly from the inside, the unceasing energy of the fruit, the bees, the drippings of cider, the songs of gnats and swallows, the endless bloomings, and – forever – the Brownian motion of the mind continually asserting agency in a universe flushed by human concern.

But to approach even closer to the poems of Keats that the anthologies deny, we might look at patterns of thought and image and even assumptions about language and the use of the poetic line: the ten-syllable line prominent in Keats's more elegiac poetry:

> Beauty is truth, truth beauty – that is all
> Ye know on earth and all ye need to know.

The lines are long and, particularly the second, sonorous and full: complete, bespeaking the transcendent nature of wisdom. This poetry of closure seems written from the perspective of completion. By contrast, consider some examples of a poetry of aperture or openness or presentness – sometimes in the ten-syllable but more often in an eight-syllable line – what Robert Bly calls 'leaping poetry,' that seeks not the roundedness of completeness but the expression of energy itself and that captures what Shelley referred to as poetry's 'vitally metaphorical' nature. To quote Bly:

> thought of in terms of language ..., leaping is the ability to associate fast. In a great ancient or modern poem, the considerable distance between the association, the distance the spark has to leap, gives the lines their bottomless feeling, their space, and the speed of the association increases the excitement of the poetry.[1]

The emphasis on the *energy* of the leaping poem echoes Charles Olson's

> *kinetics* of the thing. A poem is energy transferred from where the poet got it (he will have some several causations), by way of the poem itself to, all the way over to, the reader. Okay. Then the poem itself must, at all points, be a high energy-construct and, at all points, an energy-discharge.'[2]

Olson associates Keats with at least a perception of the relationship between poetry and energy and associates Keats's criticism of Wordsworth's and Milton's egotistical sublime with a 'non-projective' poetry which, he says, 'persists, at this latter day, as what you might call the private-soul-at-any-public-wall.' In terms of poetics, poetry of the egotistical sublime would, presumably, show its energies at the beginning and ending of a poem, stanza, or line, where the poet would exploit his/her control over the material. Consider, for example, any of Wordsworth's perfectly modulated stanzaic poems such as 'I wandered lonely as a cloud' or 'The Solitary Reaper.' By contrast, a poem showing its energies 'at all points' would be attempting to access the world relatively unimpeded by the conscious efforts of the poet to shape and control material to the needs of the social person. In Keats any of his 'list' poems will instance this more open form in which the poem does not particularly build towards a close, such as 'Fancy' or 'Where's the Poet?' or – within the stanza – the catalog of flowers in the 'Ode to a Nightingale' (V) or the 'Ode on a Grecian Urn' (I). In these instances one can say that pressure moves from within outward, threatening to burst the formal structure.

Was Keats a leaping poet? I don't think so, but I think that, more than any other poet of the English early nineteenth century (except

Blake) he wanted to be one, to push to overcome Wordsworthian inhibitions about the leaping poet within him:

> Oh, sweet Fancy! let her loose... .
>   Break the mesh
>   Of Fancy's silken leash;
>   Quickly break her prison-string
>   And such joys as these she'll bring, –
>   Let the winged Fancy roam,
>   Pleasure never is at home.

Bly says that leaping poets make leaping associations; Keats gives the Fancy wings for flying associations. But how much can he fly? Or, how much can he only speak of flying, or try to urge it into being? Surrounding the Fancy is, for Keats, a world of inhibition and tragedy. In such a world Fancy becomes escape, 'merely' play, an avoidance of the serious activity of making peace with tragedy and inhibition. This is the view of Sperry, Stillinger, Freistat, and others: Fancy, the faculty of association and list-making, may help the 'immature' Keats establish his poetic energies, but ultimately it gives way to an imagination that consolidates and 'crystallizes' the more disinterested, sublime view of life as tragedy. But I want to think that Keats is at least pointing to the strenuous poetic activity of leaping across consciousnesses. If we look for it (e.g. 'Fancy'), we will find evidence of his wanting to open up to a different consciousness, so that he can fly. Very often he heads this way with octosyllabic (or less) rhyming couplets.

In poems like 'Fancy' Keats writes in playful rhyming seven-syllable lines that jingle and hobble along, not leading in any apparent direction, and at times, one feels, stopping when the poet tires of the game.

Probably the most famous tetrameter couplets in English are Milton's in *L'Allegro* and *Il Penseroso*, but Keats's bear little resemblance to them. Rather, they seem more like the tetrameter couplets of eighteenth-century women poets such as Clara Reeve, Susanna Blamire, Lady Sophia Burell, or Mary Savage. Not Milton's elegant verses, these possess what Susanna Blamire calls a 'hobbling rhyme,' written as verse epistles to (usually other women) friends, with childlike, apparently frivolous rhymes, often full of 'feminine' endings (to add insult to injury). Clara Reeve speaks of women's writing but seems to mean primarily those very tetrameter verses:

> In all and each of these you find
> Strong markings of the female mind,
> Still superficial, light and various;
> Loose, unconnected, and precarious:
> Life and vivacity I grant,
> But weight and energy they want;
> That strength that fills the manly page,
> And bids it live to future age.... .

An excellent example comes from Mary Robinson's 'January, 1795':

> Pavement slippery, people sneezing,
> Lords in ermine, beggars freezing;
> Titled gluttons dainties carving,
> Genius in a garret starving.
>
> Lofty mansions, warm and spacious;
> Courtiers cringing and voracious;
> Misers scarce and wretched heeding;
> Gallant soldiers fighting, bleeding...
>
> Poets, painters, and musicians;
> Lawyers, doctors, politicians;
> Pamphlets, newspapers, and odes,
> Seeking fame by different roads.... .

Robinson uses the rhyming octosyllabics to create the monstrous but humorous correspondences of the varieties of life and wealth, of moralities, in the modern city; there's never enough time (from one line to the next) to judge anyone but only to mark the energies of these bizarre urban combinations.

Keats, in a similar meter, writes similarly about poetry and the conjoining of opposites, correspondences, and the discovery of instinctive energies that bind them:

> Where's the Poet? Show him! show him!
> Muses nine, that I may know him!
> 'Tis the man, who with a man
>   Is an equal, be he King,
> Or poorest of the beggar-clan,
>   Or any other wondrous thing

> A man may be 'twixt ape and Plato;
>   'Tis the man who with a bird,
> Wren or eagle, finds his way to
>   All its instincts; – he hath heard
> The Lion's roaring, and can tell
>   What his horny throat expresseth;
> And to him the Tiger's yell
>   Comes articulate, and presseth
> On his ear like mother-tongue;

In the usual readings of Negative Capability and the camelion poet, the poet 'has no identity,' 'is nothing,' as Keats himself says; and I could easily attach these notions to this fragment – the poet can 'inform' or enter and disappear in King and beggar, ape and Plato. The poet that the Muses nine may show is disinterested, there and not there, 'equal' in the attention he gives to everyone and everything. But 'equal' here means being any one of us in our *difference*, our *variety*. And this is one of the great functions of poetry, to conserve across time the image or the voice of individuals whose voices and images are not readily heard. In realizing this function the poet stands not above the world but is immersed in it and as such finds his way to the world-as-desire-and-instinct. He belongs with us and partakes of desire. Beggar, ape, lion, tiger are figures of instinct. Thus the oppositions in the poem exist not to be reconciled or transcended and the poet is not a cipher of sensitivity and self-sacrifice. Keats, in this regard and in his own way, uses the tetrameters in a manner similar to Mary Robinson, who places herself in the midst of urban contradictions without trying to transcend them. The poet, moreover, journeys, discovers, in his writing. 'Finds his way' is like the nightingale's song that 'finds a path,' sensuous, exploratory, aggressive. The poet finds his way to instincts, hearing an eternal fierce destruction ('Epistle to Reynolds') in the roars of lions and tigers, sounds that are utterances, that carry a meaning – cries of the other pressing straight to the poet's organ of receptivity. 'The tiger's yell / Comes articulate, and presseth / On his ear like mother-tongue.' The articulate roars and yells disclose a pre-syntactic language, unsublimated, not directed towards a social construction of legitimacy. It's the suppressed language of a mother tongue, a language of instinct and desire and wildness. Will the Muses nine authorize such language? Or does it reside in the margins of discourse?

'Where's the Poet' instances a poetics of *aperture*, and it is this position that needs to be valued more in Romanticism as well as in Keats, both where it actually exists and where its characteristics are implied or suggested. Here the poetic event does not stand in mournful or hopeful relationship to anything else; if the poetics of closure foregrounds individual subjectivity, the poetics of aperture identifies poetry with 'participation.' The poet streams into the collectivity of images and references called the world in space and time. And the world streams out of the poem, often in the form of lists, an exfoliating of world references, a potentially infinite documenting of phenomena under the sign of the world's love for itself.

This is seen everywhere in the cataloguing or listing of images streaming through the prophetic works of Blake and, in America, of course, in the works of Whitman. But it may be implicit in Keats's Negative Capability and camelion poet formulations in which the loss of self into the body of the object perhaps should be stated as a loss of self 'into the potentially multiple bodies of objects.' In his 'Ode to Psyche,' for example, Keats postulates a comic-visionary gardener-poet 'Who breeding flowers will never breed the same.' The poem, in this sense, turns away from the subjectivity of its maker in order to enact a proliferation of world resources, and, by naming and defining and describing them, celebrates individual identities and their diversity.

We find this proliferation of diverse elements in Mary Robinson's London poems, and in much of Byron's *Don Juan* which Peter Manning has described as follows: 'The poem functions not so much centripetally, directing attention to its uniqueness (though it does so gleefully), as centrifugally, returning each reader to the complex of private and public experiences that make up his particular life.'[3]

Behind this poetics of fecundity and diversity lies a belief in the principle of energy as required for the strenuous reach to a comic vision of the prolific and as granted through the poem for the engaged reader: poetry, in this Romantic sense, is the site of the creation of new energy in the world. Blake, again, is perhaps the most systematic advocate of the principle of energy, but one sees it in all the Romantics, even in Wordsworth's requirement for the poet that he or she 'give pleasure,' and surely it resides in Shelley's belief in poetry's 'vitally metaphorical' nature. To both terms in Shelley's phrase I would now like to turn.

He refers here to the *correspondent* nature that I have been presenting and that I find fundamental to poetry – the capacity of poetry to associate one thing with another or with many things. Behind this is the belief that poetry refuses to allow persons to remain in their isolated uniqueness nor that the world remains merely atomized and random. The value of metaphor-as-correspondence is not that it creates comparisons but that it envisions identity for and relatedness between persons and coherence in the cosmos. Historians of poetics have observed the apparent decline of metaphor in modern poetry. Donald Wesling, for example, has noted that experimental poetry in the late nineteenth century begins the process of turning away from traditional figures of speech altogether, including metaphor, turning towards the opportunities granted to language, grammar, and syntax.[4] Metaphor, which sets up a hierarchy of importance between tenor and vehicle and which thus appears to support the Coleridgean 'elitist' imagination, gives way to the non-perspectival and non-hierarchical correspondences, the sheer associating of objects or phenomena in the world, an activity belonging largely to the poetry of aperture which exists as a locus of energy – the 'vitally' in Shelley's 'vitally metaphorical.' Summing up 'vitally metaphorical' in contemporary terms is Jerome Rothenberg who says: 'Every new correspondence acts on its subject, which it changes, & on the entire field; every change a measurable burst of energy.'[5] These correspondences or combinations he finds as the basis for much of the world's poetry from the *I Ching* to surrealism.

In such poetry we have come far from the serenity proposed by Keats's admirers. They argue in their sonnets and quatrains again and again that we should allow the poet to rest in peace, which, I believe, is a recipe for how we should read his poems. But a poetry of play, aggression, and instinct, of the energies of experience requires a different sort of attention.

A CASUAL COMMENTARY ON A CASUAL POEM

> Welcome joy, and welcome sorrow,
>> Lethe's weed and Hermes' feather,
> Come to-day, and come to-morrow,
>> I do love you both together!

Tetrameters, in the first three lines of this 'Fragment' by Keats, each split down the middle, announce a poem of opposites and balance – or *correspondences*. Some Bantu theorists (cited in Rothenberg's *Technicians of the Sacred*) say that the farther combinations are separated from each other in their domains, the more interesting and thrilling is the energy emitted. This, of course, sounds like the principle of the conceit in early seventeenth-century English poetry, but T. S. Eliot and the New Critics championed those conceits as a triumph of aesthetic closure (the synthesis of disparate objects and possibly strident combinations into a pleasing unity). Jerome Rothenberg, the Bantu theorists, and the Surrealists refer less to an aesthetic unity in the poem (an instance of artistic and imaginative *control* over materials) and more to a set of associations or relationships in the cosmos, a principle of open-form poetry. The whole first sentence 'welcomes' and 'loves' opposites. It seems and sounds neat and clean: the cleanliness of synthesizing by transcending the binary oppositions, with the implication that poetry is the noble site of closing synthesis. But Keats likes to play in his tetrameters which contain their own daemon of mischief. The Hermes of line 2, Keats's favorite god, isn't apparently 'opposite' to Lethe – that is, forgetfulness vs. what? – not memory. Thresholds, yes. Hermes signals deception and trickery in the crossing, also the hermetic, the secretive, the poetically beautiful, also the transformative. Lethe would negate all this. In this combination lies the crisis of the lyric (particularly Keats's lyric and his consciousness of his death-seeped life): without poetry there is Lethe or forgetfulness and oblvion; with it lies the possibility of a memory and a transformation.

Similarly does 'today' anticipate 'tomorrow' or stand opposed to it as a combination or correspondence? Does the poet accept linear time or can he stand in the same relation to both present and future? Do these 'opposites' merely sound, by the poem's melody, opposite? Indeed, is this poem heading towards a 'meaning' or is it simply poetic play?

> I love to mark sad faces in fair weather,
> And hear a merry laugh amid the thunder;
> Fair and foul I love together;

Pure Keatsian doctrine: the camelion poet, who can enter an Iago as well as an Imogen, supposed to indicate a healthy, heroic disinterestedness; these lines (from the poem and the more or less contemporary 27 October 1818 letter), with their emphasis on love and delight, might indicate a kind of bisexuality or perhaps a playful defense against sexual confusion.

> Meadows sweet where flames burn under;

The apparent opposites suddenly fold into each other: the second underlines the first eerily; the Elysian field has Hell beneath it. How can I keep them separate, even as the poetic line does? The line lists toward the reality, the finality of Hell.

> And a giggle at a wonder;
> Visage sage at pantomime;

Perhaps the line just remarked on a wonder, something amazing and not dire at all. Yet the wonder is dissolved of awe by a giggle, subjectivity again is out the window: giggles and wonders, unattached to persons, merely signify affects. Sagacity marks an intensity, also an expansiveness of self into the world, a grasp on reality. But 'sage' is telescoped in its modifier 'visage,' or countenance or appearance, trivializing the apparent paradox of a sage, who sees into reality, observing a pantomime or impersonation. All is appearance; there is no depth, no penetration of the subject into reality.

> Infants playing with a skull;
> Morning fair and stormwrecked hull;
> Night-shade with the woodbine kissing;
> Serpents in red roses hissing;

Images, images, and death. The paradox in the first and third lines is knitted together not just by the poetic line but by the verbal within the line. Which do we honor? – the play of images or the sense of lurking danger?

> Cleopatra regal dressed
> With the aspic at her breast;

The appearance marks the queen with the death-instrument at the source of life and desire. For the first time in the poem an image of eros joins the images of appearance and death. Eros brings a formal expansiveness, the contraries occur over *two* lines. And the couplet summarizes a play – by Shakespeare, to be sure, so it's a 'real thing' (according to Keats).

> Dancing music, music sad,
> Both together, sane and mad;
> Muses bright and Muses pale;
> Somber Saturn, Momus hale,
> Laugh and sigh, and laugh again,

Literary play: chiasmus, parallelism – references to invocation, to myth and the gods, to the prosaic and the manic.

> Oh! the sweetness of the pain!

A *volta* in the poem, a turn. Hints of Bacchic pleasure, intensity, crossing a threshold: the verbal play of paradox and oxymoron, touches the poet. This particular oxymoron, familiar in Keats, seems to reveal an experience of genuine literary discomfort and power. The stakes of the game rise.

> Muses bright and Muses pale,
> Bare your faces of the veil,

A Keatsian invocation. From this perspective, the poem is a casting of a spell, the poet caught in his own sensual music.

> Let me see, and let me write

The first prayer is for desire, the anticipation of the sight; the parting of the veil by the poet creates the condition of desire which also discovers desire in the play of words. Seeing and writing: contraries? or does the second extend desire into poetry, unsettling because with desire unveiled, the play of opposites and contraries implies the condition of being, the point at which will dissolves before the power of the god.

> Of the day, and of the night,

Night is the time of eros, but Keats doesn't ask for a hymn to the night; more erotic because more confusing is

Both together, –

Redundant, explosive, or rather *im*plosive. Subjectivity, now evident in the poems, asks to be disallowed from subjectivity's gift — to make choices: a or b. ('Both together' appears now for the third time, a motif of ultimate strain and power.)

> – let me slake
> All my thirst for sweet heart-ache!

The poet cries out for poetry to become the intensity of passionate desire, reverting to a physiological index of desire (thirst), an image more primitive than poetry, and yet (another contrary) itself figurative, a metonymy of desire.

> Let my bower be of yew,
> Interwreath'd with myrtles new,
> Pines and lime-trees full in bloom,
> And my couch a low grass tomb.

Keats ends with a vision of 'easeful death,' the erotic pleasure of ease leading to death: 'Death intenser, death is life's high meed.' As the contraries continue right to the end, and multiply, they reveal the origins of and the poet's engagement with signifiers in desire and death.

In this poem runs a current of autoeroticism or pre-conversationalism. The other (reader, interlocutor, god) is not formed (as it is in Romantic pentameter verse). But neither is the voice-as-subject. Perhaps the oppositions driving on from line to line spark an archaism of feelings of desire and repulsiveness, longings and distancings. Death would be the realm of final containment for this pre-subjective terror of one's too fluid fluidity . . . when the poet dares to dwell in the high-energy zone of pure correspondence.

> . . . con alas que no vuelan en el aire,
> que vuelan en la luz de la conciencia
> mayor que todo el sueño
> de eternidades e infinitos
> que estan despues, no mas que ahora yo, del aire.
> (. . . with wings that do not fly in the air,

but fly in the light of consciousness,
larger than any dreams of eternities and infinities
that arrive, with no more than I have now, later than
      the air.)

Juan Ramon Jimenez

Leaping poetry leaps from one consciousness to another; it makes a leap of vision. If we look for it, we will find evidence of Keats's wanting to open up to a different consciousness, so that he can fly. This would constitute a poetic liberation, if consciousness were not kept tightly reined in on one level. For Bly such refusal to leap to another consciousness is a sexual refusal and, in the eighteenth century, is associated with the pervasive notion of a childhood 'innocence' devoid of sexuality and passion. Bly quotes Blake's 'Nurse's Song' in which children, whose natural passions are respected by an enlightened (or self-respectful) muse, 'leaped and shouted and laugh'd / And all the hills echoed.' (At a celebration for Allen Ginsberg and the Beat Generation at the Naropa Institute in July 1994, Ginsberg concluded the week-long festivities with all the famous poets and the audience singing the 'Nurse's Song' repeating endlessly as a refrain 'And all the hills echoed.') Keats, perhaps more than any of his contemporaries, sought to become a leaping poet, but the *problem* of sexuality wouldn't go away. Fancy in the poem of the same name seems associated with escape; if Fancy requires pleasure, it won't find it at home, *here*. But more severe:

> At a touch sweet Pleasure melteth,
> Like to bubbles when rain pelteth; . . .
> O sweet Fancy! let her loose;
> Summer's joys are spoilt by use,
> And the enjoying of the spring
> Fades as does its blossoming;
> Autumn's red-lipp'd fruitage too,
> Blushing through the mist and dew,
> Cloys with tasting: . . .
>   Oh, sweet Fancy! let her loose;
> Every thing is spoilt by use:
> Where's the cheek that doth not fade,
> Too much gaz'd at? . . .

So the leaping faculty, the faculty of association, finds a source of its energy, the pleasure of the senses (taste and touch as well as sight), also a source of sorrow and disappointment. Grief, say the visionary poets, causes the leaper to stumble. Rumi spoke of two compassions – the compassion in the realm of grief and a compassion beyond it. Lorca, in an idiom vastly different from Keats's, might have helped the young death-and-grief-soaked Romantic bring Fancy, untethered, home (and, incidentally, out of the eighteenth century):

> Friend,
> wake up, for the hills are still not breathing,
> and the grass in my heart has gone off somewhere.
> It does not matter if you are full of sea-water.
> I loved a child for a long time
> who had a tiny feather on his tongue
> and we lived a hundred years inside a knife.

O, that Keats would have heard a Lorca speaking to him! But there were no such voices within earshot, except that of Blake, of course, to whom so few could or wanted to listen in 1818–19. Psyche, also 'winged,' Keats noted, he invoked but then turned from, to the Nightingale who sang in full-throated ease. But he could not listen to that winged energy and follow it into his own leaping poetry without feeling death and grief:

> It is a flaw
> In happiness to see beyond our bourn –
> It forces us in summer skies to mourn:
> It spoils the singing of the nightingale.

> ('Epistle to Reynolds')

Dorothy Van Ghent's hypothesis about the Odes reverses the rigidly held tendency of the tradition that finds 'Psyche' relatively superficial and introductory to the other more 'tragic' Odes. She sees in them a sequence of the hero's journey as the poet's crisis. For her (denying that such psychically and archetypally rich poems should be given their usual chronological or biographical significance) 'the *winged* Psyche,' breaking past tragedy, enacts the final (correspondent) comedy of the Odes. Keats, as I will suggest at the end of this book, constructed a version of this comedy of correspondences and metonyms when he ordered the Odes and some of the tetrameter poems for publication in his 1820 volume.

THE RAT-TRAP

Keats's letters are usually quoted for the vivid formulations of poetic activity or positioning, of individual growth and identity; their evocations of tragic and jealous love; their heroic protests against dying. Writing letters to a friend, however, often seems to place him at greatest ease. At this point he abandons the grand march of his intellect and associates, or fills up a frame with fragments of impressions, or quotes and echoes a clutter of voices and vocabularies, and in this sense his letters seem one with the poetics I have been describing. In such letters the poet's subjectivity blends easily with a 'going out of his own nature,' so that the reader feels that he or she has wandered into a lyric democracy. Keats trusted that his reader would make sense of it:

> . . . some kind of letters are good squares others handsome ovals, and others some orbicular, others spheroid – and why should there not be another species with two rough edges like a Rat-trap? I hope you will find all my long letters of that species, and all will be well; for by merely touching the spring delicately and etherially, the rough edged will fly immediately into a proper compactness, and thus you may make a good wholesome loaf, with your own leven in it, of my fragments – If you cannot find this said Rat-trap sufficiently tractable – alas for me, it being an impossibility in grain for my ink to stain otherwise: If I scribble long letters I must play my vagaries. I must be too heavy, or too light, for whole pages – I must be quaint and free of Tropes and figures – I must play my draughts as I please, and for my advantage and your erudition, crown a white with a black, or a black with a white, and move into black or white, far and near as I please – I must go from Hazlitt to Patmore, and make Wordsworth and Coleman play at leap-frog – or keep one of them down a whole half holiday at fly the garter – 'From Gray to Gay, from Little to Shakespeare' – Also as a long cause requires two or more sittings of the Court, so a long letter will require two or more sittings of the Breech wherefore I shall resume after dinner. –

Have you not seen a Gull, an orc, a sea Mew, or any thing to bring this Line to a proper length, and also fill up this clear part; that like the Gull I may *dip* ['Keats begins to "cross" his letter at this point.'[6]] – I hope, not out of sight – and also, like a Gull, I hope to be lucky in a good sized fish – this crossing a letter is not without its association – for chequer work leads us naturally to a Milkmaid, a Milkmaid to Hogarth Hogarth to Shakespeare Shakespeare to Hazlitt – Hazlitt to Shakespeare and thus by merely pulling an apron string we set a pretty peal of Chimes at work – Let them chime on while, with your patience, – I will return to Wordsworth. . . .

(3 May 1818 to J. H. Reynolds)

No siege, this is the *game* of contraries (or correspondences) with – he hopes – John Hamilton Reynolds, minor poet and good friend, playing along with him. Everything is words, words, words; all is in the writing; the materiality of correspondences is striking: the grain, the crossing of the letter, the ink, the sheets of paper recall the crossing of the letter containing the Paolo and Francesca dream and sonnet. Here Keats knows that crossings (even if done to save paper) produce correspondences or associations: 'a pretty peal of Chimes.' As a poetics, the energies of correspondences belong to material nature and cannot be controlled by mind, ego, and wish. In his (somewhat sinister) rat-trap the words become a thing with rough edges that can trap you, squeeze and crush you to death if you touch the rat-trap at all clumsily. If you are not a smart fish, the gull will get you. The underside of happiness and play is aggression (and here we move, finally, to Keats's 'Epistle' to the same Reynolds):

> I was at home,
> And should have been most happy – but I saw
> Too far into the sea; where every maw
> The greater on the lesser feeds evermore: –
> But I saw too distinct into the core
> Of an eternal fierce destruction,
> And so from happiness I far was gone.
> Still I am sick of it: and though to-day
> I've gathered young spring-leaves, and flowers gay
> Of Periwinkle and wild strawberry,
> Still do I that most fierce destruction see,

> The shark at savage prey – the hawk at pounce,
> The gentle robin, like a pard or ounce,
> Ravening a worm. –

The rat-trap-player is one thing: be delicate and you will survive and survive with pleasure. But aggressive looking will produce a vision of aggression in the world, with the best play 'savage.' Usually readers of Keats talk of pleasure turning to sadness or pain, beauty dying, but here *play* turns to life red in tooth and claw. Rousseau's periwinkle – that so transformed and organized his moment – here sinks into the dependent clause, subsequent to the ravening shark, hawk, and even the gentle robin.

The play of opposites – gentle robin: pard or ounce. It's play to bring them into each other's orbits since they are just words. The 'Epistle' began with that game, just as the rat-trap letter celebrates it. But in this game the gentle robin has *become* pard-like, and the game has taken on the devouring aspect of species survival. The whole experience Keats sums up in that most un-Romantic rhetoric: 'I am sick of it,' rocketing between the ponderous vision of existential dis-ease and adolescent petulance. Yet many of his poems dwell in this world of wordplay and correspondences; his difficulty is to accept it as a preferred (modern) poetics, a difficulty perhaps resulting in his converting 'play' from asserting its own values to become an early stage in a poetic 'development' or 'maturation.'

Mark Halliday was picking up on particularly the first and last parts of the 'Epistle,' both imitating and commenting upon Keats's poem and, I believe, remarking on its (and similar-minded poems in the work of Keats) current relevance to poets. The Epistle begins:

> Dear Reynolds, as last night I lay in bed,
> There came before my eye that wonted thread
> Of shapes, and shadows, and remembrances,
> That every other minute vex and please:
> Things all disjointed come from north and south,
> Two witch's eyes above a cherub's mouth,
> Voltaire with casque and shield and habergeon,
> And Alexander with his night-cap on –
> Old Socrates a tying his cravat;
> And Hazlitt playing with Miss Edgeworth's cat;
> And Junius Brutus pretty well so so,
> Making the best of's way towards Soho.

Few are there who escape these visitings –
P'rhaps one or two, whose lives have patient wings,
And through whose curtains peeps no hellish nose,
No wild boar tushes and no mermaid's toes: . . .

And it ends:

Away ye horrid moods,
Moods of one's mind! You know I hate them well,
You know I'd sooner be a clapping bell
To some Kamschatkan missionary church,
Than with these horrid moods be left in lurch.
Do you get health – and Tom the same – I'll dance,
And from detested moods in new romance
Take refuge. . . . Of bad lines a centaine dose
Is sure enough – and so 'here follows prose.'

Keats writes to Reynolds about a world all disjointed, comically crazy, the half-frightening world of nightmares, a world which he would gladly leave behind him. The standard reading of the opening passage accords with the view that Keats begins with dreams and associations but abandons or subdues them as he learns to face reality.[7] But from a modern or even postmodern point of view he may through his opening disjointed dream be noticing a certain feature of reality, that the social world is full of such bizarre and contradictory pairings. If you write about the way things are, however, you risk taking pot-shots at revered figures like Hazlitt and Voltaire and at revered perspectives, in one case Hazlitt as the unrelenting cultural critic who, as Keats wrote in reference to his published comments on Maria Edgeworth, 'has damned . . . the bluestockinged.' Keats in his disjointed visitings transports the illustrious dead and living from a 'there' of reputation (like the one he soon would acquire) to a 'here' of realities. But again, he has invoked the poetics of correspondences which, somewhat like the use made of them by Mary Robinson, reveals the contradictions of urban society and civilization. Indeed the final quoted phrase, 'here follows prose,' comes from *Twelfth Night*, surely a play taking delight in confusion and disjointedness. Keats understands that correspondences (made available to consciousness through dream and the Fancy) offer the possibility of an inversion or dispersal of hierarchies, like a flirtation in which a new possibility – both for understanding and for gratification – presents itself, something which he at once fears but also seems to relish.

In describing 'There' as a place where 'tenure is freely granted though you're off your toes,' Halliday links inevitably the need for a 'there' with the temperament of academic critics and scholars. It is a place of the abandonment or perhaps of the simplification of consequences, responsibilities, and debts, of passion and consciousness and language itself. How brilliant to play upon a poem that purposely mires itself in materiality, in moods, in play, in contradiction, in aggression. Moreover, the rhyming couplets in the 'Epistle,' which Halliday exaggerates with his repetition of the rhyme, were here and even more in the earlier *Poems 1817* volume a source of consternation for conservative reviewers (as William Keach has shown) who found his couplets in their looseness and relentless enjambments not only to make a travesty of the Popian couplet but to reflect their author's own political looseness (i.e. left-wing, 'Cockney' predispositions). 'There' is a world where none of these issues is engaged, but 'here' – and here in this poem of couplets – they, along with the other features of a risked life, become all there is.

13

Afterthought to 'There':

Keats's 'Ode to Maia'

Sometimes one gets so caught up in an *argument* about poetry that the poem in its luminous simplicity and generosity – its love of the world – sinks beneath thought. The time comes for some Wordsworthian wise passiveness or Keatsian delicious diligent indolence that at once brings one closer to the living, intimate elements, the love-of-craft. But I don't need to go to Keats; he comes – after so many years – to me. Thinking about Halliday's 'There,' I realize that, as with so many of the themes and emphases of the tribute poems, his and the tradition's 'there' is guaranteed in part by Keats himself.

> Bards of Passion and of mirth,
> Ye have left your souls on earth!
> Have ye souls in heaven too,
> Double-lived in regions new?
> Yes, and those of heaven commune
> With the spheres of sun and moon;
> With the noise of fountains wond'rous,
> And the parle of voices thund'rous;
> With the whisper of heaven's trees
> And one another, in soft ease
> Seated on Elysian lawns
> Brows'd by none but Dian's fawns; ...
> Where the nightingale doth sing
> Not a senseless, tranced thing,
> But divine melodious truth;
> Philosophic numbers smooth; ...
> Where your other souls are joying,
> Never slumber'd, never cloying... .

And to George and Georgiana in North America right after the death of Tom, he says: 'I have scarce a doubt of immortality of some nature or other – neither had Tom' (16 December 1818). Here along with the here and there in the 'Ode to a Nightingale' are just a few instances of Keats's elysian dream: how natural for similarly inclined worshippers to build for Keats a home in a heaven, too. The earlier 'Ode to Maia' produces such a site of summer ease into which the poet can imagine creation and his own absorption/salvation:

> Mother of Hermes! and still youthful Maia!
> May I sing to thee
> As thou wast hymned on the shores of Baiae?
> Or may I woo thee
> In earlier Sicilian? or thy smiles
> Seek, as they once were sought, in Grecian isles,
> By bards who died content in pleasant sward,
> Leaving great verse unto a little clan?
> O give me their old vigour, and unheard,
> Save of the quiet primrose, and the span
> Of heaven, and few ears
> Rounded by thee, my song should die away,
> Content as theirs,
> Rich in the simple worship of a day.

The poem is an invocation and a prayer for poetic vigour for a remarkably precise outcome: to write a poetry of contentment and to be thus made content, to write a flirtation with the goddess who inspires and historically has inspired an (archaic) Arcadian poetic fecundity, and to write a secretive 'Hermetic' poetry known only to the happy few. But whereas 'Maia' imagines that Arcadian peace as a 'there' (in Halliday's sense), it concludes with an Arcadian ('rich' but 'simple') take on an essential poetic function, the praise ('worship') of a day. The vigour will derive from its Vergilian and Theocritean sources but will settle finally in the present and the quotidian. At the same time beauty – the form worship will assume – will radiate, in a spirit-language that bypasses the quotidian consciousness, to the primrose, the heavens, and the necessarily few sympathetic 'ears.'

Keats embedded 'Maia' in a letter to Reynolds (3 May 1818) in which he is meditating on the place of 'knowledge' in learning to console oneself for the evils and tragedies of the world such as the death or sickness of a friend and queries the possibility of both a personal and a historical development in such knowledge. It isn't at all clear how 'Maia' fits into his exploration. Apparently a retreat from a world of self-conscious striving in an iron age of pains and troubles into an invocation of a golden age, the poem also seeks a gratification ('may I woo thee?'), an occasion where the quest for knowledge may be beside the point. 'With respect to the affections and Poetry you must know by a sympathy my thoughts that way; and I dare say these few lines will be but a ratification... .' The reading of this poem ('by a sympathy') does not merely draw one into a golden age mindlessness, but rather gives a beautifully rich account of the poet's longings in the history of poetry and his anti-nostalgic, sensuously driven hunger to elevate, to make extraordinary the ordinary day.

Formal elements conspire with thematics. The poem is sonnet length, but with some lines drawn back from the decasyllabic expectation, opening up rich silences. Read as an early anticipation of 'organic form,' the short lines invite the inflowing of energies from afar, in this case from that blessed verse and song that the May-goddess may offer.

In its vision of secretive song, the poem still, to the goddess, opens its face and to me overhearing.

14

The Walking Tour of Scotland, 1818:
The Play of Poetic Forms*

We tend to characterize Keats's summer 1818 walking tour to Scotland with Charles Brown as a transition. Given readers' inclinations to map a complete life onto his 25 meager years, they and we have stamped youth, optimism, mawkishness, and 'Leigh Hunt' onto what came before Scotland, and maturity, experience, complexity, 'Dante,' and death onto what happened after. The walking tour North – its strangeness, physical testing and hardship, bad weather, and absorption into the orbit of Robert Burns, a poet dead too soon and a sacrifice of his life to his art – is said to have increased the tensile strength of Keats's poetry and his being. After all, *Hyperion*, *The Eve of St. Agnes*, 'La Belle Dame,' and the Odes came in the wake of this trip. To a degree Keats wanted this: Scotland should give him new images for poetry. But also the tour became defined under the category of Death – his brother Tom's sure decline from before the tour to his death on 1 December 1818, and Keats's own sinister sore throat 'which came of bog trotting in the island of Mull.' As a transition, as an event of life that exists less in the present and more in the before and after, as a time that produced no 'great' poems, therefore, the tour lacks its own substance; at most it's a 'dream of cold beauty,' more evident in its after-effects: brilliant, 'mature' poetry, passionate love, and death. The great value of Carol Kyros Walker's book is that it *frames* the tour, making one notice it for itself.

It is therefore significant that Walker's book is elegantly presented: glossy pages, large type, imaginative placing of text,

*This chapter is my review of Carol Kyros Walker's *Walking North with Keats* (New Haven, Conn.: Yale University Press, 1992) which was originally published in *The Wordsworth Circle* (Autumn 1992) and which I have slightly expanded for this book.

commentary, and photographs, beautiful photographs (over 150 in color and black and white). The reader walks through this pleasure three times: (a) an introductory essay – biographical sketches of Keats, his family, and Charles Brown; history, including the 1818 Westmorland election that greeted Keats in the Lake District; the 'walking tour' in literature and particularly a sketch of tour books of northern England and Scotland in the decades preceding Keats's tour; (b) the photographs, taken by Walker (1979–81), that follow precisely the steps of the Tour as described by Keats in his letters and Brown in his letters and journal and that attempt to catch the date or season, the time of day, the weather conditions that Keats and Brown actually experienced; and (c) Keats's and Brown's letters and journals presented as a contribution, in their own right, to early nineteenth-century travel literature of Scotland. The photographs are glossed mainly with quotes from Keats and Brown, and the letters and journals are annotated by Walker.

She observes that when Keats left the Lake District on his way north to Scotland, he stripped himself generally of the Wordsworthian influence. Although, of course, 'Wordsworth' appears in Keats's poetry and letters of 1819, he does seem a presence from which Keats is trying to free himself. If for 'Wordsworth' we substitute 'the sublime,' Walker's point by and large carries. Keats, as several readers have noted, after being astonished by the sight of Windermere and the mountains of Cumbria, slowly becomes more absorbed by Scottish behavior and custom – by culture and society and politics – than by the lonely, slate-blue power of the Highlands and Scottish lakes. More and more he eschewed the kind of identification, the wonderment appropriate to travelling in Scottish nature, for a more playful, skeptical, literary, social, politically liberal, urban response. It is a response – à la Marjorie Levinson – of the outsider to the tradition of the eighteenth-century well-to-do literary English connoisseur of Scottish tours. He, for example, opens his letter to Reynolds (11, 13 July 1818):

> I'll not run over the Ground we have passed; that would be merely as bad as telling a dream – unless perhaps I do it in the manner of the Laputan printing press – that is I put down Mountains, Rivers, Lakes, dells, glens, Rocks, and Clouds, with beautiful enchanting, gothic picturesque fine, delightful,

enchancting [*sic*] Grand, sublime – a few Blisters &c – and now
you have our journey thus far ....

The list of subjects are, in Keats's prose, simply the codewords for
subjects as traditionally and (often) boringly presented in tour
writing. With reference to Swift's Laputan printing press that
scrambles words in new unforeseen combinations, Keats indicates
that his own tour writing will not be enslaved by the tonal require-
ments of the genre.

The striking fact about the poems written on the Tour is their
variety of form and consistency of subject (i.e. stimulated by occasions and associations from the tour itself). Although continually
bobbing and weaving through Scotland in his writing – in a kind of
anxiety in relation to the material – his poetry and letters serve the
cause of his own linguistic freedom and his ease with received
genres and help to concentrate the function of poetry within him as
the search for poetic knowledge. 'There was a naughty boy' (that
line itself suggesting quietly his refusal to play by the rules of his
parents in poetry) ends with 'He stood in his / Shoes and he
wonder'd.' Poetic knowledge turns out to elude him through the
traditional organ of the sublime – the eye – while some new epistemological sensation centers in the *feet*. When all is confusion, he can
feel the certainty of the ground beneath him:

> Here are the craggy stones beneath my feet;
> Thus much I know, that, a poor witless elf,
>   I tread on them; that all my eye doth meet
> Is mist and crag – not only on this height,
> But in the world of thought and mental might.

For all the jaunty playfulness of some of the poems and letters
and for all the skepticism of others – with a curious mixture of
defiance, whimsy, and defensiveness – Keats gives plenty of evidence of being absorbed by his journey, by the scenery, the people's
customs, and economic conditions, by the memory of poets. Tour
guides behind him, he feels each new encounter on his pulses. The
reader of Walker's book is allowed to meditate on Keats's engagement largely through the photographs. A number of them are
framed by windows, doorways, natural apertures, or suggest such
framings. Apparently we are to feel, as we are supposed to imagine
Keats would feel, the encounter onto the new scene or occasion

with the eye of the wanderer *naif* (a bit like Yeats's Keats with nose pressed against the sweetshop window); this I find mildly irritating since the letters and poems intimate a far deeper engagement. But mostly the photographs beautifully allow us to realize how Keats was drawn out of the tame (relative to this) nature and culture of Hampstead and therefore how he might seek out the 'gentle anchor pull' of the one sure thing in the journeyer's repertoire, the foot's contact with the ground, while he might continually court the unfamiliar and the vast. One senses the power both of the landscape and of the figure of Robert Burns to pull him into 'other sensations,' to lead him imaginatively across the boundary of the familiar, which at times appears as the boundary between life and death. Crossing that boundary or approaching it and fantasizing it is deeply bound up with the poem and with poets. The Burns memorials he encounters – the grave and house – act on him like the edge of a precipice to which he is fearfully drawn. They are to him, in some precise way, the site of the true poetry, the extreme distance from the quotidian, and as such surprise him in their effect on his vision of the real:

> All is cold beauty; pain is never done
> For who has mind to relish, Minos-wise,
>   The real of beauty, free from that dead hue
>   Sickly imagination and sick pride
>   Cast wan upon it!

And similarly (at Burns's cottage):

> My eyes are wandering, and I cannot see,
>   Fancy is dead and drunken at its goal;
> Yet can I stamp my foot upon thy floor,
>   Yet I can ope thy window-sash to find
> The meadow thou hast tramped o'er and o'er, –
>   Yet can I think of thee till thought is blind,
> Yet can I gulp a bumper to thy name –
> Oh, smile among the shades, for this is fame!

But it is in 'Lines Written in the Highlands after a Visit to Burns's Country' that he defines the pleasure and simultaneous fear of 'footing slow' to the cottage of Burns 'beyond the bourn of care.' The pilgrimage to Burns occurs also in the mind and psyche, involving in this case a willingness to identify with the dead poet, described in a beautiful metonymy, 'when weary feet forget themselves,' the mind having given over its controls to the instinct of the feet that also give over through forgetfulness to the call of the 'there' of the poet.

> Aye, if a madman could have leave to pass a healthful
> day,
> To tell his forehead's swoon and faint when first began
> decay,
> He might make tremble many a man whose spirit had gone
> forth
> To find a bard's low cradle place about the silent
> north.
> Scanty the hour and few the steps beyond the bourn of
> care,
> Beyond the sweet and bitter world – beyond it unaware;
> Scanty the hour and few the steps, because a longer
> stay
> Would bar return and make a man forget his mortal way.

That foot, a metonymy for the sure knowledge of the senses, at the same time for the fearful advance beyond the securely familiar, may also have been a metonymy for sexual knowledge and possibility, its own new adventure and its own confusion. At what may be the emotional core of the tour stands Keats remarking his confusions about women (see 18, 22 July to Benjamin Bailey), his feelings of suspicion and smallness as well as desire, presented with the sudden frankness of self that comes upon one far from home. Then there was his walking mate Charles Brown who – as Aileen Ward noted – was at least inclined towards homosexuality.[1] The range of probable fantasies about Keats's own sexuality erupting at this time may have matched the range of verbal play ('He took / In his knapsack / A book / Full of vowels / And a shirt / With some towels') and poetic varieties.

The Scottish tour might teach one that *confusion* of sexual and poetic and vocational (and, perhaps, class) identities marks Keats's career above all, not just at this season of summer in 1818 but in the preceding and succeeding years as well. Is this terribly surprising for someone with a double parent-loss in late childhood, the meaning of which was undoubtedly confirmed by the death of his brother over which he presided? The resistances to change (the power of fixation) and exploration, growth, diversification of identities (not just one) must have been enormous. How impressive, therefore, in the confusion and 'mist' of his experience are the commitments in poetry to poetic play (a book full of vowels), to the representation of indolence and ecstasy (extreme psychic states), to the willingness to ground his poetry in a chthonic materialism (just the opposite of a mad struggle to escape).

Walker and others tend to associate the Scottish tour with the onset of Keats's terminal disease. Though certainly true, the association has had the effect of limiting the meaning of 'death' for the poet to the demise of his body. Yes, Keats uncannily foresaw his own death with the line 'This mortal body of a thousand days,' but other references intimate death as the absorption of the self into a reality 'beyond the sweet and bitter world.' I suspect that Scotland recast itself in his mind as this visionary dreariness: thus the appealing 'strange mood, half asleep' of the sonnet on visiting the tomb of Burns. To identify with the dead poet is what Keats must have thought the poet should do, in the sense that death belongs properly to the poet's song. He seems to have situated himself and his self-representation at the 'adieu' towards the familiar and at the 'adieu' to the unfamiliar, what would 'make a man forget his mortal way ....' With this in mind, the most powerful of Walker's continually evocative photographs comes near the end of her (and Keats's) sequence: two men appear on the top of Ben Nevis *in a mist*; bent over by backpacks, they travel on away from the viewer, made half-indistinct by the graininess of the picture. Why not call the men Keats and Brown, who at this moment seem very near? In context it is an image of the Death-of-the-Poet.

15

Memos on Keats for the Next Millennium

Writing is the opposite of imagining.

Edmond Jabes

Of all our poets, excepting Shakespeare and Milton, and perhaps Chaucer, [Keats] has most of the poetical character – fire, fancy, and diversity.

... there is an effluence of power and light pervading all his works ....

Walter Savage Landor

What follows, from here to the end of this study, is not an argument but rather three observations, or memos, that open up to view a Keats by now familiar to readers of this book but submerged in the Keats still prevailing in most discussions today. Memos: notes or reminders of something one might easily forget in the normal course of events. The memos – about Keats's sexuality, his February–May 1819 journal letter and open forms, and the *1820* arrangement of his short poems – refer to the presence of a poetics of aperture in Keats's thinking and reinforce this with the sense of a more 'open' sexuality than that usually granted Keats. They do not presume a causal connection between sexuality and poetics (although the possibility of this is not denied) so much as they assume that with reading Keats a revision of our view of sexuality may need and coincide with a revision of our view of his poetics. Finally, permeating the second and third memos is an implicit answer to the question of how – as the tradition of eulogy poems and subsequent criticism insists – Keats's is a poetry of death, a response to the poet's challenge: oblivion. It is not, as Neil Freistat and others suggest, a 'confrontation' against 'enchantment' or 'escape' through Fancy, nor is it 'skepticism' about Fancy and (as some imply) poetry altogether. Instead it points towards a poetics in which the primacy of the self, with its anticipation of the 'end of the world,' is submerged and reinvisioned in a sense of cosmic relations and permanence, which, from the point of view of 'self,' is, in Thomas McGrath's formulation, a postponing of the end of the world.

If it has in this sense traditionally been read as elegiac, that is, about the death of the person and subsequent consolations, and if an elegiac poetry typically in English resorts to and is expressed in closed or abstract forms in which the self is preserved and set off against the world into which it otherwise dissolves at death, then Keats's poetry, or its driving impulse that I wish to isolate, seeks to define and locate itself less along the axes of self and more along the axes of world.

EXTRAVAGANCE AND SEXUAL CONFUSION

Recent scholars of Keats have lifted the ban on questioning Keats's sexuality. Lionel Trilling insisted upon the poet's 'mature masculinity,' but now we may observe Keats's femininity, his infantilism and the early critics' delight in pointing it out, and his autoeroticism. But who talks about the homoeroticism of Keats? Consider, for example:

(a)   The Chapman's Homer sonnet. Two young men spend the night together poring over a book. Then the poem written down obviously with passion and delight the next morning concludes with all of Cortez's men staring not at the Pacific (the placid but eroticized woman) but at each other: a homosocial 'wild surmise.'

(b)   The masculine complicity of the narrator and Porphyro in *The Eve of St. Agnes*. Both are obviously *taking pleasure together* in viewing Madeline's undressing.

(c)   The slippage in the epithets for the Urn. An 'unravished bride' in the first line, it becomes a cooler, masculine 'friend to man' at the end, speaking finally an aphoristic wisdom of 'masculine' authority.

(d)   The sensuous language of, particularly, the early Keats ('slippery blisses'). Usually associated with the feminine or the infantile, this language appears to me now extraordinarily 'user-friendly' to Keats. If it were really the language of the feminine, that is, the other, would not this male poet treat it with less ease than he does?

(e)   The nightingale itself. It 'pours forth' its song in such an ecstasy. And it 'found a path' through the sad heart of Ruth. The poet's longing to fly to the bird is for a male object. Perhaps the vision of a homoerotic communion dislodges a fantasy of hetero-sexual violence (as in Charles Lamb's *Rosamund Gray*).

(f)   Biography. See Keats's extreme ambivalence towards women, including his wish that they not even read his poetry. See also the early absence of his father and the intense ambivalence towards his mother who, in death when he reached adolescence, must have become a figure of terror, betrayal, and mistrust, while his father, longer dead, may have grown into a figure of desire.

(g)   The intense homosocial bonding with his friends: Reynolds, Bailey, Woodhouse, Severn, Brown, and his two brothers. As a poet, moreover, he would be right in line with the other contemporary male pairings, Wordsworth–Coleridge and Shelley–Byron: query – might Romantic poetry reveal a defining stratum of homoerotic desire?

Oscar Wilde's sonnet to Keats is clear at least in the fantasy of what he wanted Keats to be: St Sebastian, the favorite saint among homosexuals. The identification was strong enough so that Wilde could give himself the alias of Sebastian during his last days in France. In the other direction he named one of his houses, Keats House; Keats seemed to be his favorite among English poets. At Keats's grave, he began his sonnet:

> The youngest of the martyrs here is lain,
> Fair as Sebastian, and as early slain.

Wilde was thinking specifically of a favorite painting, Guido Reni's *San Sebastian* which he saw on the same 1877 trip to Italy, in Genoa's Palazzo Rosso, that took him to Keats's grave. He wrote a note to the poem:

> As I stood beside the mean grave of this divine boy, I thought of him as of a Priest of Beauty slain before his time; and the vision of Guido's St. Sebastian came before my eyes as I saw him at Genoa, a lovely brown boy, with crisp, clustering hair and red lips, bound by his evil enemies to a tree and, though pierced by arrows, raising his eyes with divine, impassioned gaze towards the Eternal Beauty of the opening Heavens.

The 'evil enemies' only join the painting as two thin arrows, one entering above the right nipple and the other through the lower back: otherwise the painting is even more intensely erotic than Wilde's passionate vision of it, with a cloth tied suggestively around the genital region of a body frontally extended upward and with a bright gleam of the saint set against the darkness of the trees and sky in the background.

Wilde would have lain prostrate on Keats's grave at age 23, about the same year in life that Keats wrote his finest poetry, so the identification – and the understanding of Keats through identification – must have been particularly intense and, given Wilde's recent and awestruck introduction to Pope Pius IX earlier in the same day, confusing (and not un-Keatsian). Richard Ellman says of Wilde:

> ... before the grave of Keats, 'the holiest place in Rome,' he prostrated himself on the grass. It was a humbler obeisance than he had offered to the Pope, and irritated Hunter Blair [Wilde's travelling companion] because of its confusion of aesthetic and religious postures. To submit to a poet as one should submit to a prelate was to undermine the meaning of submission.[1]

Wilde's association of Keats and Sebastian is similarly interesting for its sexual and aesthetic extravagance and for its more typical placing of Keats in a Hellenic/Christian Heaven. During the same period Wilde spoke of Keats's and Swinburne's 'effeminacy and languor and voluptuousness which are the characteristics of that "passionate humanity" which is the background of true poetry.'[2] We have by and large forgotten the powerful Pre-Raphaelite reading of Keats, but its discovery of extravagance and extremity in the midst of sexual confusion seems to me far more at the heart of his accomplishment than as a poet of 'identity' and containment or maturity. How striking (and wonderfully predictable) that Wilde's understanding of Keats should emerge in an outburst of post-adolescent, gay passion and that Wilde's tribute to Keats should undermine with eroticism the serene spiritualized eternity into which the tradition has placed him!

Keats is that poet upon whose grave Wilde threw himself in a state of ecstatic grief! Must we not read Wilde's passionate identification as an interpretation of the work?

A STRUGGLE WITH POETICS: JOURNAL LETTER, FEBRUARY–MAY 1819

If there exists a general view of Keats's dazzling February–May 1819 journal letter to George and Georgiana Keats, it belongs rougly to Lionel Trilling's account and assessment of it: we are to read it 'in terms of the self.' The letter begins, he says, in 'trifles' and 'moves towards its climax' in the vale of soul-making passage: the early intuition about Negative Capability has 'yielded doctrine' about the self and spiritual salvation. The letter begins amid the grey emptiness and muted despair pervading the aftermath of Tom's recent death and rounds out three months later with the spring-time 'Ode to Psyche.' As the season warms, so do his energies, his intellect, and his poems. But the movement towards the climax does more than register the correspondence of nature's vicissitudes to Keats's temperament (although he does say in February, 'I must wait for the spring to rouse me up a little'): he embodies also, in his words, 'an ellectric [*sic*] fire in human nature tending to purify – so that among these human creatures there is continually some birth of new heroism.' Trilling has read the letter as a heroic instance of psychological and moral maturation, a coming to terms with death and with the problem of evil; it becomes a paradigm of the shape and drama of Keats's life, culminating in what he and countless other readers of Keats have admired, what Trilling referred to as that 'hard core of self,' the ability to endure (a kind of happy warrior), to establish and center himself amid a world of pains and troubles. Keats, from one perspective, is an 'image of health,' from another, the archetypal hero. His greatness is singular, the coalescence of a chaotically tragic and disparate life into an identity.

In more recent times criticism has looked more closely and technically at this identity finding it less stable, with respect to sexuality, to women, and generally to various parameters of psychological achievement. Marjorie Levinson has, without avoiding the issue of psychology and selfhood, ventured boldly into the realm of the poetry itself, finding that the basic impulse for poems is not singular and originary but pastiche, a tissue of quotation and fragment exploiting Keats's sense of literary marginalization from the tradition. But, as I have been urging here, the tradition of admiring Keats as a succeeded person in spite of or because of his early death and severe treatment by the critics goes hand in hand with a poetics of closed forms and of elegy, of completed actions fully formed. Here I will instead reread this extraordinary letter ('dazzling' is Trilling's word) with an eye to a poetics of multiplicity and dispersal. Hazlitt, whose comments on poetry and power figure centrally in the letter, helps Keats to locate the possibility of a new poetics of power, one based not – as Hazlitt suggests – on monarchical and tyrannical hoardings and misuse of power but on a power dispersed through a democracy.

Little of this last, however, is direct. Keats, as he says, straining at particles of light amid a great darkness, writes in a three-month trance, testing and playing out words, words, words – anecdotes, recollections, images, propositions, states of mind and body, and poems. From remarks made early in the letter, he apparently had no idea that it would be more than a day or two long. He seems silently, at some point, to have agreed with himself to let it proliferate, to let himself, like his gardener Fancy of May, breed flowers endlessly, never the same. Regardless of the heroism of personality displayed here, the profile of poetic change is what needs to be graphed in a new way: the point is not change to a poetry of tragic reality (the way the Odes are often read) but one one of comic fecundity.

A subdued nihilism, a consciousness of emptiness, an unvisionary dreariness, what Keats will call an uneasy indolence, marks the first half of this letter:

> I see very little now, and very few Persons – being almost … tired of Men and things –
>
> The Literary world I know nothing about –
>
> I have not been in great cue for writing lately –
>
> We lead verry [*sic*] quiet lives here –
>
> During the evening nothing passed worth notice
>
> I know not why Poetry and I have been so distant lately
>
> I cannot bear a day annihilated in that manner

And then, as a healthy irritated summary of the above:

> to have nothing to do, and to be surrounded with unpleasant human identities; who press upon one just enough to prevent

one getting into a lazy position; and not enough to interest or arouse one; is a capital punishment for a capital crime .... I do not know what I did on monday – nothing – nothing – nothing ....

At about this point, 19 March, the nothing and the emptiness seem to be less an absence and the sinking into a forgetfulness and more the presence of absence, the texture of oblivion seen as a challenge. One can easily refer this change to successful self-therapy. I, however, want to think of it as potentially a *poet's reaction to the problem of oblivion*: acknowledging it in his life, Keats begins to represent it in his poetry in order to perform, but potentially in a new way, its defeat in poems that counter oblivion.

Keats shows a preoccupation with the vanishing of persons that can be referred simultaneously to his life and his poems – from his sonnet 'When I have fears' to his obsessive image of Fanny Brawne: 'I eternally see her figure eternally vanishing.' The language of dullness and emptiness and uneasy indolence displaces this onto the loss of consciousness and of acknowledgment. Poetry insists upon a counter-statement, a reversal of the entropy of neglect and of the abandonment of the person to oblivion. Poetry, in a phrase to which I have already referred, 'postpones the end of the world.' The February-to-May journal letter can be read as an effort (probably unconscious) to chart out such a poetics of postponement, or, put simply, a poetics relying less upon elegiac, closed forms emphasizing scarcity and loss and the precariousness of self and accessing more the language and syntax of abundance, a proliferation of world elements. Nothingness and emptiness pose the visionary problem for the poet. Even 'La Belle Dame sans Merci,' composed and included in the midst of this letter, can perhaps best be read in context as a nightmare about his commitment to 'gap'ing emptiness, scarcity, starvation, and gloom, in short a withering mind of winter, as the poet's problem. The poem, about the loss of consciousness in love, the inverse of the Psyche myth addressed in the 'Ode' near the end of the letter, nonetheless represents the recovery of images, the refusal to allow the final success of the oblivion implied in the strange magic of the kiss as a kind of epitome of experience. The poem dramatizes the radical alienating intensity of the lyric moment (the need, with an eye to the critics, to temper the infinity of kisses – 'score' – with moderation: 'four') with the resultant assignation of the poet to a palely loitering, or uneasy-indolent, permanence.

Another way of looking at the nightmare is that attention is brought to bear upon the uniqueness, the singularity, the *integer* of identity of the knight, to invert part of Keats's epithet for Wordsworth, an egotistical inferno. The camelion poet, as I've previously suggested, seeks multiple identities and voices: the only unity is that which the poem offers as a set of cosmic correspondences to ensure the postponement of the always imminent oblivion of the singular human subject. This contest, between the singularity and the multiplicity of identity, is, I believe, what drives the journal letter through nearly three months of intense and playful exploration. It is during these months that Keats abandons his poet-deity Apollo, in *Hyperion*, at the moment of the achievement of godhead and that he also distinguishes himself from the 'ideal' of disinterestedness, granting that capacity primarily to Socrates and Christ. In all these instances the heroic figure has the capacity to gather the world into a single, powerful identity that, on the human scale, Keats must associate with the predilection for oblivion (in some sense the supremely powerful may be supremely isolated) and in poetry would be associated with the power inherent in the monarchical and tyrannical rulers of a society. Both of these associations get reinforced or stimulated by Keats's model in cultural criticism, William Hazlitt, who appears in the letter through lavish quotation.

In the earlier 16 December 1818 to 4 January 1819 journal letter to George and Georgiana, Keats was so impressed with Hazlitt's account of Godwin's St Leon that he quoted the critic extensively, including:

The faces of Men pass before him as in a speculum; but he is attached to them by no common tie of sympathy or suffering. He is thrown back into himself and his own thoughts. He lives in the solitude of the world. *His is the solitude of the Soul, not of woods, or trees or mountains* – but the desert of society – the waste and oblivion of the heart. He is himself alone.[3]

The association of an unsympathetic solitude with words like 'oblivion' and 'desert' seems to enunciate a type of person that Keats would like to repudiate, a singular identity imploding upon itself, taking the rich foliage of the world into it, creating thereby his own oblivion with his loss of connection to anything else. As such, the passage seems to interest Keats for its psychological insight, but then one notices that it is sandwiched between two tetrameter poems quoted in full: 'Fancy' and 'Bards of Passion and of Mirth.' Taken together these three elements indicate a concern at least as much with poetics as with psychology; the poems present an alternative to Godwin's novels in which, says Hazlitt as Keats has quoted it, 'There is little knowledge of the world, little variety, neither an eye for the picturesque, nor a talent for the humourous ....' There is, in other words, imaginative power in Godwin but not imaginative variety. 'Fancy' and 'Bards of Passion' speak of an imagination of fecundity and proliferation. The second poem is then followed shortly by another, 'I had a dove and the sweet dove died,' a brief lyrical elegy about someone – to paraphrase Blake – who destroys the winged life by binding to himself a joy: 'it was tied / With a silken thread of my own hands weaving.' Keats, during the months following Tom's death, may be struggling to discover (or rediscover) a counter-poetic to the elegiac one, a poetic that kisses the joy as it flies.

In the passages quoted from Hazlitt's open letter to the reviewer Gifford about the latter's 'invincible pertness, ... mercenary malice, ... impenetrable dullness, ... barefaced impudence,' and so on, Keats is taken with four features of Hazlitt's writing: he responds first to Hazlitt's energy for intelligent invective, second to his theory of poetry, third to his 'feeling for the costume of society,' and fourth to his style. Keats likes the 'force and innate power with which [the essay] yeasts and works itself up.' 'To yeast' perhaps refers to Hazlitt's driving paratactic style, brilliantly exhibited in these passages, as an endlessly expansive imagination that catches, among other things, the costumes of society in its path. Hazlitt's theory of poetry – 'the sense of power abstracted from the sense of good' – would appear to Keats as acknowledging the political stakes inherent in poetry, stakes denied by Gifford in his attack. The young poet might have sensed that two kinds of power were embedded in these passages: the first the association of an exclusionary, class-limited power in poetry that Hazlitt describes, and second the power manifest in Hazlitt's own prose, style and content: here power is returned to 'the sense of good' and returned, so to speak, to the people from whom it had been unjustly taken. Is it not possible that Keats might have begun to associate Hazlitt's parataxis with a power directed to the people and not to their oppressors? And by extension, such a poetry – not imagined by Hazlitt – could also be 'anti-oblivious'? It would be a poetry of the world, a visionary poetry of abundance, not of scarcity, a poetry delighting in an

Iago as much as an Imogen, a poetry delighting in all sorts of juxtapositions and correspondences, of things all disjointed coming from north and south, a poetry potentially of a democratic variousness; formally, a poetry of lists and sequences, kissing the joys as they fly. It would be a poetry freed from the ego in order to emanate from the world.

There is more of this kind of poetry, or at least more poetic exercises in this direction, than readers of Keats usually notice, from the early 'Cockney Couplet' poems like 'I stood tiptoe' and *Sleep and Poetry*, to parts of *Endymion*, to the 'Epistle to Reynolds,' to the playful six- and eight-syllable-line poems of 1818 and 1819, even to parts of the Odes. In this regard consider the months of December through May as a time of pointed experiment with short poems, or lyrics with potentially more open forms, and more specifically experiments with that most closed and abstract of forms, the sonnet. (The earlier Scottish tour was another such period of lyric experiment.) After copying out 'Fancy' and 'Bards of Passion' in the December–January journal letter, Keats explains his current infatuation with these tetrameter poems: 'these are specimines [*sic*] of a sort of rondeau which I think I shall become partial to – because you have one idea amplified with greater ease and more delight and freedom than in the sonnet ….' He continues in this predictive manner: 'It is my intention to wait a few years before I publish any minor poems – and then I hope to have a volume of some worth – and which those people will relish who cannot bear the burden of a long poem ….' A poetry of amplification, delight, and freedom – hardly *Hyperion*, hardly *The Eve of St. Agnes*; instead he imagines a project of short lyrics, postponing oblivion or the end of the world with a syntax of delight and freedom. Of course, one could look at the entire spring journal letter as one long, three-month paratactic glide – on every level of detail. What he observes in Coleridge – running through topics one after another – is just what Keats does. The sonnets sprinkled throughout seem on the one hand part of this larger sequencing, but in terms of the strict, unpliable boundaries they individually propose, they stand for a different mentality, even a different set of ethical choices, which is why Keats experiments with them.

After writing 'La Belle Dame' and the tetrameter poems 'Lines on the Mermaid Tavern' and 'Robin Hood' and the dimeter 'Two or three Posies' to his sister Fanny, Keats turned in April, a few weeks before the 'peeping of the first rose,' to pump out four more sonnets, but, with one exception, each tampers with sonnet form. In

March he had written the Paolo and Francesca sonnet which apparently disappointed him: 'There are fourteen lines but nothing of
what I felt in it ....' This is the sonnet with which I began, with the
crossing of the final couplet ('melancholy storm') over the 'delightful enjoyments' of his dream. The April sonnets break the form in
the rhyme scheme while keeping 14 ten-syllable lines. One can
view this as a compromise with opening the form completely or,
more interestingly, as a formal element in the twisting of thoughts,
in Zukofsky's phrase, 'thoughts' torsion.'[4] Keats's proverbial epi-
graph to the first 'Fame' sonnet is: 'You cannot eat your cake and
have it too.' But this, I think, is precisely the poetics that Keats is
trying to devise this spring: the representation of oblivion (eating
your cake) and its postponement (have it too), all under the sign of
pleasure. He doesn't like the legitimate (Italian) sonnet for its
pouncing rhymes or the Shakespearian for its *abab* quatrains which
are 'too elegiac,' that is, too much under the sign of the end of the
world. The Fame and Sleep sonnets are about the release of the
ego's control, the mind's policeman; if you bid adieu to Fame and
Fame then follows, you in effect enter the social and collective
matrix of multiple identities. Implicit here and spelled out in the
'Ode to Psyche' is the proliferating tendency coming from such a
paradoxical, or perhaps oxymoronical, gesture. Note again the
plural formulation in Zukofsky: 'the actual twisting / Of many and
diverse thoughts.'[5]

Just before copying the sonnets and the 'Ode to Psyche' Keats
had written the Vale-of-Soul-making passage much of which is
stated in the plural: 'a Place where the heart must feel and suffer in
a thousand diverse ways! ... As various as the Lives of Men are – so
various become their souls, and thus does God make individual
beings.' The variety of souls in Keatsian doctrine becomes the
triumph of the gardener Fancy in the 'Ode to Psyche,' who breeding flowers will never breed the same. Here is the wish of the poet
who will not let this heathen goddess be neglected, who will postpone the end of the world through the encouraging of as yet name-
less images in new and endless combinations.

POETICS IN KEATS'S *1820* VOLUME: POSTPONING THE END OF THE WORLD

The first Ode published in Keats's 1820 volume is the 'Ode to a
Nightingale,' and, therefore, the first words of the Odes published

together are 'My heart aches.' I like to think of them as a quotation, lifted from the tales and poems about the fated bird, of the nightingale's pain – the first and last utterance, erupting to die, caused by the thorn of its violation leaning into its breast. It is a voice with nowhere to go; it marks the end of a consciousness.

At the same time it is the voice of the poet identifying with the tragedy of the myth. It is the crisis of the Ode and of the Odes: how to go on, in the human scale? The history of reading these poems proceeds in the tragic mode: Keats effectively cleaves to the tragic identification – himself being borne towards death – to produce a poetry of heroic proportions, establish a lyric proof of the 'hard core of self' that the modern poem supposedly embodies. The heroic protagonist of the Odes, like Wordsworth's Happy Warrior or the heroines of Schiller's dramas, endures the long tragedy like a burden, like Shelley in the 'Ode to the West Wind' whom 'A heavy weight of hours has chained and bowed.'

A poem written and interpreted in this register refers to a sense of past experience; the poem records the speaker's success with the battles for identity, for reaching a psychic landing place; its form is closed (regular stanzas), the atmosphere is elegiac: whatever succeeds does so by acknowledging loss and mutability and a fundamental scarcity of the repertoire of world elements accessible to the subject. It should be said that our tradition of reading the Romantic lyric follows this pattern, laid out by readers of the Wordsworth lyric as well as those of Keats's Odes. Clearly in what has preceded this section I have claimed another possibility for Keats; the test case, however, is the Odes, themselves written during a springtime clouded by the over-resonant death of Tom.

Wordsworth's 'Lucy' poem, 'She dwelt among the untrodden ways' – as a poetic instance that infiltrates Keats's Odes – occasions the same possibility for reading according to death, pastness, and closure *or* death and praise and presence: the poem of 'emergency.' Lucy, who is neither seen nor known (except by the poet's metaphors: violet, star) is dead, and this 'difference' affects the poet radically as a terrible absence. This is a poem of loss and grief. Moreover, her beauty, registered through the metaphors that overflow the middle stanza, comes with the most terrible price, her death, thus fulfilling the feminist critique of the poem's aesthetics: beauty in poetry equals the death of the woman. But I can read this poem in a different key altogether (and in a way that anticipates my reading of Keats's Odes). Lucy, the poem says in its third line, was 'A Maid whom there were none to praise.' She has no social identity; there is no account of her. Before the poem she has been consigned to oblivion. Oblivion is precisely the enemy of poetry. Oblivion is 'the end of the world,' a moment and condition that does not require the fanfare of cosmic apocalypse but can simply be the act, as it were, of forgetting, of not acknowledging, a life. It is negligence, moral entropy, and it is natural, as in the phrase from Wordsworth's 'The Ruined Cottage': 'the calm oblivious tendencies of nature.' The first of the poem's three brief stanzas registers her proximity to oblivion and marks the crisis of the poem.

The second stanza starts the engine of the poem's and the poet's functions – to usher Lucy into the world of discourse, of the community – in a spectacular way, with a starburst of two powerful, unanticipated correspondences:

> A violet by a mossy stone
> Half-hidden from the eye!
> – Fair as a star when only one
> Is shining in the sky.

When these lines are read as metaphor or comparison – Lucy is like a violet, Lucy is like a star – they serve to reinforce the elegiac temperament imputed to this lyric, for the poet, like the community, attempts to substitute beautiful images for the young girl now dead, a tragically futile exercise. If, however, the images appear as correspondences, that is, as the insistence that the girl has a place – along with a violet, a mossy stone, a perceiving eye, a star, and the sky – in the cosmos, then she *comes into being* by virtue of these newly established relationships. And the cosmos, potentially emptied of its objects by the overwhelming presence of human loss and forgetfulness, flourishes again, now enlivened by Lucy's place amid the correspondences. There *is* now someone to praise Lucy, the speaker-poet, which brings 'She dwelt among untrodden ways' into the orbit of world praise-poems that exist not to mourn but to coax life into being, to acknowledge presence. Indeed, alongside the overt praise of stanza two works a repetitive, nearly ritualized insistence on her unknownness: no one trod to her home, no one praised her, few loved her, she was half-hidden, far away, and again 'She lived unknown, and few could know.' Jerome Rothenberg would say that such repetition 'exhausts the burden'[6] of the word or image, the casting of a spell that casts out the jaundice in the diseased body, that casts out the unknownness, the oblivion of the woman:

> Lucy ceased to be.

Lucy is named at the moment her death is announced. Notice that the long 'e' sound threads through the whole line – from the name to her death to her presence: the length of the vowel, the fact that no other sound in the line stops its final articulation – 'be' – lifts it into, if not permanence, at least the postponement of its ending and converts absence into presence. The final verse pair –

> But she is in her grave, and oh,
> The difference to me –

shows a similar conversion: the trimeter ('But she is in her grave') is here the line of oblivion; the postponement of its end, 'and oh,' extends existence into the consciousness of the speaker-as-poet for whom 'difference' marks the stimulation of the poet's vocation of countering the oblivious tendency, of world forgetfulness, with praise.

For Wordsworth the conservation of the image and the naming of the other (one of poetry's traditional functions) is constrained – by an identification of the poet with his alienated subjects in *Lyrical Ballads* – to inhabit the same space as that of the speaker poet. Keats, working from his Wordsworthian model but also alive to the substantiality of mythic apparitions as at once different from the subject yet part of his psycho-religious makeup, tries to recover the older form of praise that leaves the speaking subject 'darkling' and the unfolding of world images in the sun.

When the Odes have been read as a group or suite of poems, they appear sequentially in rough, projected order of composition, beginning with the 'Ode to Psyche,' often leaving out the 'Ode on Indolence' (except Helen Vendler who places it before 'Psyche'), and concluding, inevitably as well as chronologically, with 'To Autumn' assumed – though not called by Keats – an ode. This sequence is useful, of course, for the elegists since it progresses from spring to autumn, comedy to tragedy, 'imperfect' ('Psyche') to 'perfect' ('Autumn'). In every way the quintessence of Keats's *oeuvre* marks the *maturation* into *tragic* lyric *acceptance*.

But when he presented these poems in his 1820 volume, Keats and his publisher ordered them differently: 'Ode to a Nightingale,' 'Ode on a Grecian Urn,' 'Ode to Psyche,' 'Fancy,' 'Ode' ('Bards of Passion and of Mirth,'), 'Lines on the Mermaid Tavern,' 'Robin Hood,' 'To Autumn,' and, last, 'Ode on Melancholy.' Presumably the book would have ended here but Taylor and Hessey sneaked in the unfinished *Hyperion* as well – a deed which didn't please the dying poet. This sequence, I believe, tells a story different from that of chronology. First of all, the cluster of Odes does not exclude other kinds of poems: tetrameter poems, playful, which are at times 'list' poems, calling attention away from the elegiac, commemorative function of odes. Moreover, they offer relief from and propose an alternative to the massive English pentameter line written on the human, potentially elegiac, scale.

And second, the 'Ode to Psyche' – the most comic of the Odes – is placed centrally, looking back to the two more 'tragic' Odes and forward immediately to the jaunty tetrameter poems, while the 'Ode on Melancholy' and not 'To Autumn' rounds out the suite. This order, I have come to believe, directs us to read the Odes not as poems of death and tragic acceptance but as visionary structures that 'postpone the end of the world,' that demonstrate a proliferative imagination: the gardener Fancy, breeding flowers who never breeds the same, beams forward and backwards over the sequence (and the poem 'Fancy' follows 'Psyche' pushing the point home).

But in speaking about chronological versus published sequences and about Keats's intentions, I have been making Romantic assumptions about authorship and book production which need examination: that this poet wrote what he intended and published exactly what he wrote – 'full blown.' Did Keats actually choose the *1820* ordering of poems? did he choose it in serious consultation with his friend Richard Woodhouse and publisher John Taylor? or did the latter two (Keats being very sick in the spring and early summer of 1820 when the book was with the editor and then the printer) make all serious decisions? and if they did exert final control over the ordering, would their own conservative literary politics (in contrast to Keats's more liberal ones) have prevailed at some level of the editorial choices made? These questions come to mind precisely because the work of Keats's most authoritative twentieth-century editor, Jack Stillinger, has documented the active editorial presence of Woodhouse and Taylor in the making of *1820*, a presence that contravened the poet's intention of where in the volume to place *The Eve of St. Agnes* and of whether or not to include the unfinished *Hyperion* at all.

The view of Stillinger on the production of *1817* and *Endymion* as well as *1820* (acknowledged and supported by Neil Freistat in the volume previously cited) seems to boil down to this: 'There is plentiful evidence ... that Keats had a hand in the texts of these three volumes while they were being printed and that ... he was free to accept or reject his friends' changes in them.'[7] In a later book, however, Stillinger says that 'it is highly likely that, once he had prepared the volume, Keats did not see the poem until it was set in type . . ,' and he quotes Woodhouse: 'Keats left it to his Publishers to adopt which [readings] they pleased, & to revise the Whole.'[8] Nothing, therefore, can be determined precisely about who ordered the short poems in *1820*, but the evidence finally suggests that Keats would have had a say in the ordering of these poems even if it was a collaborative effort with his friend and publisher. And it is clear – from his stated wish about having no preface for the volume and from his negative comments about the placement of *The Eve of St. Agnes* – that Keats was not above asserting strong views. The publication, against his will, of *Hyperion* in *1820* notwithstanding, there is every reason to believe that Keats fully accepted and probably determined the short poems' ordering, and that therefore we can assume that the meaning of the present sequence, to the extent that it has one, Keats would have assented to. This assurance allows Neil Freistat his reading of the sequence and will allow my – different – one.

Freistat insists, and this is important and more or less unique in criticism, that the Odes be read in conjunction with the tetrameter rhyming poems embedded in the suite. Moreover, he acknowledges in these tetrameter poems a 'playfulness.' But stamped upon the meaning he finds in the group is the familiar myth of Keats's maturation into a 'confrontation' with 'reality,' an acceptance of death, a growing perception of projective, expansive, 'enchanting' mental faculties as escapist, and the simultaneous cultivation of a more skeptical imagination that aggrandizes its heroic achievement by acknowledging its own limits to shape reality. 'Fancy' (following the Coleridgean hierarchy) takes the poet away ('Away! Away! for I shall fly to thee!') from the human mind and heart, while the preferable Imagination tolls the poet back to the painful world of the sole self. Imagination, following Stillinger and Sperry, asserts a heroic, Victorian resistance of the ego against the 'flow' of collective and disparate life. Formally, this coalescence of self against world is demarcated in closed, abstract lines or stanzas; it is the model of the lyric of closure, which awakens the reader to a distinct, individuated and somewhat alienated lyric subject.

The drama of the sequence, according to Freistat, belongs largely to a figure of the poet: 'In the Odes [and implicitly the other poems of the group] Keats is to isolate and examine in closer detail the question of the poet's proper relationship to poetry and to his world.'[9] In particular, Keats examines the values and, finally, serious limitations of 'enchantment,' associated with Fancy. The triumph of the sequence, in this sense, is in the acceptance of 'disenchantment' and its sequellae. The lineaments of the 'Ode to a Nightingale' establish the model: 'Already with thee!' (enchantment), 'But here there is no light' (disenchantment), 'Thou wast not born for death, . . my sole self.' This pattern (and this poem), according to Freistat's quoting of Sperry, displays Keats's 'insistence on the integrity of the creative process'[10] and the poet's wish to cover the 'entire imaginative spectrum' of poetry 'from a lark with fancy to the concrete richness of the vision in "To Autumn"' (and, says Freistat, moving past the short poems, 'to the abstract "Hyperion"').[11]

Three initial questions: how do we know that, with the exception of 'Bards of Passion' and the 'Ode to Psyche,' Keats is writing about 'the poet' who is, the argument implies, the speaking subject of these poems? And, are the poems about 'the creative process,' and if so, do we know what the creative process is, and is there only one, and one preferred one, of them?

To me, the speaking or lyric subject in these poems hovers at the point where the ego of ordinary consciousness tries to release its crippling and illusory sense of control by establishing its connection to larger modes of being, in nature and the vision of myth. This is not exclusively the project of the poet whose task is to write poems but rather that of a person whose life is found meaningful only when it risks the loss of its ready-made, familiar, categories, and, indeed, risks the loss of itself as an entity distinct from and superior to the worlds into which it dissolves. And it suggests a less tragic and decidedly more comic vision of life than that in Freistat's summary:

> The world presented by the volume seems knowable only by transposing the physics of Newton's third Law of Thermodynamics into psychic terms: for every motion of the mind the world responds

with an equal and opposite motion. The more the mind desires the more it will be frustrated; the more it seeks pleasure, the more it will be given pain; the more it retreats into its own fictions, the more it will be destroyed by reality.[12]

The history of modern poetics instructs us again and again that the poetry of radically expanded consciousness – as opposed to the vision just presented, one of limitation and a psychic and meta-physical economics of scarcity – is marked by a shift towards more open forms. Thus the issue of 'the poet' here, I believe, is at least as much a formal as a thematic one: the 'play' that Freistat observes in 'Fancy' and the rondeaus, the persistant *listings* that could go on forever, call attention to an incipient poetics of aperture, in which Fancy would (as Hazlitt implies in several essays including 'On Poetry in General,' 'On Going a Journey,' and 'The Fight') dominate over Imagination: the infinitely fecund source of associations and correspondences would dominate over the capacity of the mind to assert synthetically the tragic superiority of the human mind over and against the relentless world. The term 'creative process' seems to refer to this, latter, darkly athletic exercise, but clearly there is at least one other creative process in the Romantic tradition:

It seems that we can think but of one place at a time. The canvas of the fancy has only a certain extent, and if we paint one set of objects upon it, they immediately efface every other. We cannot enlarge our conceptions; we only shift our point of view.... We measure the universe by ourselves, and even comprehend the texture of our own being only piece-meal. In this way, however, *we remember an infinity of things and places* [emphasis mine].[13]

A final comment on Fancy: it should not, I think, be precisely equated with 'enchantment,' which does involve leaving the world for a different, preferred, domain. Fancy typically names the world's elements in a set of correspondences that (as Hazlitt suggests) could accumulate infinitely. The connection between Fancy and enchantment lies in the focus of each *away* from the preoccupation with self.

To return now to the concerns of the sequence, the *1820* ordering of poems refigures the problem of death as specifically the problem of 'the long night of oblivion' (Horace). In this ordering 'Lethe' brackets the poems ('Nightingale,' 'Lethewards had sunk';

'Melancholy,' 'Go not to Lethe'): oblivion, forgetfulness, custom, death. Every one of the Odes is driven by the presence, fear, or expectation of some form of negation, a *concentration* of nothing. In the 'Ode to a Nightingale' it is the drowsy numbness, an opiate-like forgetfulness; in the 'Ode on a Grecian Urn' it is the Urn's silence that, if not challenged, will carry history and feeling into oblivion; in the 'Ode to Psyche' it is the more-than-millenial unworshipped and therefore unacknowledged presence of the goddess; in 'To Autumn' it is the absence of the 'songs of Spring' and the implied numbness brought by the approaching winter months; and in the 'Ode on Melancholy' it is the exhortation to counter the oblivious tendencies and a recipe for doing so. Leaving out the 'Ode on Indolence' is consistent in that that poem courts forgetfulness and unconsciousness, the end of the world as easeful death. That the line 'No! No! Go not to Lethe' opens the final poem encourages us to read it as an Afterword to the sequence, a frame or motto applicable to each of the preceding poems. It, moreover, marks out the response to oblivion as a crisis that poetry is to address.

Thomas McGrath in 'The End of the World'[14] suggests that the end's postponement came to him when he heard the 'careless, irreverent laughter' of a beer-drinking neighbor from the next block. The end of the world was a fantasy – summoned from the collective imagery of the Judeo-Christian tradition – that needs to be *broken* by a sensuous interference: the sound of laughter. Perhaps the prescription – 'Or if thy mistress some rich anger shows, / Emprison her soft hand' – creates the same counter-Lethewards gesture. The senses, that landmark focus in Keats's poetry and letters (how early in 1819 does he rhapsodize the luxury of his palate affair with claret!), may be that which breaks the fantasy of the end of the world or at least postpones it. But postponement shifts attention away from oblivion and death to a new flourishing: how else to explain the rush felt as one wanders in the middle stanzas of the 'Ode to a Nightingale.' The crisis is met with an 'emergent' energy and vision and a *naming* of elements:

> I cannot see what flowers are at my feet,
>   Nor what soft incense hangs upon the boughs,
> But, in embalmed darkness, guess each sweet
>   Wherewith the seasonable month endows
> The grass, the thicket, and the fruit-tree wild;
>   White hawthorn, and the pastoral eglantine;
>   Fast fading violets cover'd up in leaves;

And mid-May's eldest child,
The coming musk-rose, full of dewy wine,
The murmurous haunt of flies on summer eves.

Darkling I listen; and, for many a time
I have been half in love with easeful Death,
Call'd him soft names in many a mused rhyme,
To take into the air my quiet breath;
No more than ever seems it rich to die,
To cease upon the midnight with no pain,
While thou art pouring forth thy soul abroad
In such an ecstasy!
Still wouldst thou sing, and I have ears in vain –
To thy high requiem become a sod.

('Ode to a Nightingale')

Thou still unravish'd bride of quietness,
Thou foster-child of silence and slow time,
Sylvan historian, who canst thus express
A flowery tale more sweetly than our rhyme:
What leaf-fring'd legend haunts about thy shape
Of deities or mortals, or of both,
In Tempe or the dales of Arcady?
What men or gods are these? What maidens loth?
What mad pursuit? What struggle to escape?
What pipes and timbrels? What wild ecstasy?

('Ode on a Grecian Urn')

O Goddess! hear these tuneless numbers, wrung
By sweet enforcement and remembrance dear,
And pardon that thy secrets should be sung
Even into thine own soft-conched ear:
Surely I dreamt to-day, or did I see
The winged Psyche with awaken'd eyes?
I wander'd in a forest thoughtlessly,
And, on the sudden, fainting with surprise,
Saw two fair creatures, couched side by side
In deepest grass, beneath the whisp'ring roof
Of leaves and trembled blossoms, where there ran
A brooklet, scarce espied:

'Mid hush'd, cool-rooted flowers, fragrant-eyed,
    Blue, silver-white, and budded Tyrian,
They lay calm-breathing on the bedded grass;
        Their arms embraced, and their pinions too;
        Their lips touch'd not, but had not bade adieu
As if disjoined by soft-handed slumber,
And ready still past kisses to outnumber
        At tender eye-dawn of aurorean love:
            The winged boy I knew;
        But who wast thou, O happy, happy dove?
            His Psyche true!

                                      ('Ode to Psyche')

Yes, I will be thy priest, and build a fane
    In some untrodden region of my mind,
Where branched thoughts, new grown with pleasant pain,
    Instead of pines shall murmur in the wind:
Far, far around shall those dark-cluster'd trees
    Fledge the wild-ridged mountains steep by steep;
And there by zephyrs, streams, and birds, and bees,
    The moss-lain Dryads shall be lull'd to sleep;
And in the midst of this wide quietness
A rosy sanctuary will I dress
With the wreath'd trellis of a working brain,
    With buds, and bells, and stars without a name,
With all the gardener Fancy e'er could feign,
    Who breeding flowers, will never breed the same:
And there shall be for thee all soft delight
    That shadowy thought can win,
A bright torch, and a casement ope at night,
    To let the warm Love in!

                                      ('Ode to Psyche')

Season of mists and mellow fruitfulness,
    Close bosom-friend of the maturing sun;
Conspiring with him how to load and bless
    With fruit the vines that round the thatch-eves run;
To bend with apples the moss'd cottage-trees,
    And fill all fruit with ripeness to the core;
        To swell the gourd, and plump the hazel shells
    With a sweet kernel; to set budding more,
And still more, later flowers for the bees,

Until they think warm days will never cease,
    For Summer has o'er-brimm'd their clammy cells.

                        ('To Autumn')

    Where are the songs of Spring? Ay, where are they?
        Think not of them, thou hast thy music too, –
    While barred clouds bloom the soft-dying day,
        And touch the stubble-plains with rosy hue;
    Then in a wailful choir the small gnats mourn
        Among the river sallows, borne aloft
           Or sinking as the light wind lives or dies;
    And full-grown lambs loud bleat from hilly bourn;
        Hedge-crickets sing; and now with treble soft
        The red-breast whistles from a garden-croft;
           And gathering swallows twitter in the skies.

                        ('To Autumn')

No, no, go not to Lethe, neither twist
    Wolf's-bane, tight-rooted, for its poisonous wine;
Nor suffer thy pale forehead to be kiss'd
    By nightshade, ruby grape of Proserpine;
Make not your rosary of yew-berries,
    Nor let the beetle, nor the death-moth be
        Your mournful Psyche, nor the downy owl
A partner in your sorrow's mysteries;
    For shade to shade will come too drowsily,
        And drown the wakeful anguish of the soul.

But when the melancholy fit shall fall
    Sudden from heaven like a weeping cloud,
That fosters the droop-headed flowers all,
    And hides the green hill in an April shroud;
Then glut thy sorrow on a morning rose,
    Or on the rainbow of the salt sand-wave,
    Or on the wealth of globed peonies;
Or if thy mistress some rich anger shows,
    Emprison her soft hand, and let her rave,
        And feed deep, deep upon her peerless eyes.

                    ('Ode on Melancholy')

'Never, never canst thou kiss,' in the poet's visionary logic, meta-
morphoses into a 'forever,' 'Forever wilt thou love, and she be
fair!' As Van Ghent says, the Odes are 'the advent of a new form
of perception.'[15]

Reading the Odes with a Wordsworthian emphasis, one would
incline towards viewing the fecundity in the above passages as an
'abundant recompence,' finding consolation for the losses in 'what
remains behind.' But Keats, as my reading of the spring journal
letter proposes, takes a more radical position towards death and
loss than does Wordsworth – thematically and poetically: the Odes
are praise poems; their aim is to urge these apparitions – goddess,
bird, urn – from the collectivity of world images – into being, to
confront the emptiness with presences, to counter the calm oblivious tendencies with namings and apostrophes:

> Thou, light-winged Dryad of the trees
> Thou still unravished bride of quietness
> Who wast Thou, O happy happy Dove?
> His Psyche true!
> Season of mists and mellow fruitfulness –

to name them and find them *good*. These are poems of beginnings,
of filling the world over the void, which exists in the world but also
in the mind. In this sense the Odes seem typically Romantic and
modern. The site of poetic crisis is in the mind but only because of
the mind's own oblivious, Lethewards tendencies. The goal of the
poems, however, is a negatively capable one: to praise the world is
to demonstrate its significance for persons.

> The end of the world provoked
> Out of the dark a single and melancholy sigh
>
> From my neighbor who sat on his porch drinking beer in the
>   dark.
> No: I was not God's prophet. Armageddon was never
> And always: this night in a poor street where a careless
>   irreverent laughter
> Postpones the end of the world: in which we live forever.

> (Thomas McGrath's, from 'The End of The World')

The visionary element in Thomas McGrath's poem lies not in the
end of the world but in the ability to detect and mark the end's

postponement. First of all he projects a faith, that the end of the world 'provokes' its undoing, the personification a way of asserting the human-centeredness, even when not apparent, of both and that oblivion is not the only possible outcome for human exertions. After the Homeric hero steps out of the crowd for his *aristeia*, he gets absorbed back into his anonymity among soldiers, but the poet marks the unstable isotope of heroic personhood. Here the poet announces the melancholy sigh and careless irreverent laughter of the neighbor before they are swallowed up in the endlessly repeated end of the world.

The end of the world is real in its effects – people and events are regularly forgotten, their outlines vanish – but phantasmal, metaphysical in its origins: I am struck by how, in this poem, the postponement is registered first through the senses. The sigh, the laughter *intrude* upon the silence. More positively they are culled by the ready and sensitive poet. In 'To Autumn' the anxious, unimaginative voice forgets the moment in defining the season by the wintry end to follow in order to ask the conventional question of elegiac hope: where are the songs of spring? The question is constructed out of a belief in the end of the world. But the antiphonal voice that concludes the poem is the visionary one: thou hast thy music too. The exhortation is to *listen*, and the lines that follow *list* the sounds in a gathering that only the constraints of the stanza bring to a close. In this regard the closed form reminds one that there is an end which the poet exerts against and postpones. Similarly the retrospect instructions in the 'Ode on Melancholy' advise countering the fantasy-driven tendency towards oblivious death with the senses: *glut* thy sorrow on the morning rose...Emprison [thy mistress'] soft hand. Feed deep, deep upon her peerless eyes. The speaker hears the nightingale, observes the urn, sees feelingly the lovers Cupid and Psyche embedded in grass.

Notice that typically in the Odes the activation of the senses produces these namings and listings; the senses work with the winged Fancy, labile and endlessly excursive.

The apparent insertion of the four tetrameter (or 'Fancy') poems into the Odes group suggests that Keats was – in the manner of Wordsworth – constructing a book (or section of a book) of poems, with its own particular logic. 'Mermaid Tavern' and 'Robin Hood,' written over a year before the Odes, clearly don't belong to an 1819 chronology but do belong to the 1820 book-making imagination. What do these four poems accomplish in this sequence? – poems introduced, so to speak, by the prayer-manifesto 'Ode to Psyche':

And in the midst of this wide quietness
A rosy sanctuary will I dress
With the wreath'd trellis of a working brain,
   With buds, and bells, and stars without a name,
With all the gardener Fancy e'er could feign,
   Who breeding flowers, will never breed the same: ...

'Fancy,' in Keats's long strip of a poem (like Shelley's 'To a Skylark'), needs to be released from prison; the 'mind's caged door' needs opening. Read biographically, this poem, coming on the heels of Tom's death, means escape and confirms the conventional wisdom that the 'winged Fancy' is a less profound and conclusive poetic faculty than the synthesizing (Coleridgean) imagination; moreover, Keats knew this in his sad, resigned opening couplet: 'Ever let the fancy roam, / Pleasure never is at home,' and in the succeeding line: 'At a touch sweet pleasure melteth... .' But Hazlitt's brilliant essay, definitive, I believe, for Keats's developing poetics, 'On Poetry in General,' reverses the priority. Fancy is the primary faculty for the best poetry, encouraging the representation and the release of passion; it courts excess and range and variety and naming-the-world and speed, anticipating Olson's dictum that the poet must move quickly from perception to perception, 'INSTANTER.' 'Fancy' is less a nineteenth-century update of the mutability topos and more a manifesto of poetic fecundity and regeneration. 'She will bring, in spite of frost, / Beauties that the earth has lost.' Oblivion, again, is the enemy to poetry. Fancy records the world as correspondences, not singular but multiple entities: 'She will mix these pleasures up / Like three fit wines in a cup, / And thou shalt quaff it... .' Anticipating the visionary 'To Autumn' (the next Ode in the collection), Fancy discovers the renewing life beneath the ends of life:

         thou shalt hear
Distant harvest-carols clear;
Rustle of the reaped corn;
Sweet birds antheming the morn;
And, in the same moment – hark!
'Tis the early April lark... .

When Keats says, 'let her loose; / Every thing is spoilt by use: / Where's the cheek that doth not fade, / Too much gaz'd at?' he is declaring his version of Blake's tetrameter dictum, his ethics for poetry as well as for life:

> He who binds to himself a joy
> Doth the winged life destroy
> But he who kisses the joy as it flies
> Lives in Eternitys sun rise

Stillness in poetry is death; it's less than passivity; it is a binding, an imprisonment. Instead, give us a poetry of liberation, a kiss on the wing. The quick, musical rhyming tetrameters seem the perfect vehicle.

The remaining three tetrameter poems seem at first glance nostalgic invocations of 'Souls of poets dead and gone,' but part of the recovery that Keats attempts is for a livelier more luxuriant thematics and poetics and a remaking of poetry into a 'new old sign': Chaucer, the writers of the French rondeau or dance-poem, the Fletcher of *The Faithful Shepherd* (admired by Hazlitt for its 'luxurious and delicate' lyrics), and Milton's 'L'Allegro' and 'Il Penseroso.' (Perhaps, too, Keats had read the 'hobbling rhyme' tetrameters of the women poets of the eighteenth century.) He celebrates not tragic poets like Shakespeare but the 'Bards of Passion and of Mirth,' like Beaumont and Fletcher who, according to Hazlitt, 'had a great and unquestioned command over the stories both of fancy and passion.' Keats imagined an English, popular collective in the Mermaid Tavern, repeated the gathering-place of some Elizabethan poets who loved to confound popular and classical tradition over their wine, 'pledging with contented smack / The Mermaid in the Zodiac.'

The spirit in these poems tends towards what Marjorie Levinson sees as the appropriation of aristocratic forms (the rondeau, a courtly dance) for a more democratically directed poetry and by a poet who feels outside that literary aristocracy. In this sense Robin Hood, mentioned in 'Mermaid Tavern' and the subject of the companion poem, fits with the method of appropriation: he robs the rich to give to the poor! And part of the impulse to recover these poets and old times stems from Keats's distaste for the exploitative conditions of modern capitalism:

> [Robin] would swear, for all his oaks,
> Fall'n beneath the dockyard strokes,
> Have rotted on the briny seas;

[Marian] would weep that her wild bees
Sang not to her – strange! that honey
Can't be got without hard money!

The popular element in these poems and their critical politics is at one with their sexual and sensuous energies. The Fancy comes from an imagination of the body, a passion in the mind, and in Keats's view it pinpoints the protest against an aristocratic poetry, just as Keats, on his Scottish tour of 1818, took the Kirk to task for banishing puns and kissing among its poorer subjects. His critique differs little from Blake's in the quatrain quoted above. A poetry that lives in Eternity's sunrise, like that of Bards whose souls are in heaven, lives in the excess of desire and fruitfulness.

Turning from the tetrameter poems back to the next major Ode, 'To Autumn,' one is struck less by its associations with a Greek mythology (the Apollonian autumn) and more by Keats's remarks in his letter to Reynolds about the poem in which he associates with Chatterton's 'pure' English as opposed to the artiness of Miltonic inversions: English, he says, 'ought to be kept up.' But how, in this conjunction of jaunty tetrameter poems and mellow pentameter Odes, is one to justify the connection formally? It is worth noting that 'Bards of Passion' is called an 'Ode' and that in one transcription Brown referred to the 'Ode to Fancy.' And, of course, Keats does not refer to 'To Autumn' as an ode. All these pieces to one degree or another are praise poems. Moreover, two of the Odes, 'Nightingale' and 'Psyche,' contain lines of substantially less than ten syllables. For these reasons the sets of poems move closer to each other.

The tetrameter poems, then, begin to appear as simple, more naive versions of the Odes: their form is freedom without constraint, a form that does not impose itself upon the subject but that is in fact shaped by it and by its energies. The freedom vs. constraint issue comes to the surface in the sonnet on the sonnet ('If by dull rhymes') written roughly the same time as the 'Ode to Psyche' which, along with the later Odes, is clearly written with the sonnet form (and the sonnet line, the pentameter) in mind. It is possible to look upon Keats's brief career in terms of a perpetual liberalizing of form: from the 'Cockney couplets' of *Sleep and Poetry* that loosen the Popian couplets, to the tetrameter poems that loosen the couplets of *L'Allegro* and *Il Penseroso* and the strict form of the early rondeau, to the flagrant release of the sonnet from its rhyme-scheme bondage both in 'If by dull rhymes' and then in the Odes. So far the arguments given to explain this refer to the politics of aesthetics: the loosening of Pope's couplets is analogous to the loosening of morals and lifestyles of the liberal Leigh Hunt and his friends. But 'If by dull rhymes' raises the question: why, if one wishes formal freedom, should one try to use the highly constrained form of the sonnet at all? It is not enough, I think, to say that poetry has always done this, has always survived on the conflicts between form and syntax. Certainly the modern history of a thriving free verse and organic form poetics shows that poetry can sustain itself on a *poetics of congruence* as well as if not better than on a poetics of conflict. Keats's relationship to the latter seems particularly pointed.

I go back to the lines in 'Fancy': 'She will mix these pleasures up / Like three fit wines in a cup / And thou shalt quaff it.' Keats takes such mixings very seriously and at all levels of poetic concern. The thematic level is perhaps most evident – the mixing of light and shade, Iago and Imogen, spring and autumn, joy and sorrow. He, following Hazlitt, is inclined to mix 'high' and 'low' culture, Latinate and English language and intonation. In form, moreover, Keats mixes the impulse for the formless and free with the impulse for the highly constrained and abstract (the sonnet), to mirror what Louis Zukofsky calls 'the actual twisting / Of many and diverse thoughts.'[16]

In his poem 'Mantis' Zukofsky has written about an insect found in a New York subway that stands for 'the poor.' But the conjunction of this poem's subject matter – the unspoken image of poverty – with the form the poem takes – a sestina, aristocratic, Italianate – produces 'the new world,' an image of remaking the *familiar* knowledge and discourse of poverty by acknowledging 'thoughts' torsion': the simultaneity of tradition and forms, sustained over centuries, with the entropic, oblivious tendencies of poverty. For Zukofsky this stunning juxtaposition models the *putting to use* of materials and perceptions, a mind set in motion to act upon poverty's neglected familiarity. I think that Keats, in a mode perhaps less conscious than Zukofsky's, nonetheless intuited a socially regenerative possibility for poetry which, at one level or another from 1817 to 1820, he practiced through the simultaneous loosening of and adherence to traditional forms, a poetry of thoughts' torsion, of the new world.

The poets who eulogized Keats by and large did not respond to his death as a problem of poetics or a problem of defamiliarization.

The visionary poet recognizes that death for him or her challenges poetics and categories. So many of the eulogy poets worked within the sonnet, accepting form as a comfort or consolation, a grave to commemorate *by containing* the poet's work. These sonnets are tame, compared to some of Keats's, or, later, Hopkins's, which push so hard against the forms that they project the possibility of the dissolution of abstract form as a tomb into a new beginning altogether. A poetry of listing and mixing can be an answer to the problem of oblivion. The translocation of Keats, from his small, pinched gravesite in Rome, to the abode of the Eternals, to membership in a constellation of poets including Homer and Dante and Shakespeare has its correlate in Keats's own formal and visionary extravagances.

The opposite of Keats's poetics of postponing the end of the world may be found in Theognis's lines (from the *Greek Anthology*):

> The best of all things it were, never to be born,
> Never to know the light of the strong sharp sun;
> But being born,
> The best of all is to pass as soon as may be
> To Hades' gate,
>   there to lie dead,
> Lost, locked close beneath the world's huge weight.[17]

Death, here, determines all discourse and creates the poem's only familiarity. Eduard Roditi, writing about the German-Jewish poet Alfred Lichtenstein who died in the First World War at age 25, Keats's age, says of poetry's speech:

> From womb to tomb, the poet's tongue
> Is his home to which he's bound.

Not a prison, though working in the closed dust-to-dust circuit, the poet's speech is a nurturing source, and what better and more pleasant thing to do at home than breed new flowers?

AN ENDING

Keats: around me at the moment are Lu Chi's *Wen Fu* or *The Art of Writing*, Kenneth Rexroth's *Love and the Turning Year: One Hundred More Poems from the Chinese*, two anthologies – *Surrealist Poetry in*

English and *The Poetry of Survival: Post-War Poets of Central and Eastern Europe* – and the *Selected Poems of Marina Tsvetaeva.* The world of poems has changed so radically since Keats's day both in so far as vast numbers of new poems have been written – not just poems but 'poetries' – and because, through the technologies of mechanical reproduction and translation, we can 'hear' so many more poetic voices old and new that (inevitably) ought to affiliate to Keats, the ended one. The profusion of poems is overwhelming. Where do I begin?

I think first of a poem by Brecht in *The Poetry of Survival,* 'Bad Time for Poetry,' a manifesto-lyric about his drive to exclude from poetry what does not point to injustice, the impossibility of a light-and-shade poetry:

> Inside me contend
> Delight at the apple tree in blossom
> And horror at the house-painter's speeches.
> But only the second
> Drives me to my desk.[18]

From this I foresee a familiar narrative: the 'innocence' of Keats leads to the severe, ungiving knowledges forced upon an honest twentieth-century poet – perhaps true but, I believe, not useful in a generative way for us as readers or writers. I can't get out of my mind a lyric (trans. Kenneth Rexroth) by the Poetess Li Ch'ing Chao (1084–1142):

> The gentle breeze has died down.
> The perfumed dust has settled.
> It is the end of the time
> Of flowers. Evening falls
> And all day I have been too
> Lazy to comb my hair.
> The toilet articles are there,
> But the man is gone away.
> All effort would be wasted.
> When I try to sing, my tears
> Choke me. I dreamed my flower boat
> Carried me to him, but I
> Know so fragile a vessel
> Won't bear such a weight of sorrow.

The middle lines are a condition from which poems spring: entropy, an oblivious tendency. The poet doesn't shirk the reality but describes it along with her dream of recovery and along with a beautiful framing line of cosmic order:

> It is the end of the time
> Of flowers.

The dream doesn't defeat the reality, but the poem does, by including both, and in this sense it resembles Brecht's; each poem (a presence) is more than the negativity of the speaker's condition. This 'more' sends me to a passage from the *Wen Fu* (written after a military defeat, the death of brothers, and in exile):

> The poet stands at the center of the universe,
> contemplating the enigma, ...

And another (about the poet's initial creative activity):

> . . . our spirits ride
> to the eight corners of the universe,
> mind soaring a thousand miles away; . .
>
> It is like being adrift
> in a heavenly lake
> or diving to the depths of seas.
>
> We bring up living words
> like fishes
> hooked in their gills, leaping from the deep.... .
>
> We gather words and images
> from those unused by previous generations.
>
> Our melodies have been unplayed
> for a thousand years or more.... .
>
> Past and present commingle:
> Eternity in the single blink of an eye!

This begins to sound like Keats, that drifting, diving, fishing, gathering poet of not only the 'Ode to Psyche' or the playful short-lined rhyming poems but 'I stood tiptoe' with its 'wide wandering for the greediest eye,' with its pleasure in the chaos of life-elements and words and images and melodies unplayed for years and centuries:

> To picture out the quaint and curious bending
> Of a fresh woodland alley, never ending;
> Or by the bowery clefts, and leafy shelves,
> Guess where the jaunty streams refresh themselves.
> I gazed awhile, and felt as light, and free
> As though the fanning wings of Mercury
> Had played upon my heels: ...

But what, I wonder in this closing statement, has such a passage to do with death – the death announced again and again by the poems in praise of Keats? Surely this is not a poetry of 'the end of the time/Of flowers.' The answer is in the acknowledgment of death – oblivion, entropy, forgetfulness – as the condition from which poems spring. Keats's is a poetry of spring and of springing, of fecundity, even in its most crisis-laden moments; it is the 'still-forever' of death-haunted love:

> No – yet still stedfast, still unchangeable,
>   Pillow'd upon my fair love's ripening breast,
> To feel for ever its soft swell and fall,
>   Awake for ever in a sweet unrest,
> Still, still to hear her tender-taken breath,
> And so live ever – or else swoon to death.

Appendix

A Selection of Poems written to or about John Keats: 1821–1994

CONTENTS OF APPENDIX

The following poems are present in rough chronological order of publication or composition, beginning with Clare (1821).

TO THE MEMORY OF JOHN KEATS

The world, its hopes, and fears, have pass'd away;
   No more its trifling thou shalt feel or see;
Thy hopes are ripening in a brighter day,
   While these left buds thy monument shall be.
When Rancour's aims have past in naught away
   Enlarging specks discern'd in more than thee,
And beauties 'minishing which few display –
   When these are past, true child of Poesy,
Thou shalt survive. Ah, while a being dwells,
   With soul, in nature's joys, to warm like thine,
With eye to view her fascinating spells,
   And dream entranced o'er each form divine,
Thy worth, Enthusiast, shall be cherish'd here,
   Thy name with him shall linger, and be dear.

John Clare

IN MEMORY OF KEATS

Mute minstrel of the Eve, pale, mystical
When one by one comes forth the pensive train
Of things not born for worldly strife and pain,

That cannot fade, though doomed perchance to fall;
Fond Cherisher of passions, fancies, all
Whose essence fills a poet's flower-like home –
I saw but now, within your distant dome,
A cloud that cast its transitory pall
Across the quivering light: and I did think
That moment on the cold and shadowing shame
With which thy starry spirit hath been crowned.
How vain their torturings were! for thou didst sink
With the first stone cast at thy martyred fame;
How like the snow that's ruined by a sound!

                                        1823

                    S. Laman Blanchard

WRITTEN IN KEATS'S 'ENDYMION'

I saw pale Dian, sitting by the brink
    Of silver falls, the overflow of fountains
From cloudy steeps; and I grew sad to think
    Endymion's foot was silent on those mountains,
And he but a hushed name, that Silence keeps
    In dear remembrance, – lonely, and forlorn,
Singing it to herself until she weeps
    Tears that perchance still glisten in the morn; –
And as I mused, in dull imaginings,
    There came a flash of garments, and I knew
The awful Muse by her harmonious wings
    Charming the air to music as she flew –
Anon there rose an echo through the vale,
    Gave back Endymion in a dream-like tale.

                                    Thomas Hood

ON KEATS

A garden in a garden: a green spot
    Where all is green: most fitting slumber-place
    For the strong man grown weary of a race
Soon over. Unto him a goodly lot

Hath fallen in fertile ground; there thorns are not,
  But his own daisies; silence, full of grace,
  Surely hath shed a quiet on his face;
His earth is but sweet leaves that fall and rot.
What was his record of himself, ere he
  Went from us? 'Here lies one whose name was writ
  In water.' While the chilly shadows flit
Of sweet St. Agnes' Eve, while basil springs –
  His name, in every humble heart that sings,
Shall be a fountain of love, verily.

18 January 1849 (Eve of St. Agnes)

Christina Rossetti

FROM *AURORA LEIGH*

By Keats's soul, the man who never stepped
In gradual progress like another man,
But, turning grandly on his central self,
Ensphered himself in twenty perfect years
And died, not young, (the life of a long life
Distilled to a mere drop, falling like a tear
Upon the world's cold cheek to make it burn
For ever;) by that strong excepted soul,
I count it strange and hard to understand
That nearly all young poets should write old,
That Pope was sexagenary at sixteen,
And beardless Byron academical,
And so with others. It may be perhaps
Such have not settled long and deep enough
In trance, to attain to clairvoyance, – and still
The memory mixes with the vision, spoils,
And works it turbid.
               Or perhaps, again,
In order to discover the Muse-Sphinx,
The melancholy desert must sweep round,
Behind you as before. –
              For me, I wrote
False poems, like the rest, and thought them true
Because myself was true in writing them.
I peradventure have writ true ones since
With less complacence.

Elizabeth Barrett Browning

POPULARITY

Stand still, true poet that you are!
 I know you; let me try and draw you.
Some night you'll fail us: when afar
 You rise, remember one man saw you,
Knew you, and named a star!

My star, God's glow-worm! Why extend
 That loving hand of his which leads you,
Yet locks you safe from end to end
 Of this dark world, unless he needs you,
Just saves your light to spend?

His clenched hand shall unclose at last,
 I know, and let out all the beauty:
My poet holds the future fast,
 Accepts the coming ages' duty,
Their present for this past.

That day, the earth's feast-master's brow
 Shall clear, to God the chalice raising;
'Others give best at first, but thou
 Forever set'st our table praising,
Keep'st the good wine 'til now!'

Meantime, I'll draw you as you stand,
 With few or none to watch and wonder:
I'll say – a fisher, on the sand
 By Tyre the old, with ocean-plunder,
A netful, brought to land,

Who has not heard how Tyrian shells
 Enclosed the blue, that dye of dyes
Whereof one drop worked miracles,
 And colored like Astarte's eyes
Raw silk the merchant sells?

And each bystander of them all
 Could criticise, and quote tradition
How depths of blue sublimed some pall
 – To get which, pricked a king's ambition;
Worth sceptre, crown and ball.

Yet there's the dye, in that rough mesh,
 The sea has only just o'er whispered!
Live whelks, each lip's beard dripping fresh,
 As if they still the water's lisp heard
Through foam the rock-weeds thresh.

Enough to furnish Solomon
  Such hangings for his cedar-house,
That, when gold-robed he took the throne
  In that abyss of blue, the Spouse
Might swear his presence shone

Most like the centre-spike of gold
  Which burns deep in the bluebell's womb
What time, with ardors manifold,
  The bee goes singing to her groom,
Drunken and overbold.

Mere conchs! not fit for warp or woof!
  Till cunning come to pound and squeeze
And clarify, – refine to proof
  The liquor filtered by degrees,
While the world stands aloof.

And there's the extract, flasked and fine,
  And priced and salable at last!
And Hobbs, Nobbs, Stokes and Nokes combine
  To paint the future from the past,
Put blue into their line.

Hobbs hints blue, – straight he turtle eats:
  Nobbs prints blue, – claret crowns his cup:
Nokes outdares Stokes in azure feats, –
  Both gorge. Who fished the murex up?
What porridge had John Keats?

                    Robert Browning

TO THE SPIRIT OF KEATS

Great soul, thou sittest with me in my room,
Uplifting me with thy vast, quiet eyes,
On whose full orbs, with kindly lustre, lies
The twilight warmth of ruddy ember-gloom:
Thy clear, strong tones will oft bring sudden bloom
Of hope secure, to him who lonely cries,
Wrestling with the young poet's agonies,
Neglect and scorn, which seem a certain doom:
Yes! the few words which, like great thunder-drops,
Thy large heart down to earth shook doubtfully,
Thrilled by the inward lightning of its might,

Serene and pure, like gushing joy of light,
Shall track the eternal chords of Destiny,
After the moon-led pulse of ocean stops.

James Russell Lowell

ON KEATS'S GRAVE

He said that the greatest delight of his life had been to watch the growth
of flowers. And when dying 'I feel them growing over me'.

They waited not for showers
But made a garden in the dark above him,
– Stayed not for summer, growing things that love him.
Beyond the light, beyond the hours,
Behind the wind, where Nature thinks the flowers,
He entered in his dying wandering.
And daisies infantine were thoughts of his,
And different grasses solved his mysteries.
He lived in flowers a snatch of spring,
And had a dying longing that uncloses
In wild white roses.

Down from the low hills dark with pines
Into the fields at rest, the summer done,
I went by pensive ways of tombs and vines
To where the place I dream of is;
And in a stretch of meditative sun
Cloven by the dark flames of the cypresses
Came to the small grave of my ended poet.
– I had felt wild things many a dreamy hour
Pushing above him from beyond the sea,
But when I saw it
It chanced there was no flower;
And that was, too, a silent time for me.

O life of blossoms – Prosperine!
O time of flowers where art thou now,
And in what darkness movest thou?
In the lost heart of this quiet poet of mine
So well-contented with his growth of flowers?
Beyond the suns and showers
Stirrest thou in a silence that begets
The exquisite thought, the tuneful rhyme –

The first intention of the violets,
And the beginnings of the warm wild-thyme?
Indeed the poets do know
A place of thoughts where no winds blow,
And not a breath is sighing,
Beyond the light, beyond the hours,
Where all a summer of enchanted flowers
Do mark his place, his dying.
Sweet life, and is it there thy sceptre passes
On long arrays of flowering grasses
And rows of crimson clover?
Are these the shades thou reignest over?
Come ere the year forgets
The summer her long lover.
O Prosperine, November violets!

– Where art thou now?
And in what darkness movest thou
Who art in life the life of melodies?
Within the silent living poet's heart
Where no song is,
Where, every one apart,
Arrays of the morn fancies err
Vaguer than pain in sleep, vaguer than pain,
And no winds stir; –
Over these shadows dost thou reign?

See now, in this still day
All winds are strayed and lost, wandered away,
Everywhere from Soracte to the sea.
All singing things muse in the sun,
And trees of fragrant leaves do happily
Meditate in their sweet scents every one,
The paeans done.
All olives turn and dream in grey at ease,
Left by the silver breeze.
Long smiles have followed the peal of mirth.
– But silence has no place for me,
A silent singer on earth.
Awake!

And thro' the sleeping season break,
With young new shoots for this young poet's sake,
With singing lives for all these dreams of mine,
O darkened Prosperine!
Out of the small grave and the thoughts I love
Stir thou in me and move,
If haply a song of mine may seem a dim

Sweet flower grown over him.
Oh come from underground and be
Flowers for my young dear poet and songs for me.

November 1869

Alice Meynell

KEATS

The young Endymion sleeps Endymion's sleep;
    The shepherd-boy whose tale was left half told!
    The solemn grove uplifts its shield of gold
    To the red rising moon, and loud and deep
The nightingale is singing from the steep;
    It is midsummer, but the air is cold;
    Can it be death? Alas, beside the fold
    A shepherd's pipe lies shattered near his sheep.
Lo! in the moonlight gleams a marble white,
    On which I read: 'Here lieth one whose name
    Was writ in water.' And was this the meed
Of his sweet singing? Rather let me write:
    'The smoking flax before it burst to flame
    Was quenched by death, and broken the bruised reed.'

Henry Wadsworth Longfellow

THE GRAVE OF KEATS

Rid of the world's injustice, and his pain,
    He rests at last beneath God's veil of blue:
    Taken from life when life and love were new
The youngest of the martyrs here is lain,
Fair as Sebastian, and as early slain.
    No cypress shades his grave, no funeral yew,
    But gentle violets weeping with the dew
Weave on his bones an ever-blossoming chain.
O proudest heart that broke for misery!
    O sweetest lips since those of Mitylene!
    O poet-painter of our English Land!
Thy name was writ in water – it shall stand:

And tears like mine will keep thy memory green,
As Isabella did her Basil-tree.

Rome

Oscar Wilde

JOHN KEATS

The weltering London ways where children weep
　　And girls whom none call maidens laugh, – strange road
　　Miring his outward steps, who inly trode
The bright Castalian brink and Latmos' steep: –
Even such his life's cross-paths; till deathly deep
　　He toiled through sands of Lethe; and long pain,
　　Weary with labor spurned and love found vain,
In dead Rome's sheltering shadow wrapped his sleep.

O pang-dowered Poet, whose reverberant lips
And heart-strung lyre awoke the Moon's eclipse, –
　　Thou whom the daisies glory in growing o'er, –
Their fragrance clings around thy name, not writ
But rumor'd in water, while the fame of it
　　Along Time's flood goes echoing evermore.

Dante Gabriel Rossetti

POST MORTEM

I

It is not then enough that men who give
　　The best gifts given of man to man should feel,
　　Alive, a snake's head ever at their heel:
Small hurt the worms may do them while they live –
Such hurt as scorn for scorn's sake may forgive.
　　But now, when death and fame have set one seal
　　On tombs whereat Love, Grief, and Glory kneel,
Men sift all secrets, in their critic sieve,
Of graves wherein the dust of death might shrink
　　To know what tongues defile the dead man's name
　　With loathsome Love, and probe that stings like shame.

Rest once was theirs, who had crossed to mortal brink:
No rest, no reverence now: dull fools undress
Death's holiest shrine, life's veriest nakedness.

II

A man was born, sang, suffered, loved, and died.
Men scorned him living: let us praise him dead.
His life was brief and bitter, gently led
And proudly, but with pure and blameless pride.
He wrought no wrong toward any; satisfied
With love and labour, whence our souls are fed
With largesse yet of living wine and bread
Come, let us praise him: here is nought to hide.
Make bare the poor dead secrets of his heart,
Strip the stark-naked soul, that all may peer
Spy, smirk, scoff, snap, snort, snivel, snarl, and sneer,
Let none so sad, let none so sacred part
Lie still for pity, rest unstirred for shame,
But all be scanned of all men. This is fame.

III

'Now what a thing it is to be an ass!'
If one, that strutted up the brawling streets
As foremen of the flock whose concourse greets
Men's ears with bray more dissonant than brass,
Would change from blame to praise as coarse as crass.
It is natural note, and learn the fawning feats
Of lapdogs, who but knows what luck he meets?
But all in vain old fable holds her glass.
Marked and reviled by men of poisonous breath,
A great man dies: but one thing worst was spared;
Not all his heart by their base hands lay bared.
One comes to crown with praise the dust of death;
And low, through him the worst is brought to pass.
Now, what a thing it is to be an ass!

IV

Shame, such as never yet dealt heavier stroke
On heads more shameful, fall on theirs through whom
Dead men may keep inviolate not their tomb,
But all its depths these ravenous grave-worms choke.
And yet what waste of wrath is mine, to invoke
Shame on the shameless? Even their natural doom,
The native air such carrion breaths perfume,
The nursing darkness whence vermin broke,
The cloud that wraps them of adulterate ink,
Hath no sign else about it, wears no name,

As they no record in the world, but shame.
If thankfulness nor pity bids them think
   What work is this of theirs, and pause betimes,
   Not Shakespeare's grave would scare them off with rhymes.

A. C. Swinburne

KEATS' CRITICS

He deems himself superior to man,
   Hath somewhat of the seraph in his look;
The poet's lines he well knows how to scan,
   And how to damn the author of a book.

He could not write a worthy word himself,
   Nor couple reason once with any rhyme;
But he is Judgement throned upon a shelf,
   To dust the book that dares the test of time.

His pin-point eyes detect the fine defects,
   His ready pen is much a microscope,
The dotless 'i' this organ quick detects,
   Though in the dark its guardian had to grope.

Perry Marshall

TO KEATS

On a magical morning, with twinkling feet
And a song at his lips that was strange and sweet,
Somebody new came down the street
   To the world's derision and laughter.

Now he is dumb with no more to say,
Now he is dead and taken away,
Silent and still, and leading the way,
   And the world comes tumbling after.

Lord Dunsany

TO A LIFE MASK OF KEATS

(The day the mould was made)

Pain's withering kiss had not been pressed
Upon your singing mouth that day,
Nor anguish silenced in your breast
The glad heart's lay.
With scent of the hedges' bitter bloom
And a misted blow from sea
The English air was sweet to breathe
And laughter free.

So with earth's music in your throat
And the winds of youth for breath,
Love's hand preserved this replica
Of you, forgetting death.

Yet where the faint smile's loveliness
Makes beauty in your face;
Where whimsy turns a question
And yearning leaves a trace,
Three griefs oppress the eyelids
And little shadows lie;
Where lip and little shadows meet
Three piteous sorrows cry –
The loneliness of life unloved,
The agony of songs unwrote,
The waste that youth's sweet voice must die
Still calling its eternal note.

Anne Elizabeth Wilson

ON THE DRAWING DEPICTING JOHN KEATS IN DEATH

Between the face of the still praise-and-blesser
and open distance there is no more tension,
so all the pain that passed our comprehension
falls back again upon its dark possessor;

which as it was when contemplated pain
transfigured it to this supreme creation,

it still remains: in new-found mitigation
disdaining equally both wax and wane.

Whose face? Not that of features still combined
with the same understanding as before.
Eye, that will not wring beauty any more
out of terrestrial things you've now declined!
Song's open door,
Young mouth, young mouth, eternally resigned!

Only the forehead seems to be achieving
A lasting bridge across those liquefying
relationships, as though it were belying
the locks that cling about it, gently grieving.

Rainer Maria Rilke

TO KEATS

Stretch me, dear Keats, thine absent spirit hand;
    For I do love thee when I sometime read
Thy pensive lines, and in whatever land
    Thou art, would wish thee back my steps to lead –
But that thy melancholy must return
    With thy return to earth, and in thy breast
Must rise again the anguish and the pain
    That sped thy pen; – for all the old unrest
That once within thy tender heart did burn,
    Would, with this life, come back to thee again.

Where wanderest thou? Upon what green hillside?
    What look thine eyes upon? What fills thy soul
With the full joy that here thou wast denied –
    So high was heaped thy flowing cup with dole?

Is all made clear that once was dark with death:
    Night so dissolved in day's eternity,
That haply thou forget'st the spirit's rack
    Here on the narrow earth, where every breath
Strives to be freer? Yet howe'er it be,
    Too well I love thee, Keats, to wish thee back.

Louise Morgan Sill

A BROWN AESTHETE SPEAKS

No: I am neither seeking to change nor keep myself;
Simply acting upon new revelations.

There was a time,
I own,
When I fared, quite pleased with myself,
With my unkempt curls, unhealthy pores – myself;
When Jenny Lind,
In song that brought your tears,
Was like morphine, teasing me to sleep and dream;
When Beecher's cadences stirred no shout in me,
And when I thought it a miracle that
    your visage flushed with delight
    as you recited Aeschylus and Homer.

But since that time, I met Keats and Poe.
(Wisdom can evolve a simple taste,
And love is a feeling deep and universal.)
Now, I perceive:
Ah, you had tasted Beauty!
Now I understand you;
Can interpret you;
Try you by myself, –
Now that Beauty is religion in my soul!
I fired your furnaces,
Served your parties,
Washed your dishes;
Yes, on my knees and hands like a quadruped creature,
I scrubbed your kitchen floor –
That I might learn of Beauty,
Of Keats and Poe.
And why shall I not love Keats and Poe?
Feel their genius,
Marvel at their fire,

Pity their fates,
Laud their martyrdom,
Love the art they loved?
Did I carp when you created beautiful curls,
Becoming curls, to deck your Marcian Bob?
Or of the Bob itself?
Or of how you smiled to hear me sing
Of how Malindy sings?
Or when you required of me the sad songs of my fathers?
Or when your body lilted to the sway of new folk music?
And your nimble feet tangled in the

double-quick movement of my
   body-wriggling, syncopated dance?
Did I charge that you were aping me?
(Why should I
Or why should anyone?)
I only thought that you were questioning Beauty.

Oh friend, let's be kind to one another!
Let us be mutual teachers,
Mutually questioning El Dorado;
Lovely Arcady;
Those are wonderful Hands that fashioned us!
Handle those cosmetics softly;
I would more beautify these curls,
This skin,
Would refine this brain.
Oh chide me not if I met Keats and Poe,
If I met Keats and Poe –
And love them!

Mae V. Cowdery

IN AN AUCTION ROOM

(Letter of John Keats to Fanny Brawne, Anderson Galleries, 15 March 1920)

To Dr. A. S. W. Rosenbach.

How about this lot? said the auctioneer;
One hundred, may I say, just for a start?
Between the plum-red curtains, drawn apart,
A written sheet was held… . And strange to hear
(Dealer, would I were steadfast as thou art)
The cold quick bids. (*Against you in the rear!*)
The crimson salon, in a glow more clear
Burned bloodlike purple as the poet's heart.

Song that outgrew the singer! Bitter Love
That broke the proud hot heart it held in thrall –
Poor script, where still those tragic passions move –
Eight hundred bid: fair warning: the last call:
The soul of Adonais, like a star… .
Sold for eight hundred dollars – Doctor R.!

Christopher Morley

IN REMEMBRANCE OF THE ODE TO A NIGHTINGALE

(A sonnet to Keats, Mozart, and Schubert)

This poet died too young – and with him, these
Who followed Orpheus. Down in early death
Sank their great spirits. Hollow-eyed disease,
Comfortless poverty, destroyed their breath,
Froze the warm motions of their gallant hearts,
And stopped the lightning movements of their minds!
Yet would I not have chosen (in the hearts
Of their own day) to take the crusts and rinds
Flung down to them to meet their human needs
To bear the hunger, the despair, the same
Dark fate, just to have been the deathless reed
For such a music, wick for such a flame! –
Just to have wrought one ode, that day beneath
The garden plum tree there by Hampstead Heath!

Katharine Shepard Hayden

ON READING KEATS IN WAR TIME

As one long lost in no-man's-land of war
Dreams of a cup of pure forgetful wine,
Dark waters deeper than the ancient Rhine
Where Saturnalian maidens swam before
The age of knowledge, and all your golden lore
Held in the splendor of a castle's shine
At sunset on a crag of somber pine –
But wakes to death and thirst and cannon's roar;

So I have come upon your book and drunk
Even to the dregs of melancholy bliss
Your poetry, Keats, and smoothing down your page,
Thought how a soldier leaner than a monk
Still loves, though time without the lover's kiss
Pours out its viscous hemlock on your age.

Karl Shapiro

A ROOM IN ROME

For Vera Cacciatore

I

The water-poet lay down with flowers above
And the half-sunken boat below his head.
Bitter with young and unrespondent love
Poetry lay foundering on the Italian bed

Vision and terror held him while he bled
Himself of character and identity.
Upon the coffered ceiling his soul fed
Festoons of roses to his fevered eye.

Friends from afar watch over every breath,
Friends in the room receive his last asides,
Sleep and poetry, charactr'y and death
Stand by the pillow as he outward rides.

Poets of all times and ages come and go
Here where Keats died. The boat sinks on below.

II

The house looks rich; this was no starving poet,
And nowadays a millionaire can't buy it.
The famed boat-fountain lying just below it
Is a bad joke. At least the plash is quiet.

The Spanish Steps sweep upward like a skirt
To the effeminate church that squats on high.
What did he think, lying in mortal hurt,
Of all that grunting in the lovers' sty?

Now he's a library and a sacred name,
Voices take off their shoes when here they tread,
And quite a few remember the belle dame
Who sidewise leant beside his glowing head

When to his healthy friend he turned and said,
Severn, please don't be frightened, and was dead.

9-16-94 Vienna

Karl Shapiro

POSTHUMOUS KEATS

The road is so rough Severn is walking,
and every once in a while, since the season is
beautiful and there are flowers on both sides,
as if this path had just been plowed,
he picks by the handful what he can

and still keep up. Keats is in the carriage
swallowing blood and the best of the bad food.
It is early November, like summer,
honey and wheat in the last of the
daylight, and above the mountains a clear

carnelian heartline. Rome is a week
away. And Severn started to fill
the carriage with wildflowers – rust, magenta,
marigold, and the china white of cups.
Keats is floating, his whole face luminous.

The biographer sees no glory in this,
how the living, by increments, are dead,
how they celebrate their passing half in love.
Keats, like his young companion, is alone,
among color and a long memory.

In his head he is writing a letter
about failure and money and the ten-
thousand lines that could not save his brother.
But he might as well be back at Gravesend
with the smell of the sea and cold sea rain,

waiting out the weather and the tide –
he might as well be lying in a room,
in Rome, staring at a ceiling stylized
with roses or watching outside right now
a cardinal with two footmen shooting birds.

He can still remember the meadows near
St. Cross, the taste in the air of apples,
the tower and alms-square, and the River
Itchen, all within the walk of a mile.
In the poem it is Sunday, the middle

of September, the light a gold conglomerate
of detail – 'in the same way that some pictures
look warm.' He has closed his eyes.
And he is going to let the day close down.
He is thinking he must learn Italian.

By the time they reach the Campagna the wind
will be blowing, the kind that begins at the sea.
Severn will have climbed back in, finally a
passenger, with one more handful to add
to what is already overwhelming.

                                        Stanley Plumly

SCIROCCO

In Rome, at 26
    Piazza di Spagna,
at the foot of a long
    flight of
stairs, are rooms
    let to Keats

in 1820,
    where he died. Now
you can visit them,
    the tiny terrace,
the bedroom. The scraps
    of paper

on which he wrote
    lines
are kept behind glass,
    some yellowing,
some xeroxed or
    mimeographed ....

Outside his window
    you can hear the scirocco
working
    the invisible.
Every dry leaf of ivy
    is fingered,

refingered. Who is
    the nervous spirit
of this world
    that must go over and over
what it already knows,
    what is it

so hot and dry
   that's looking through us,
by us,
   for its answer?
In the arbor
   on the terrace

the stark hellenic
   forms
of grapes have appeared.
   They'll soften
till weak enough
   to enter

our world, translating
   helplessly
from the beautiful
   to the true ....
Whatever the spirit,
   the thickening grapes

are part of its looking,
   and the slow hands
that made this mask
   of Keats
in his other life,
   and the old woman,

the memorial's
   custodian,
sitting on the porch
   beneath the arbor
sorting chick-peas
   from pebbles

into her cast-iron
   pot.
See what her hands
   know –
they are its breath,
   its mother
tongue, dividing,
   discarding.
There is light playing
   over the leaves,
over her face,
   making her

abstract, making
   her quick

and strange. But she
    has no care
for what speckles her,
    changing her,

she is at
    her work. Oh how we want
to be taken
    and changed,
want to be mended
    by what we enter.

Is it thus
    with the world?
Does it wish us
    to mend it,
light and dark,
    green

and flesh? Will it
    be free then?
I think the world
    is a desperate
element. It would have us
    calm it,

receive it. Therefore this
    is what I
must ask you
    to imagine: wind;
the moment
    when the wind

drops; and grapes,
    which are nothing,
which break
    in your hands.

                    Jorie Graham

JOHN KEATS AT THE LOW WOOD HOTEL DISCO, WINDERMERE

His girls dance under
iridescent snakes
and chop away

their territory
with flattened hands
indifferent to his fatalism.

Outside the mountains fade
insubstantial as cloud
their crumbling seems
blue as the dusk that hides them.

To prove he don't
need human love
he moves to go, says
nothing too polite,
rage grooming in his eye.
At once they follow
link his arms
fold with him into night.

Wilko Johnson once asked Basil Bunting to tell him which poet was the best to read in a 'Southron' accent (Basil had insisted that neither his nor Wordsworth's poetry should be mauled by voices that refuse to rhyme 'waters' with 'chatters'). '.Ah now', replied the discriminating author of Briggflats, 'Keats – he's your poet ...'

This poem is written for a Cockney voice.

There is no documentary evidence that Keats encouraged troilism during his brief visit to the Lake District in 1818, However, we do know that his mind was tinged with the sort of pessimism that could have led him into many such unusual situations. As he wrote to Ben Bailey in the year before his northern tour: 'I scarcely remember counting upon any Happiness – I look not for it if it be not in the present hour nothing startles me beyond the Moment'.

Peter Laver

VOYAGES

On April twenty-seventh, 1932, Hart Crane
walked to the taffrail of the *Orizaba*
took off his coat, and leaped. At seventeen,
a changeling from among the tire-and-rubber

factories, steel mills, cornfields of the Ohio
flatland that had absentmindedly produced him,
on an enthralled first voyage held looked into
the troughed Caribbean, and called it home.

Back where held never been at home, he'd once
watched the early-morning shift pour down South Main –
immigrant Greeks eager to be Americans –
and then tried to imagine Porphyro in Akron

(Greek for 'high place'): the casement, the arras,
the fabricated love nest, the actual sleet storm,
the owl, the limping hare, the frozen grass,
Keats's own recurring dream of being warm –

who'd been so often cold he looked with yearning even
into blacksmiths' fires: 'How glorious,' he wrote
of them, shivering (with Stevens) to see the stars put on
their glittering belts: of what disaster was that

chill, was that salt wind the imminence? The cold-
a-long time, lifetime snow man did not know.
Beside the Neva, Osip Mandelstam wrote of the cold,
the December fog-blurs of Leningrad. O to throw

open (he wrote) a window on the Adriatic! – a window
for the deprived of audience, for the unfree
to breathe, to breathe even the bad air of Moscow.
Yet on the freezing pane of perpetuity,

that coruscating cold-frame fernery of breath,
harsh flowerbed of the unheated rooms of childhood,
even from the obscurity that sealed it off, his breath,
his warmth, he dared declare, had already settled.

The dream of being warm, its tattered cargo
brought too late to Italy, a mere dire fistful
of blood (the sea had soaked his heart through):
the voyage, every voyage at the end is cruel.

In February 1937, from exile to flatland
Voronezh, a kind of twin of Akron, Mandelstam
wrote, in an almost posthumous whisper, of round
blue bays, of sails descried – scenes parted from

as now his voyage to the bottom of a crueler
obscurity began, whose end only the false-haired
seaweed of an inland shipwreck would register.
Untaken voyages, Lethean cold, O all but unendured

arrivals! Keats's starved stare before the actual,
so long imagined Bay of Naples. The mind's extinction.
Nightlong, sleepless beside the Spanish Steps, the prattle
of poured water. Letters no one will ever open.

                                        Amy Clampitt

A KUMQUAT FOR JOHN KEATS

Today I found the right fruit for my prime,
not orange, not tangelo, and not lime,
nor moon-like globes of grapefruit that now hang
outside our bedroom, nor tart lemon's tang
(though last year full of bile and self-defeat
I wanted to believe no life was sweet)
nor the tangible sunshine of the tangerine,
and no incongruous citrus ever seen
at greengrocers' in Newcastle or Leeds
mis-spelt by the spuds and mud-caked swedes,
a fruit an older poet might substitute
for the grape John Keats thought fit to be Joy's fruit,
when, two years before he died, he tried to write
how Melancholy dwelled inside Delight,
and if he'd known the citrus that I mean
that's not orange, lemon, lime or tangerine,
I'm pretty sure that Keats, though he had heard
'of candied apple, quince and plum and gourd'
instead of 'grape against the palate fine'
would have, if he'd known it, plumped for mine,
this Eastern citrus scarcely cherry size
he'd bite just once and then apostrophize
and pen one stanza how the fruit had all
the qualities of fruit before the Fall,
but in the next few lines be forced to write
how Eve's apple tasted at the second bite,
and if John Keats had only lived to be,
because of extra years, in need like me,
at 42 he'd help me celebrate
that Micanopy kumquat that I ate
whole, straight off the tree, sweet pulp and sour skin –
or was it sweet outside, and sour within?
For however many kumquats that I eat
I'm not sure if it's flesh or rind that's sweet,
and being a man of doubt at life's mid-way
I'd offer Keats some kumquats and I'd say:
You'll find that one part's sweet and one part's tart:
say where the sweetness or the sourness start.

I find I can't, as if one couldn't say
exactly where the night became the day,
which makes for me the kumquat taken whole
best fruit, and metaphor, to fit the soul
of one in Florida at 42 with Keats
crunching kumquats, thinking, as he eats
the flesh, the juice, the pith, the pips, the peel,
that this is how a full life ought to feel,

its perishable relish prick the tongue,
when the man who savours life 's no longer young,
the fruits that were his futures far behind.
Then it's the kumquat fruit expresses best
how days have darkness round them like a rind,

life has a skin of death that keeps its zest.

History, a life, the heart, the brain
flow to the taste buds and flow back again –
That decade or more past Keats's span
makes me an older not a wiser man,
who knows that it's too late for dying young,
but since youth leaves some sweetnesses unsung,
he's granted days and kumquats to express
Man's Being ripened by his Nothingness.
And it isn't just the gap of sixteen years,
a bigger crop of terrors, hopes and fears,
but a century of history on this earth
between John Keats's death and my own birth –
years like an open crater, gory, grim,
with bloody bubbles leering at the rim;
a thing no bigger than an urn explodes
and ravishes all silence, and all odes,
Flora asphyxiated by foul air
unknown to either Keats or Lemprière,
dehydrated Naiads, Dryad amputees
dragging themselves through slagscapes with no trees,
a Shirt of Nessus fire that gnaws and eats
children half the age of dying Keats …

Now were you twenty five or six years old
when that fevered brow at last grew cold?
I've got no books to hand to check the dates.
My grudging but glad spirit celebrates
that all I've got to hand's the kumquats, John,
the fruit I'd love to have your verdict on,
but dead men don't eat kumquats, or drink wine,
they shiver in the arms of Proserpine,
not warm in bed beside their Fanny Brawne,
nor watch her pick ripe grapefruit in the dawn
as I did, waking, when I saw her twist,
with one deft movement of a sunburnt wrist,
the moon, that feebly lit our last night's walk
past alligator swampland, off its stalk.
I thought of moon-juice juleps when I saw,
as if I'd never seen the moon before,
the planet glow among the fruit, and its pale light
make each citrus on the tree its satellite.

Each evening when I reach to draw the blind
stars seem the light zest squeezed through night's black rind;
the night's peeled fruit the sun, juiced of its rays,
first stains, then streaks, then floods the world with days,
days, when the very sunlight made me weep,
days, spent like the nights in deep, drugged sleep,
days in Newcastle by my daughter's bed,
wondering if she, or I, weren't better dead,
days in Leeds, grey days, my first dark suit,
my mother's wreaths stacked next to Christmas fruit,
and days, like this in Micanopy. Days!

As strong sun burns away the dawn's grey haze
I pick a kumquat and the branches spray
cold dew in my face to start the day.
The dawn's molasses make the citrus gleam
still in the orchards of the groves of dream.

The limes, like Galway after weeks of rain,
glow with a greenness that is close to pain,
the dew-cooled surfaces of fruit that spent
all last night flaming in the firmament.
The new day dawns. O days! My spirit greets
the kumquat with the spirit of John Keats.
O kumquat, comfort for not dying young,
both sweet and bitter, bless the poet's tongue!
I burst the whole fruit chilled by morning dew
against my palate. Fine, for 42!

I search for buzzards as the air grows clear
and see them ride fresh thermals overhead.
Their bleak cries were the first sound I could hear
when I stepped at the start of sunrise out of doors,
and a noise like last night's bedsprings on our bed
from Mr Fowler sharpening farmers' saws.

                                                    Tony Harrison

THERE

For Keats

Peace is where the body finally goes
after trying all the moves its fever knows;
asylum where your debt for what you chose

need not be paid and the interest never grows;
bower where no one's lips look like a rose
and no one hopes you'll take off all your clothes.
Preferment's not an issue there, you strike no pose:
tenure is freely granted though you're off your toes.
It's where the river Lethe darkly flows
(except it doesn't). No one comes to blows.
The lover there lies safe in perpetual doze –
woman who has no dreams of lusty beaus
and thro' whose curtains peeps no hellish nose;
man unthinkably unworried by his foes.
All sound there would be blank as endless oh's;
no messy voice can say 'here follows prose.'

Mark Halliday

OATMEAL

I eat oatmeal for breakfast.
I make it on the hot plate and put skimmed milk on it.
I eat it alone.
I am aware it is not good to eat oatmeal alone.
Its consistency is such that its better for your mental health if
    somebody eats it with you.
That is why I often think up an imaginary companion to have
    breakfast with.
Possibly it is even worse to eat oatmeal with an imaginary
    companion.
Nevertheless, yesterday morning, I ate my oatmeal – porridge, as
    he called it – with John Keats.
Keats said I was absolutely right to invite him: due to its
    glutinous texture, gluey lumpishness, hint of slime, and
    unusual willingness to disintegrate, oatmeal must never be
    eaten alone.
He said that in his opinion, however, it is perfectly OK to eat
    it with an imaginary companion,
and he himself had enjoyed memorable porridges with Edmund
    Spenser and John Milton.
Even if eating oatmeal with an imaginary companion is not as
    wholesome as Keats claims, still, you can learn something from
    it.
Yesterday morning, for instance, Keats told me about writing the
    'Ode to a Nightingale.'
He had a heck of a time finishing it – those were his words-
    'Oi 'ad a 'eck of a toime,' he said, more or less, speaking
    through his porridge.

He wrote it quickly, on scraps of paper, which he then stuck in
　　his pocket,
but when he got home he couldn't figure out the order of the
　　stanzas, and he and a friend spread the papers on a table, and
　　they made some sense of them, but he isn't sure to this day if
　　they got it right.
An entire stanza may have slipped into the lining of his jacket
　　through a hole in the pocket.
He still wonders about the occasional sense of drift between
　　stanzas,
and the way here and there a line will go into the configuration
　　of a Moslem at prayer, then raise itself up and peer about,
　　and then lay itself down slightly off the mark, causing the
　　poem to move forward with God's reckless wobble.
He said someone told him that later in life Wordsworth heard
　　about the scraps of paper on the table, and tried shuffling
　　some stanzas of his own, but only made matters worse.
I would not have known about any of this but for my reluctance
　　to eat oatmeal alone.
When breakfast was over, John recited 'To Autumn.'
He recited it slowly, with much feeling, and he articulated the
　　words lovingly, and his odd accent sounded sweet.
He didn't offer the story of writing 'To Autumn,' I doubt if
　　there is much of one.
But he did say the sight of a just-harvested oat field got him
　　started on it,
and two of the lines, 'For Summer has o'er brimmed their clammy
　　cells' and 'Thou watchest the last oozings hours by hours,'
　　came to him while eating oatmeal alone.
I can see him – drawing a spoon through the stuff, gazing into
　　the glimmering furrows, muttering – and it occurs to me:
maybe there is no sublime; only the shining of the amnion's
　　tatters.
For supper tonight I am going to have a baked potato left over
　　from lunch.
I am aware that a leftover baked potato is damp, slippery, and
　　simultaneously gummy and crumbly,
and therefore I'm going to invite Patrick Kavanagh to join me.

　　　　　　　　　　　　　　　　　　　　　　Galway Kinnell

PEGASUS JOCKEY

Born over a stable, a stableboy's son,
A boxer in my youth, tiny as Tom Thumb,
With a naval officer in the family,

Apprenticed as an apothecary,
Later on is proposed to me that
I become a commercial man in the hat
Or tea trades, or write popular plays,
Or become a doctor in the high seas,
Plying plasters on an Indiaman,
But I spare myself confinement in all
Those yawning quarters by throwing
Myself completely into the nervous
Excitement of riding the little horse
Poetry, with its shoes kicking in the stars.

Tom Clark

ENDYMION

Endymion: it is all one moon who in
The innumerable phases of women

Turns to kiss him. And when, guilty over
His serial betrayals, he feels muddled,

It is the mawkish young author who rushes
In to assist him. We hold our breath for him.

His dreams fill up with melting women who
Will have their way with him, in the dark

They are all alike. He may not wake up soon,
No one may ever wake up again.

For fear all women will stop sleeping
With him, nature presses a finger to her lips.

Tom Clark

A POCKET APOLLO

The thrush or nightingale that began calm-throated
Lifted the curtain on a tragic play that opened
Like an evening glory, with Vega in the Summer
Triangle, poised overhead to be sung

As Aeschylus sang the god on Delos discovering
Poetry in a mimetic touching of the strings
Which serendipitously charms every thing.
That forward spring Keats stood beneath Brown's plum

Tree, head cocked alertly as the listening forest
Faun in a tragic masque strains to pick up
Distant chords unheard by the mortal players,
A modal continuum of quiet minor song

That keeps the Ring Nebula in Lyra spinning
And swimming, an incandescent sea of gas
That surrounds its central star the way grief
And lament echo and engulf suffering. Dying

Back into ambient underground rustling, then rising,
Birdsong continued to flow from the covert glade,
Drowning Brown's garden in a grief-drenched shade.
Mortality like a fist closed in Keats' throat

While the golden lyre lying at his side,
Touched by no one, tuned to no human register,
Poured out liquid notes to the unwearied underground
Ear of the alert listening forest, smooth,

Clear as claret out of a cell a mile
Deep. All through that aching starlit spring
In Hampstead the god kept being born
As the stunned, exhausted player was abandoned.

Tom Clark

IT IS GETTING LATE

Half bottle of claret drunk alone – a soft
Dusk falls in this dragon world of men
Who cannot see what flowers are at their feet
Once the swarming of phenomena begins

Better perhaps to guess than to see
Those flowers of death's close growth and breathing,
Lustrous, fragrant, spongy, aethereal,
Shadowy thought left to supply its own

Earth-figuring text finds this evanescent
Diffuse sense efflorescing, this slow
Faint luminous phosphorescence rising
From the forever speculative ground

The moving waters at their priestlike task,
Polaris growing bright against the sky
Like an evening glory, with Vega
Swimming, an incandescent sea of gas

That surrounds its central star the way
A modal continuum of quiet
Keeps the Ring Nebula in Lyra spinning,
Shows the magic of chance at work:
She moves in next door, we huddle over
The doomed infatuated ones in Dante,
The burden of the mystery producing
A mimetic touching of the strings

With which we might identify
Deneb and Altair locked across the dark.

Tom Clark

THE ORE, THE FIRE, THE FABULOUS HEFT

For poets dying young I felt once
a sadness wide as their days left behind,
yet doesn't that easy pathos give off

a fragrance almost sweeter than fame?
Oh youthfully dead, are you creation's
true favorites? Many a man might prefer

dying retroactively, as if thereby
to suture a complicated wound; but then
sunlight stored up in his brain

shines forth in syllables like 'tanager,'
'hackberry,' 'mariposa,' 'tomorrow,'
and other small victories taken alive,

one at a time out of daybreak's fresh
distances. So because to envy the dead
seems desertion, utterance charged –

such as 'anguish,' 'elation' – continues
electric polarities of that inner current
the heart is slow to let suicide have.

As to creation's true favorites, who knows?
Shark? Scorpion? Bivalve? Worm? Worked
pretty well the first time, requiring

little adjustment. And we? Stitched
out of words, our gauze wings flutter us
toward horizons that pull apart as we go

escaping the truth of illusion, fed up
with shaped air whose bards turn earth
into ore; 'the fire, the smoking ingot

and fabulous heft' – of mere spoken gold.
Which sooner or later nonetheless
our every loss or salvation gets made of.

                                        Reg Saner

Notes

CHAPTER 1   INTRODUCTION

1. Christopher Ricks, *Keats and Embarrassment*. Oxford University Press, 1976.
2. Susan Wolfson, 'Feminizing Keats,' in H. de Almeida (ed.), *Critical Essays on Keats*, Boston, 1990, 217–57; Margaret Homans, 'Keats Reading Women, Women Reading Keats,' *SiR* 29(1990), 341–70.
3. Lionel Trilling, 'Why We Read Jane Austen,' in *The Last Decade*. New York: Harcourt Brace Jovanovich, 1979, p. 219.
4. Stuart Sperry, *Keats the Poet*. Princeton; NJ: Princeton University Press, 1973, p. 78.
5. Ibid., p. 80.
6. Leon Waldoff, *Keats and the Silent Work of Imagination*. Urbana: University of Illinois Press, 1985, p. 112.
7. Sperry, p. 248.
8. 21, 27 (?) December 1817 to George and Tom Keats, in *Letters of John Keats*, ed. Robert Gittings. Oxford: Oxford University Press, 1977, p. 43.
9. 27 October 1818 to Richard Woodhouse, in Gittings, p. 157.
10. Allen Grossman, *The Sighted Singer*. Baltimore, Md: The Johns Hopkins University Press, 1992.

CHAPTER 2   A GAME OF SHARDS: KEAT'S 'VITALLY METAPHORICAL' POETRY

1. *Letters of John Keats*, ed. Robert Gittings. Oxford: Oxford University Press, 1977, pp. 239–40.
2. See Jerome McGann, 'Keats and the Historical Method in Literary Criticism,' *MLN*, Vol. 96, No. 5, December 1979, pp. 988–1032. McGann discusses the question of which of three known versions of the poem is the one authorized by Keats, but the issue of authority is not particularly relevant to my observation about the letter's version which is, as it were, an unstable isotope of the poem.
3. Jean Baudrillard, *The Ecstasy of Communication*. New York: Semiotext(e), 1988, p. 50.
4. I am not suggesting that Keats was catagorizing a monolithic dominant poetics to which Shakespeare, Milton, and Wordsworth all subscribed. Indeed, he often distinguished among them and sided with one against another. But to the degree that they stood for monumental instances of closed forms, Keats – amid ambivalence and gropings, to be sure – was – this book argues – after something else.

5. Allen Grossman, *The Sighted Singer*. Baltimore, Md: The Johns Hopkins University Press, 1992, p. 248.
6. Jerome Rothenberg (ed.), *Technicians of the Sacred*. Berkeley: University of California Press, 1985, pp. 455–6.
7. See Jerome Rothenberg's and Pierre Joris's extraordinary new anthology, *Poems for the Millenium*, Vol. 1. Berkeley: University of California Press, 1995: the section of 'Forerunners' to twentieth-century avant-gardist poetries, which sees modern movements in poetry anticipated by such figures as Blake, Holderlin, Baudelaire, Hopkins, and Mallarmé.

CHAPTER 3   ENSHRININGS: PUBLIC MEMORIALS AND KEATSIAN POETICS

1. James Russell Lowell (ed.), *The Poetical Works of John Keats*, Boston: Little, Brown, 1854, p. xii.
2. Marjorie Levinson, *Keats's Life of Allegory*. Oxford: Basil Blackwell, 1988.
3. Lowell, op. cit., p. xv.
4. William Keach, 'Cockney Couplets: Keats and the Politics of Style,' *SiR*, Vol. 25, Summer 1986, pp. 182–96.
5. Keats-Shelley Memorial Association, 1973, p. 18.
6. Ibid., p. 18.
7. Hyder Rollins (ed.), *The Letters of John Keats*, Vol. II, Cambridge, Mass.: Harvard University Press, 1958, p. 372.
8. Ibid., p. 372.
9. Ibid., p. 341.
10. *Letters of John Keats*, ed. Robert Gittings. Oxford: Oxford University Press, 1977, p. 426.

CHAPTER 4   KEATS ENSHRINED IN POEMS: THE NINETEENTH CENTURY AND TRADITIONAL POETICS

1. *Letters of John Keats*, ed. Robert Gittings. Oxford: Oxford University Press, 1977, p. 426.
2. Ibid., p. 421.
3. Susan J. Wolfson, 'Keats enters history: autopsy, *Adonais*, and the fame of Keats,' in Nicholas Roe (ed.), *Keats and History*. Cambridge: Cambridge, University Press, 1995, p. 22.

CHAPTER 8   BIBLIOGRAPHY AND THE POET

1. Walter Jackson Bate, *John Keats*. Cambridge, Mass.: Harvard University Press, 1963, p. 2.

2. Aileen Ward, *John Keats: The Making of a Poet*. New York: Viking Press, 1963.

CHAPTER 9   POETRY AND/AS BIOGRAPHY: AMY CLAMPITT'S A HOMAGE TO JOHN KEATS

1. Hélène Cixous, *Three Steps on the Ladder of Writing*. New York: Columbia University Press, 1993.

CHAPTER 10   COSMIC BIOGRAPHY: TOM CLARK'S *JUNKETS ON A SAD PLANET*

1. Tom Clark, *Junkets on a Sad Planet*. Santa Rosa: Black Sparrow Press, 1994.
2. Allen Grossman, op. cit., p. x.
3. Hélène Cixous, op. cit., pp. 12–13.
4. Dorothy Van Ghent, *Keats: The Myth of the Hero*, revised by Jeffrey Cane Robinson. Princeton: Princeton University Press.

CHAPTER 11   MORE READINGS

1. Cid Corman, *Word for Word*, Vol. 1. Santa Rosa, Calif.: Black Sparrow Press, pp. 68–9.

CHAPTER 12   MARK HALLIDAY'S 'THERE: FOR KEATS' AND KEATS'S 'EPISTLE TO J. H. REYNOLDS, ESQ.: AGAINST MONUMENTAL POETRY'

1. Robert Bly, *Leaping Poetry*. Boston: Beacon Press, 1975, p. 4.
2. 'Projective Verse,' in Charles Olson, *Selected Writings*. New York: New Directions, 1966, p. 16.
3. Peter Manning, '*Don Juan* and Byron's Imperceptiveness to the English Word,' in *Reading Romantics*. New York: Oxford University Press, 1990, p. 140.
4. Donald Wesling, *The New Poetries*. Lewisburg, W. Va.: Bucknell University Press, 1985.
5. Jerome Rothenberg (ed.), op. cit., p. 458.
6. Robert Gittings (ed.), *Letters of John Keats*. Oxford: Oxford University Press, 1977, p. 94.
7. See Jack Stillinger, *The Hoodwinking of Madeline*. Urbana: University of Illinois Press, 1971, pp. 33, 35.

CHAPTER 14   THE WALKING TOUR OF SCOTLAND, 1818

1. Ward, op. cit., pp. 204–5.

CHAPTER 15   MEMOS ON KEATS FOR THE NEXT MILLENNIUM

1. *Oscar Wilde*, New York: Knopf, 1987, p. 74.
2. Ibid., p. 42.
3. Cited in Neil Freistat, *The Poem and the Book*. Chapel Hill, University of North Carolina Press, 1985.
4. Louis Zukofsky, 'Mantis' and 'Mantis: An Interpretation,' in *Complete Shorter Poetry*. Baltimore: The Johns Hopkins University Press, 1991, pp. 65–73.
5. Ibid.
6. Rothenberg (ed.), *Technicians of the Sacred*, op. cit., p. xxvii.
7. Jack Stillinger (ed.), *The Poems of John Keats*. Cambridge, Mass.: Harvard University Press, 1978, p. 15.
8. Jack Stillinger, *Multiple Authorship and the Myth of Solitary Genius*. New York: Oxford University Press, 1991, p. 41.
9. Freistat, op. cit., p. 119.
10. Ibid., p. 99.
11. Ibid., p. 100.
12. Ibid., p. 118.
13. William Hazlitt, 'On Going a Journey,' in *Complete Works*, ed. P. P. Howe. London: J. M. Dent and Sons, 1930, Vol. VIII, p. 187.
14. Thomas McGrath, 'The End of the World,' in *Selected Poems 1938–1988*, Port Townsend: Copper Canyon Press, 1988., p. 99.
15. Van Ghent, op. cit., p. 144.
16. Zukovsky, op. cit., p. 68.
17. In *Poems from the Greek Anthology*, trans. Dudley Fitts. New York: New Directions, 1956, p. 132.
18. Bertolt Brecht, 'Bad Time for Poetry,' in *The Poetry of Survival*, ed. Daniel Weissbort. New York: St. Martin's Press, 1991, p. 3.

Index